Logic in
Everyday Life

Logic in Everyday Life
PRACTICAL REASONING SKILLS

Zachary Seech
Palomar College

Wadsworth Publishing Company
Belmont, California
A division of Wadsworth, Inc.

Philosophy Editor: *Kenneth King*

Production Editor: *Lisa Danchi*

Print Buyer: *Barbara Britton*

Designer: *Donna Davis*

Copy Editor: *Greg Gullickson*

Compositor: *Graphic Typesetting Service*

Cover: *Donna Davis*

Cover Photo: *Tim Pogue*

Signing Representative: *Sue Lasbury*

Printed in the United States of America   34

  2 3 4 5 6 7 8 9 10---91 90 89 88

Library of Congress Cataloging-in-Publication Data

Seech, Zachary.
  Logic in everyday life.

  Includes bibliographies and index.
  1. Logic.   I. Title.
BL108.S35   1987   160   87-10685
ISBN 0-534-08196-7

To Valerie
And to Kyle, Trevor, and Todd

Contents

PART
TWO

Building on Logical Foundations 135

Preface

Professors are aware of the demands of tradition and convenience; these move us to teach courses in the same way they were taught to us. We also see, at times in our careers, that many of our classroom practices do not yield the kinds of practical skill-oriented results that serve students best in their continuing academic and nonacademic lives. In writing this text, I have tried to preserve some of the wisdom behind the traditional elements of logic courses while focusing simultaneously on what my students have taught me. Essentially, they have taught me that they must perceive the usability of a skill before they will fully absorb it as a tool for personal out-of-the-classroom reasoning.

I kept both of these requirements in mind as I fashioned (and refashioned) a book that combines formal and informal tools for the analysis of reasoning, delineates and relates the various skills, and feels inviting rather than forbidding to the people who will benefit from reading it.

Combination of Formal and Informal Tools of Analysis

For formal analysis, I explore patterns of deductive validity, soundness, patterns of conditional arguments, logical analogy, and Venn diagrams (in Appendix A).

For informal analysis, I discuss evidence and counterevidence, generalization, analogy, informal fallacies, language (clarity, definitions, and emotional charges), hypothesis, statistics, library research (for premise verification), decision-making, and problem-solving. I also introduce points of logical vulnerability, sidetracks in reasoning, nonfallacious fallacy look-alikes (to guard against overzealous fallacy-finding) and the R-E-T method of evaluating the inductive strength of an argument.

Formal and informal techniques are combined in the Chapter 6 skill, mapping arguments, and in the exercises in Appendix B.

Skills-Acquisition Focus

In listening to lectures, students often have difficulty discriminating between primary and secondary points. The same difficulty occurs in reading texts, when students have difficulty identifying and relating the primary points of a narrative discourse. Headings and subheadings usually help students by serving as organizational aids. In this book, however, the skills-acquisition focus further organizes the student's conceptual model of the overall task.

Twenty-one specific skills are presented in this book. Each of these skills is introduced in a special skill box that numbers, names, and describes the skill, and explains why the skill is important for clear reasoning. With the exception of chapter beginnings, which offer a brief conceptual foundation before any skills are taught, the book's focus is consistently practical and skills oriented.

By using an explicit skills-acquisition approach—identifying and delineating the skills to be learned—we avoid the undesirable student impression that there's literally "no telling" how much of a chapter-upon-chapter narrative is really important. Students can gain confidence with each skill mastered and pinpoint remedial needs.

Friendly, Helpful Format

The publisher's reviewers agree that the writing style is friendly and accessible. The opening and continuing theme underscores the reader's success at reasoning in everyday situations. We do, it seems, reason correctly more often than not. To make the text easier to use, examples are clearly set off, exercises are separated into as many as three levels of difficulty, and chapter highlights are collected in a closing section for each chapter. Suggested readings are listed and briefly described for each chapter.

The inductive/deductive distinction in *Logic and Everyday Life* follows Brian Skyrms's excellent work in *Choice & Chance* (Wadsworth, 1986) and avoids the difficulties of making the distinction on the basis of the intention of the arguer or on the basis of a contrast between generality and specificity. Venn diagrams, from Appendix A, can easily be studied at any point after the Chapter 3 presentation of deductive validity.

* * * * *

I thank Sue Lasbury of Wadsworth Publishing Company for encouraging me to write this book and for her moral support throughout the process. For their help and encouragement, I also thank the following individuals: everyone in the Behavioral Sciences Department at Palomar College; Sharon Norton, untiring research assistant; Dan Arnsan, librarian; my students, especially Charles Bacha; Palomar president George Boggs and Dean of Humanities Gene Jackson.

Ken King, philosophy editor at Wadsworth, has been optimistic and encouraging. Lisa Danchi, production editor, has been a pleasure to work with. I also want to thank the rest of the Wadsworth staff who worked on this book, including Peggy Meehan, Donna Davis, and free-lance copy editor Greg Gullickson. The text itself has been greatly improved through the observations of these reviewers: Jeffrey Berger, Community College of Philadelphia; Ralph Clark, West Virginia University; Vern Denning, Indian River Community College; Frank Fair, Sam Houston State College; Kevin Galvin, East Los Angeles College; Jerry Gravender, Clarkson College; Dale Lugenbehl, College of the Siskiyous; Mike McMahan, California State University at San Bernardino; and Marc Skuster, Victor Valley College. With appreciation, I acknowledge my debts to Irving M. Copi, author of *Introduction to Logic;* Howard Kahane, author of *Logic and Contemporary Rhetoric;* and Professor Thomas Gregory of Westminster College in Pennsylvania.

Finally, I thank Palomar College for a sabbatical leave, without which this book would have been delayed, and my friends and family. My wife, children, and parents have helped me in more ways than I will take the liberty to describe here.

Z.S.

ONE
Logical
Foundations

C H A P T E R

ONE

Being Reasonable

Dozens of times in almost every day—hundreds of times on some days—we need to reason something out. We take information that is available to us and draw conclusions. Often we act on these conclusions, and how well our lives go depends, in part, on how well we have reasoned.

Generally speaking, we are quite good at our task. We are good thinkers and the conclusions we draw are correct. Whether we are concluding that the interstate highway route will get us to grandma's house more quickly than the old river road or that the quiet and apparently shy sales clerk really *was* stealing money from the cash register, we normally know what counts as good evidence and what doesn't, and we generally know when we have enough evidence and when we don't. At times, however, we don't reason as well as we should. This is often because we've already made up our minds. When we start with an emotional commitment to one conclusion, or a prejudice against another conclusion, the chances are good that we will have a hard time being objective and thinking clearly.

POINTS OF LOGICAL VULNERABILITY

For virtually everyone, there are topics about which that person, we say, "just cannot be rational." What we mean is that this person has great difficulty in being objective on these topics. He or she finds it difficult, in some cases, to consider the evidence impartially and draw a sensible, justified conclusion. These topics are the **points of logical vulnerability** for that person.

Points of logical vulnerability vary from one person to another. While it is often recommended that we avoid the topics of religion and politics in order to keep out of nasty arguments, many other topics can bring out the fight in at least someone. In these instances, a psychological commitment to a certain belief or against another belief keeps the person from weighing fairly the evidence for each side of the question. For one person, nothing that the Democratic nominee for president could do or say would show him to be an honorable or intelligent person. For another person, nothing that the Republican nominee for president could do or say would show her to be an honorable or intelligent person. Some people would be unable to accept any significant criticism of a particular political or economic system, regardless of the merit of the criticism. Others can see nothing that is right about that same system. Sometimes the touchy topic *is* a political or a religious one, but the problem can be even closer to home. It may be that nothing can be said on behalf of my new brother-in-law to convince me that he has my sister's best interests at heart. On this point, I am probably not being rational.

What are *your* points of logical vulnerability? It is worthwhile to reflect in order to identify them. An awareness of your points of logical vulnerability can prevent you from becoming unjustifiably self-righteous and can further prevent you from managing to believe that some quite nonsensical reasoning makes sense. Such arrogance and irrationality serve only to put a person in a foolish position.

Often, when you desperately want a particular belief to be true, then almost any reasoning offered in support of that conclusion looks like good reasoning, and when you desperately want a particular belief to be false, then the reasoning that appears perfect to your neighbor may seem obviously inadequate to you. Ironically, the very same kind of reasoning may appear good to you in one context and bad in another. If you are aware of your points of logical vulnerability, you will be more likely to notice when you are inclined to shortchange yourself logically.

WINNING AND LOSING

Sometimes we have a hard time keeping an open mind simply because losing face is considered a fate worse than being wrong. In debate-like conversations with other people, we may find ourselves defending views that are not supported by the evidence, either because we simply want those views to be correct or because we started the conversation with this position (or are known for previously holding this position) and we don't want to lose the argument. We assume that it's always good to win an argument and that it's always bad to lose one. So we first choose a position, sometimes with good grounds and sometimes without, and then proceed to look for evidence to support that position, discounting or minimizing the value of evidence that opposes the position. At times we even fool ourselves into thinking that we are being objective in our assessment.

A "win, don't lose—whatever the cost" attitude is often obvious in conversation. Two minutes' worth of listening to a conversation is sometimes enough to identify those speakers who have such an approach. But a similar attitude can color a person's reading and listening as well as his or her speaking. When our mind is already made up, or we are at least inclined toward a certain position, we may take in information selectively. Listening to a political speech or reading a campaign pamphlet, listening to someone arguing that the city needs a new library or reading a letter to the editor in the local newspaper, being told why you shouldn't buy that new car or reading about the virtues of thrift—in all of these situations, we can easily dismiss or overassess the merits of the reasoning with which we are presented.

Most people will find that their tendency toward a combative stance in conversation—or in reacting to what they read or hear—is more extreme with some persons than with others. Your reaction to a particular point—even with the same wording—may vary, depending on whether it has been presented by Mom, Aunt Darcy, or that surly looking mail carrier. As with points of logical vulnerability, it is worthwhile to reflect on this with the intention of gaining insight into yourself and your habits of argumentation.

FAIRMINDEDNESS

You probably know someone who almost always "wins" in those discussions in which he or she is "arguing against" another person. It may be that this person does not arrive at better conclusions than you do; it may just be that he or she knows how to use logic and language as tools for *appearing* to prove a point. This is no assurance that the point is being presented fairly.

We can misuse the rules of good reasoning, employing them as weapons to force on others the conclusions that we want to be seen as true. When we "win" an argument in this manner, however, we learn nothing. We are combatting rather than inquiring. We cheat ourselves by eliminating the possibility of adding to our own insights.

Fairmindedness demands that, in argumentative discourse, we remain as objective as possible. Sometimes, virtually any reasoning offered in support of a statement that we want to be true strikes us as good reasoning, and almost any reasoning offered in support of a statement that we want to be false strikes us as bad reasoning. Thus, we may contrive and overstate our own reasonings, while failing to notice any merit at all in the points made by the person who is seen as an opponent.

An attitude of fairmindedness, then, requires two things of us as we approach controversy. First, we must present our own position with honesty, being just as willing to see weaknesses in our own reasoning as we would be to see weaknesses in the other's. Second, let's approach the other position with fairness and openness, being just as willing to see strengths in the other's reasoning as we would be to see strengths in our own.

STAYING ON TRACK

When we want to win more than we want to learn from the other person, when we fear "losing" more than we fear missing the other person's point, we sometimes use trickery instead of reasoning. One form of trickery in argumentation involves getting off the track of reasoning about the subject at hand by shifting the topic. Before we explore the basics of good reasoning, we must learn to recognize when we are getting off the topic. After all, we can reason well about a subject only if we are first keeping our mind on that subject.

Sometimes we purposely lead someone off track. Sometimes we are purposely led off track. At other times, however, the shift is only a result of sloppy thinking while no one has actually intended to mislead and abort the process of clear reasoning. The result, however, is the same. We are not resolving the issue *because we have simply lost track of the issue*. Now, to clarify your sense of the skill to be mastered here, turn your attention to the skill box below and examine it carefully.

There are four major "side tracks" that may lead our thinking to destinations different from the originally intended ones.

SKILL

Skill I. Staying on track

Recognize departures from the topic and identify which kind of shift has taken place.

Why this skill is important

To make progress in thinking about a topic, we must first manage to stay on that topic long enough to consider the relevant information. ■

Getting Personal

Sometimes, when one person should be directing criticisms to the reasoning or the position that another person has presented, he or she instead directs the attack toward the *person* who has presented the reasoning or position. This tactic is sometimes used when the person can think of no better criticism of the point being discussed. Here is an example.

EXAMPLE

David is discussing with his neighbor, Gary, the need for a tax cut. David says to Gary, "Taxes are much too high. I just can't believe how much is taken out of my paycheck for taxes. There's no doubt that we need a tax cut." Gary responds, "Well, I pay a lot in taxes, too. But if we're going to maintain vital services as well as reduce the national debt, a tax cut is just not possible."

The conversation continues, with each man giving reasons that his own position is the correct one. Finally, David strikes a confident pose, waving a finger at Gary and riveting his eyes on his opponent. "Okay, listen to this," he says. "On the basis of even *your own* assumptions, I can show you that, to be consistent, you must agree that I'm right. Now, follow my reasoning. . . ." David presents his reasoning carefully, ending with a challenge to "show me where I'm wrong."

Gary doesn't say anything for a moment. He looks down at his shoes and tightens his lips. Then he darts a look at David, raising his eyebrows. "You really *like* to argue, don't you?" he asks pointedly. "You don't really care about the topic when we're having a conversation like this. You're just arguing for argument's sake. I never did like that about you. Can't you ever just ease up a little?"   ∎

In this conversation, Gary has resorted to **getting personal** with David. Instead of attacking David's reasoning or the position that he is taking, Gary has shifted to a personal attack on David.

What are the results of such an attack? Certainly, different people will react differently to a particular kind of comment. In this case, the response is crucial to the direction of the whole conversation. When we are attacked personally, we commonly reach right down to that same level and respond either with a defensive and hostile justification of ourselves or by attacking the other person in a similar way. David might, for example, respond by saying, "I'm no more argumentative than you are, you hypocrite. Do you remember the time? . . ." Here David counterattacks by getting equally personal and stinging. This is most often the very worst kind of response.

First, whoever responds like this is cooperating in setting up an adversary relationship that promises more emotion than reason, more contention than insight. Secondly, both people are now off the topic. Furthermore, since attacks on the person are common when the speaker simply has nothing better to offer, by coming down to the attacker's level and responding defensively or aggressively, the second person allows the shift just when his or her point may be on the verge of being established. If, instead, he or she can maintain a balanced perspective on the conversation as a whole, holding personal emotions in check, a response that gets the conversation back on track can be offered. For example, in the situation previously presented, David could respond by saying, "Perhaps I do get argumentative. But the topic we've been discussing up to now isn't my character, it's the issue of taxes. Now, think about the point I had just made about a tax cut. Did you think there were any mistakes in my reasoning?" With such a response, David keeps himself from a demeaning emotional display and, at the same time, does what he can to revive their comparatively rational discussion—to get the conversation back on track.

Setting Up a Straw Man

"That's not what I said!" you exclaim with frustration. Sometimes our messages get twisted by the recipient.

When people are taking sides in conversational debate, misrepresentation of another person's position or reasoning is not uncommon. Sometimes this is done purposely. Another cause is careless listening. Someone responds not to the actual position or reasoning of the other person but to a different, though similar, position or sequence of reasoning. That is what happens in the following example.

EXAMPLE

Dr. Turanos, noted child psychologist, is appearing as a guest on a television talk show that is hosted by a flashy but grating interviewer. Dr. Turanos opens by commenting that "children in our society should be allowed significantly greater latitude in evaluating alternatives and making their own decisions, at least in many areas." The talk-show host narrows his eyes, smiling slightly as he looks at Dr. Turanos.

Then he turns to the camera and studio audience, shaking his head from side to side. "I thought I had heard it all. Today's guest offers the outlandish suggestion that children be deprived of parental guidance and be allowed to make all of their own decisions. This 'expert opinion' certainly defies the common sense of most of us."　　■

The position that is under attack by the sarcastic talk-show host—that children be given neither guidance nor limits in making decisions—is not the position of Dr. Turanos, who has suggested only that children be given somewhat more say in matters that concern them. How much more? He is not precise. But he has claimed neither that children should be wholly without controls nor that this freedom should extend to all decisions that a child might want to make. Presumably, Dr. Turanos will correct his host if given a chance.

In the preceding example, if some viewers in the television and studio audiences were not sufficiently attentive, they might indeed mistake the host's **straw man** position for the one actually presented in the first place. They would then be mistaking a counterfeit for the real thing, just as a scarecrow—a "straw man"—is a counterfeit that is sometimes mistaken for the real thing—a person—by hungry crows in the field.

Sometimes, surprisingly, such a misrepresentation can fool someone concerning his or her own stand! Consider whether this has ever happened to you. You are defending one view on an issue, but your friend has a different view. You discuss the issue, exchanging defenses of the favored view and attacks on the opposed view. At some point, you realize that the discussion has shifted. The view your friend is now attacking is not the view that you had been supporting at the beginning of the discussion. It seems, however, that, not having noticed the subtle shift yourself, you have been actually defending this manufactured view in which you do not really believe. You are arguing for a position you would normally reject, simply because the "straw man" version of your own view took you in. In your determination to outargue the friend, your thinking became muddled. When the friend made the shift, you should have said, "But that isn't what I've said." Instead, this shift slid right by you. Most of us can reluctantly remember occasions when we have, in this way, been victims of our own carelessness or argumentative natures.

Notice that the "straw man," whether presented intentionally or not, misleads us when the counterfeit view is similar to the original, though different in some significant way. If the two were not somewhat similar, we would not mistake one for the other. Usually, however, the counterfeit is more vulnerable to a logical or factual attack than the original.

Pursuing a Tangent

Sometimes we get off the track of the conversation by shifting the focus to a topic that is not directly related to the discussion. This is known as **pursuing a tangent**. When someone notices such a shift in focus, this comment is often made: "He's gone off on a tangent." This means that, although the person who has made the shift is neither attacking the person nor misrepresenting what the person has said, he has shifted his comments to a different topic. Like the setting up of a straw man, this shift may go unnoticed by the listener or even the speaker. In writing, it may go unnoticed by the reader or even the writer. Here is an example.

EXAMPLE

Tracy and her mother are discussing whether it would be reasonable for the sixteen-year-old to spend all of her savings on a car. If she had a car, she wouldn't have to take the bus to work after school. This would, in the end, save time so she could get her homework done and get into bed at a more reasonable time than she does now.

Tracy and her mother stay on the topic for about twenty minutes. In that time, they discuss insurance rates, maintenance costs, and the problem of where the car could be parked safely at night. (They live in a dangerous neighborhood.)

Then, with a reflective gaze and a half-smile, Tracy's mother muses, "You know, your Dad used to park his old Chevy in a different place each night when we lived at South Side. I used to ask him why he did that, but I never could get a straight answer."

Tracy then says, "Dad is generally pretty secretive, isn't he—even with you? He hardly ever explains how he feels or why he does things."

"Yes, he is. But I never realized that you noticed. Actually, you notice a lot about the way Dad and I interact, don't you? . . ."

And the conversation continues, winding along its unpredictable way. ∎

It's fine that Tracy and her mother are getting a chance to talk about the family. Sometimes a rambling conversation is very pleasurable, and even productive. If it is not necessary for Tracy and her mother to settle the car issue right now, there is no harm in the shift. Only if, for some reason, it were important that they come to a decision without delay would their lack of focus pose a problem. That kind of situation is found in the following example.

EXAMPLE

Mark hadn't wanted to take the statistics course in the first place. Now it seems to him that his concerns had been justified. Although he was good at math and had no problems with the statistics course until the past few weeks, his concern is increasing day by day. He can correctly perform any of the five "t-tests," but he is very often unable to determine which "t-test" to use for a particular statistics problem. Hypothesis testing also frustrates him. Tomorrow is the last day he can drop out of the course and he is tempted to do it.

Eric is visiting Mark tonight. Although he doesn't expect to teach Mark both skills in this one evening, he is hoping to convince him that there is a very good chance that he can master these skills in time for the test next week. Mark would certainly like to be convinced.

Mark and Eric have been looking at statistics problems for only a half hour when Eric comments that Mark should use the library's computer program that was designed to teach these skills.

"Is the software for IBM or Apple computers?" Mark asks.

"IBM."

"That's convenient for me," Mark responds. "By the way, have you read about the new IBM machine that's coming out?"

"Yes, I just found out about it today. It's supposed to be able to . . ."

The conversation goes on until Eric notices the time and apologetically insists that he must leave. ∎

Pursuing a tangent *has* posed a problem in this case. Mark needs to determine whether it is likely that he would be able to pass next week's test. Tomorrow is the last day to drop the course. The half hour spent before Mark's ominous phrase, "by the way," was insufficient. He regrets having pursued that tangent for so long.

Pursuing a tangent also generates problems in the following two situations. First, it can create a problem when the person who is pursuing the tangent is supposed to be presenting essential information. Consider, for example, the math teacher who, instead of explaining that confusing point

The activity of "going on a tangent" can be conceived in a visual way by thinking about the meaning of *tangent* in geometry. In this sense, the straight line in the following figure is considered a tangent to (touching at one point) the circle.

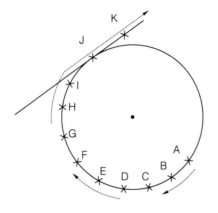

Now, if we think of the center of the circle as the topic under discussion, then points A through J can be viewed as the comments that, in the course of the discussion, relate to (or "center on") the topic. At a certain point, however (in this figure it is at point J), a comment that *does* relate to the topic is pursued in a way that is now irrelevant to that original topic. Someone has gone off (or "flown off") on a tangent.

of calculus, tells how he is "reminded of the time when . . ." and proceeds to relate a long personal anecdote. Secondly, pursuing a tangent presents a problem when, in a dispute, someone evades the issue by changing the subject subtly. When this happens, the other person may feel frustrated in his or her attempt to develop a continuous line of reasoning or may even fail to notice the shift (as with the straw man), unwittingly getting wrapped up in the discussion of the tangential point.

Shifting Ground

Try to catch a grasshopper. It's not easy because the grasshopper won't stay in one place and because it jumps so quickly from one position to another.

Sometimes we get off track by "shifting ground." Like the grasshopper, we won't stay in one position. The sidetrack of **shifting ground** appears when the reasoner changes her or his own position without acknowledging that any shift whatsoever has taken place.

When we shift ground, we do something similar to the setting up of a straw man. However, rather than misrepresenting another person's view or failing to notice that this person has misinterpreted our own view, we initiate a misinterpretation of what we have already said (or written).

Very often such a shift takes place when the reasoner recognizes a weakness in the position or reasoning that she or he has already presented. Still, as with setting up a straw man, this can be the result of mere inattention. Here is an example of the sidetrack of shifting ground.

EXAMPLE

Upset by the grade report he has just received, showing his marks for the previous semester, Samuel complains about grading in general.

"There shouldn't be any grades," he laments. "If learning is our purpose here, and grades—which don't always show how much you learned—are so overemphasized that they become almost our sole focus, what's the point?"

Although Leila understands Samuel's frustration, she is not one to stifle her own comment when she sees another side to the issue. "Well, it's true," concedes Leila. "Grades are overemphasized. Many students are more concerned with their grades than with what they learn in a class. Many *teachers*, knowing that grades are important to students, stick tightly to a schedule so that all the intended material can be covered. They pass up those opportunities to pursue a topic in depth if the digression is not scheduled and won't be 'testable.' Still, it wouldn't be such a good idea to eliminate grades altogether. Students *need* feedback. It's useful to know how well you have mastered the material. Sometimes you don't know it as well as you think you do. It would be foolish not to have a way to communicate the student's degree of success."

Leila's comments seem reasonable to Samuel. "Well, of course you need to be able to do that. I'm not saying that all grading should be abolished. My point is that a different system of grading should be used—one that avoids the problems of the system we use now. That's all I'm saying!" ∎

It seems that Samuel's game is "catch me if you can." His stated position—"there shouldn't be any grades"—is criticized, and he shifts ground to a different position—"a different system of grading should be used"— as if this were nothing more than the point he had originally intended. Perhaps Leila's criticism of this position will occasion another shift. How frustrating this must be for Leila! There is nothing wrong with changing your mind. The admirable characteristic of open-mindedness often dictates such a move. The *unacknowledged* shifts are the ones that threaten—and sometimes kill—progress in evaluating the subject under consideration. We must be willing, when appropriate, to concede that our own previous position was too extreme and that it must be modified or that we were simply wrong.

■

EXERCISES

1.1 Basic

In each of the following cases, a "sidetrack" occurs. Decide where the shift takes place and determine whether it is a sidetrack that involves (a) getting personal, (b) setting up a straw man, (c) shifting ground, or (d) pursuing a tangent.

1. Jack Smith authored an article in the *Los Angeles Times Magazine*, October 6, 1985, titled "That Lingering Glance." Consider this excerpt.

   I don't happen to believe in telepathy—the transference of ideas from one person to another by some means other than the normal sensory channels: writing, the spoken word, body language, et cetera.

   I have highly intelligent friends who do believe in telepathy, or extrasensory perception, but I suspect that they have merely imagined receiving messages from persons to whom they are very close and whose thoughts they might intuit.

   To those who are excited by the prospect of extrasensory phenomena, I merely point out that if it were really possible for us to read one another's thoughts, society would be impossible. No marriage, no friendship, no business association, no social relationship of any kind could survive such insights.*

2. Here is an excerpt from a *U.S. News & World Report* interview (September 29, 1986 issue) with Scott Helband, a college admissions officer at Yale from 1982 to 1984.

   Q: Is the essay the most important part of the application?

   A: Because each piece really weaves an application together to portray the fabric of a human being, there isn't one document that is all important.

Jack Smith, "That Lingering Glance," Los Angeles Times Magazine, October 6, 1985. Reprinted with permission of the Los Angeles Times.

3. On July 27, 1986, during the New York Yankees–Minnesota Twins baseball game, two radio announcers had the following exchange on the air. Twins pitcher Burt Blyleven had just struck out Claudell Washington for the first out in the eighth inning, and Don Mattingly had stepped up to bat:

Announcer R: Third time Washington has struck out this afternoon, and all three occasions have been called third strikes. So Washington with three strikeouts, and for Blyleven that's his fourth strikeout of the afternoon. First pitch to Mattingly, ball one.

Announcer M: But he got the right blow in at the right time. [In his third time at bat that afternoon, Washington had hit a two-run home run.]

R: That's right. Pitch is inside for a ball. Two and 0. You could strike out three times if you hit me a game-winning home run every day.

M: You'd have, ah, you'd be batting .250.

R: You'd make a million and a half dollars a year.

M: What?

R: Mattingly loops one high and deep to right field. [Tom] Brunansky moves toward the line, and this is a foul ball. Brunansky came over and ran out of room.

M: What'd you say, you'd be making a half—one and a half trillion dollars? Is that what you said?

R: No, not quite that high. You'd be making a million dollars a year.

M: A home run, a home run a day?

R: A game-winning homer just about every day.

M: Oh, you mean a game-winning homer.

R: Yeah, a game-winning homer.

M: It doesn't make any difference. A home run or a game-winning home run, do you know how many home runs that is?

R: Well—

M: They would build a stadium for you.

R: They'd—

M: And you would own two or three American League clubs yourself if you hit a home run a day.

R: But you're only a .200 hitter, though. See—

M: .250 hitter.

R: Well—

M: If you went four times, on the average they're going up four times [a game], right?

R: Well, you'd be about, between .250 and—

M: I'm closer to a million and a, I'm closer to one and a half trillion than you would be to a million.

R: One and a half trillion.

M: If a guy hit a home run a day.

R: You can't fathom a trillion.

M: Every day.

R: How much is a trillion?

M: A trillion is just a number.

R: It's a lot of money.

M: A trillion's only, a trillion's only a debt.

R: Oh, that's right.

M: That's all it is, it's a number, it's a, it's, pick a number.

R: Pick a number.

M: A trillion, right. Nobody knows how much a trillion is.

R: It's near infinity. Ball three now to Mattingly, 3 and 1.*

4. In an article published in the *Washington Post* (National Weekly Edition) on November 10, 1986, "The Nobel Prize for the Obvious," James M. Buchanan is said to have won the Nobel Prize in economics for very ordinary, unremarkable opinions. The following paragraph is taken from that article.

Buchanan opposes pork-barrel politics. Who doesn't? He's cynical about politicians afraid to raise taxes. Who isn't? Among his long-

*Reported in Harper's, *October 1986. Reprinted with permission of Adler Communications, Inc.*

held remedies for curing deficits, Buchanan joins the flat-earthers and full-mooners in calling for "the constitutional restraint" of a balanced-budget amendment. The professor, whose salary of $114,100 is $39,000 higher than that of the members of Congress whose big-spending ways he deplores, argues that we should have deficits only in times of depression or major wars.*

5. *Rubens:* All successful politicians—in whatever official position—are corrupt. You need to be willing to make moral compromises to get ahead in politics.

   Larkin: What about Mayor Atwood? When you supported him in that letter to the editor last year, you wrote that he had never been involved in dirty dealings and that, as far as you're concerned, he was entirely trustworthy.

   Rubens: That may be possible in local politics. In fact, I'm sure that the mayor is a good man. I only said that in big-time national politics, you've got to be corrupt to get ahead.

6. The manager of the college baseball team pulled aside the second baseman. "David, we have just a few minutes before the game. I want to explain what I think you can do to improve your batting and lift you from the slump you're in." David listened.
   "You have an unusual stance at the plate. I think that if you adjust your stance as I'll suggest, you'll have more success. You know, a lot of professional baseball players have actually done quite well with peculiar batting stances. Smokey Burgess was one. Smokey used to . . ." The tales of stars of the past go on until the manager is interrupted by his coach, who says it's game time.

7. *Steve:* The ancient Greeks made great strides in scientific thinking.

   Lisa: Oh, come on. Just think of the staggering multitude of advances made in the past hundred years: the harnessing of electricity and Einsteinian physics, for example. Don't these sorts of examples prove to you that the Greeks weren't the smartest people in history?

8. The high-school teacher insists that unless his student puts in more study time or gets a tutor, he'll fail the course. "You would probably like it if I failed, wouldn't you?" responds the student. "I'm not going to even talk to you about this."

---

*The Washington Post, *November 10, 1986.* © 1986 Washington Post Writers Group. Reprinted with permission of the Washington Post Writers Group.*

9. After a taste of LaMarr's morning coffee, Jess asks, "Did you do something different when you were making the coffee this morning? It tastes just a bit different."

    "Look," snaps LaMarr, "if you don't like the taste of the coffee, you can just make up a pot for yourself!"

10. Lieutenant Wren, ending a few minutes of quiet reflection, comments earnestly to her husband, "You know, I'm finding that I really respect Major Zeleny." Her husband responds, "I'm glad to hear that. It's certainly important to like the people you work with."

11. During a study break at the college library, Kent mentions his new history course to Paige. "My history course is really going to be difficult. In the first two weeks, we've covered three long chapters in the textbook. There are weekly assignments in addition to four major papers that we'll have to write."

    Paige is puzzled. "You told me before that this course was not required for graduation. I don't understand. If you don't like the course, why don't you just drop it?"

12. Professor Scolis says, "Education in the United States is sorely in need of reform. Memorization of facts is still emphasized more than creative and critical thinking skills." Professor Libris responds, "The view you advance with that comment is no better. After all, if the schools required no memorization of facts, students would not be adequately prepared in subjects like math and history."

13. After years of concern about his father, young Everett finally ventures a comment to Dad about the prospects of lung disease if he continues smoking cigarettes. Dad claims, at first, that there is no real danger. As Everett quotes statistics, Dad grows sterner. Finally, Dad says, "Everett, you are so obsessed with other people's well-being. When you grow up and are out on your own, you're going to find that you need to keep from sticking your nose into other people's business."

14. Dear George,

    I'm writing to explain more clearly why I felt I had to fire you from your job here at Phantos Corporation last week.

    Although no one could seriously fault you for failing to anticipate that the machines would not support the heavier metal casings, our concerns focus on your handling of the immediate results of that mismatch. We on the Executive Review Committee considered three specific courses of action that you might have taken. First, you might have informed Ed Hollings, who, as Second Vice-President, oversees the acquisition of new materials and the adoption of new processes. He then could have taken the responsibility for continuing the manufacture or he could have informed Andy Levine. I'm sure you haven't heard, as a matter of fact, that Andy went into the hospital for emergency surgery just two days ago. He is in serious condition and perhaps, since you were one of the people he liked best, you could send him a card or call his wife to express your concern. I'm sure that would be greatly appreciated.

It looks like Andy will be off the job for at least two months. We all wish him a speedy and complete recovery. He's a very good man.

Andy's address is Room 306B, Weinraub Memorial Hospital, in Kinsey City.

I'm sorry to send the bad news.

Regards,

Jim Leben

President

15. *Carolyn:* There aren't any places to get a decent education in this part of the state. You have to go outside the area to get quality schooling.

Sarah: The state university has a very good reputation scholastically.

Carolyn: Oh, I don't mean State. I mean the smaller local schools.

Sarah: Well, you know that Patterson College has some excellent programs. They have an archeology program that is better than most at big universities. And their art department is supposed to be excellent.

Carolyn: I don't mean that every single program is bad. It's just that these schools have a lot of weaker areas, too.

16.–17. Item 1 in Appendix B displays an article from the *Los Angeles Times* in which two sidetracks occur. For practice at locating sidetracks within a longer text, turn to Appendix B and test your skill. ■

■

CHAPTER HIGHLIGHTS

- Reasoning is not a skill that is altogether new to the average person. We normally reason quite well in everyday settings. Sometimes, however, we don't draw reasonable conclusions. This is often because of an emotional commitment for or against a particular view.

- Our *points of logical vulnerability* are those topics about which we have difficulty being objective and thinking clearly. We should be aware of them. A "win-lose" attitude can prevent us from keeping an open mind, but an attitude of fairmindedness ensures that we keep an open mind when our perspective differs from those of others.

- Staying on track—keeping to the point—is necessary if progress is to be made along a continuous line of reasoning. We can get off track in four primary ways: (1) *getting personal* instead of attacking a position or reasoning, (2) *setting up a straw man* that is a misrepresentation of another's view, (3) *pursuing a tangent* by being diverted from the original topic, and (4) *shifting ground* by misrepresenting our own prior position, thus eluding effective criticism.

For Further Reading

Adler, Mortimer. *How to Speak, How to Listen.* New York: Macmillan, 1983.
  A popular book that has several good chapters on reasonable conversation.

Chaffee, John. *Thinking Critically.* Boston: Houghton Mifflin, 1985.
  A textbook organized in a workbook format. Chapter 3, "Thinking Critically," offers exercises for analyzing "points of logical vulnerability" and "fairmindedness," although these expressions are not used.

Keyes, Ken, Jr. *Taming Your Mind.* Living Love Center, 1975.
  A simple, readable nonacademic guide to patterns of thinking that affect our perspective on everyday events. (This book was originally published by McGraw-Hill under the title, *How to Develop Your Thinking Ability.*)

St. Aubyn, Giles. *The Art of Argument.* Buchanan, NY: Emerson Books, 1962.
  A short book on reasoning in practical settings. Irrationality and prejudice are discussed in chapters 1 and 2.

Skwire, David. *Writing with a Thesis.* New York: Holt, Rinehart and Winston, 1985.
  A handbook of advice and examples focusing on logical and persuasive writing. This book touches on many of the skills in *Logic in Everyday Life.*

C H A P T E R

Premises and Conclusions

Almost all of us are good thinkers most of the time. The conclusions we draw need not be constantly revised. Still, we occasionally offer or accept reasoning that should not convince. We sense, on some of these occasions, that the reasoning is somehow faulty. However, if we do not feel confidence in our own abilities to scrutinize the reasoning and locate the step that causes the feeling of uneasiness, we are left with impressions and emotions, rather than a reliable pattern of thinking.

INFORMING VERSUS PERSUADING

Sometimes we use language, as we speak or write, to convey information. At other times we use language to persuade. Certainly the task of informing is often an important part of the task of persuading. Still, we can distinguish between these two general functions.* We most often wonder about questionable "reasoning" when the attempt is to persuade.

The press secretary to the President of the United States, as he describes to the press corps a typical day for the President, may begin by saying, "The President awakens at 5:30 A.M. and, during a brief 6:00 meeting, is updated on crucial national and international affairs by his top aides. At

---

*Other functions of language can also be identified. J. L. Austin, for example (in How to Do Things with Words, Harvard University Press, 1962 and elsewhere), describes the "performative" use of language. He observes that when we make a bet or pronounce marriage vows we thereby perform an act. Language in such cases is neither informative nor persuasive.

Furthermore, reasoning takes place in circumstances other than the typically "persuasive." We offer reasons in giving explanations (for example, suggesting a likely cause for a past event) and in making personal decisions. Still, each of these is related to persuading. Explanatory hypothesis is discussed in Chapter 8, decision making in Chapter 10.

6:20 he breakfasts with . . ." If the press secretary continues in this manner, we can see that he is informing rather than attempting to persuade. Now, it is certainly possible that under the guise of informing, he is hoping also to persuade us of something—perhaps that the President is a conscientious, hard-working person. However, the secretary's task can still be identified as primarily, or at least formally, one of informing.

When someone gives *reasons* for believing something, apparently hoping that another person will come to the same conclusion by considering those reasons, the discourse is geared toward persuasion. When the political campaign manager says, "You should vote for my candidate because he has experience and is the only honest person who is running for this office," he or she is involved in an attempt to *persuade* the listeners.

When we try to be persuasive, we should do our best to be both rational and fair. It's what we would hope for from others, and it's what we owe them as well.

Unfortunately, people are sometimes convinced with poor reasoning. Sometimes this is because they are not listening carefully. Sometimes it is because they are mystified by the reasoning but are embarrassed to admit it because they fear that the reasoning is good and they don't want to appear stupid. Often it is because one of their points of logical vulnerability is being addressed.

We can sometimes be persuasive without good reasoning. We can also have good reasoning without successfully persuading! We will have to consider, then, not only how to reason well but also how to present our position in a fair but effective way. We need to strive for correct *and* persuasive reasoning.

A basic skill, necessary for a fair evaluation of the merit of any persuasive reasoning, is that of identifying the point to be proven and the evidence offered in support of it. This important skill is discussed next.

THE POINT TO BE PROVEN AND THE EVIDENCE

Before deciding whether someone's reasoning is good, you must mentally separate the point to be proven from the evidence that is offered as support for that point. If this is not done correctly, you will be evaluating a straw man counterfeit of the intended line of reasoning. If you lose sight of this distinction between the point to be proven and the supporting evidence in reasoning that you have constructed on your own, then the danger is that you may be unable to clarify or defend the reasoning adequately.

SKILL

Skill 2. Finding the conclusion and premises

Identify the intended point to be proven and the evidence offered in support of it.

Why this skill is important

To see if the reasoning makes sense, we must find out if the evidence leads to the intended point. Thus, we must clearly recognize both what that point is and how it is supported. ∎

To develop the skill of correctly identifying these basic elements in someone's reasoning, this chapter is divided into the following sections:

The conclusion

Conclusion indicators and premise indicators

Multiple conclusions

Unstated conclusions and premises

Parenthetical statements and tangents

The Conclusion

The **conclusion,** in someone's attempt to persuade, is the statement that presents the point to be proven. Whether we are reading written material or listening to a friend talk, if the purpose of the communication is persuasion, then we should quickly scan, visually or mentally, for the conclusion. In fact, *we cannot hope to analyze the reasoning unless we can first identify the conclusion.* At this point, read the skill box above.

If someone stopped you by the side of the road and asked, "Is this the best route to get there?" you would probably respond, "To get *where?*" Similarly, we certainly can't tell if a person's reasoning leads correctly to its destination—the point to be proven—unless we know what that destination is.

Before discussing how to identify the conclusion, we should define two words: **argument** and **premise.** When we consider reasoning, the word *argument* is used to refer to the conclusion and to the statements that present the evidence—the reasons for believing the conclusion. (In this sense of the word, *argument* does not suggest the red faces and white knuckles of dispute, as it does when we speak of "having an argument with Dad.") A statement that presents a reason for believing the conclusion is called a *premise.*

By its name, it would seem that a conclusion should *conclude* an argument—that it should come at the end. Sometimes the conclusion does appear at the end of the argument. Consider, for example, the following reasoning, which ends with the conclusion that "Castro must be a ruthless leader."

> Stalin was a dictator and he was ruthless. Hitler was a dictator and he was ruthless. Castro is a dictator. So he must be a ruthless leader too.

The conclusion is presented after the evidence. There are three premises; they are the first three sentences. The final sentence states the conclusion that the speaker or writer wants you to accept on the basis of the evidence offered. Notice, however, that the argument is not a good one. Even if the premises are true—and even if the conclusion is true—the truth of the premises is insufficient, taken alone, to *prove* that the conclusion is true. This matter is discussed in chapters 3 and 4.

This reasoning could, however, be presented differently. For example, the conclusion could be stated before the premises. Consider the following presentation of the same reasoning.

> Castro must be a ruthless leader because he's a dictator. Think about other dictators: Stalin was a dictator and he was ruthless. Hitler was a dictator and *he* was ruthless. Don't you see a connection here?

Here we have the same three premises and the same conclusion. Besides the slightly different wording, the only difference is that the conclusion is presented before the premises.

Another alternative is to offer a conclusion after the beginning but before the end of the argument. Reasons for believing it are now presented both before and after the conclusion. The argument about Castro can now be seen with yet another construction.

> Castro is a dictator, so he must be a ruthless leader. Hitler was a dictator and he was ruthless. Stalin, another dictator, was ruthless as well. It's all so obvious!

Here the conclusion is presented after one premise but before the others. The conclusion, in fact, can appear almost anywhere. This is so in the short argument we have been examining, and it is so in nearly any argument you can imagine. Now, if the conclusion can appear almost anywhere in the argument, and if we cannot analyze the reasoning unless we first locate the conclusion, it is reasonable to ask "How do I find the conclusion in someone's reasoning?"

First, notice that you normally have no trouble determining what someone's point is in everyday conversation. In the process of learning the English language, you have become adept at identifying the main point and—at least generally—following the reasoning. Don't be confused by the use of the special term *conclusion*. You have been identifying conclusions virtually all your life.

Secondly, you can watch for **conclusion indicators** and **premise indicators.** Although we normally follow arguments easily, on some occasions the flow of the reasoning may not be obvious. Perhaps an unfamiliar and technical topic is being discussed. Perhaps the argument is unusually detailed and complex. Perhaps our emotions are clouding our thoughts. In such circumstances, we may need to think through an argument carefully in order to follow it.

Conclusion Indicators and Premise Indicators

We can often locate a conclusion by finding a conclusion indicator in the argument. A conclusion indicator is a word or phrase that commonly precedes a conclusion. Go back to the three versions of the argument about Castro. In two of them the same word introduces the conclusion that "Castro must be a ruthless leader." (The exception, notably, is the version in which the conclusion appears first.) The word is *so*. This word is perhaps the most frequently used conclusion indicator in everyday conversation. You should be able to think of other conclusion indicators. Among the most familiar are *therefore, thus,* and *consequently.*

These, however, are not the only conclusion indicators. Other words, such as the seldom used *hence,* also serve as conclusion indicators. There are also phrases that perform this same task of introducing a conclusion. Some examples are *it follows that . . . , we can conclude that . . . ,* and *this proves that . . . .* You may be able to think of many other ways of introducing a conclusion. So do not merely learn the words and phrases mentioned here. Listen carefully to persuasive reasoning when it is presented by people around you. Develop a sense of the variety of ways to signal the arrival of a conclusion.

Premise indicators are also helpful when you are trying to follow someone's reasoning. A premise indicator is a word or phrase that commonly precedes a premise. Most common are the words *because* and *since.* Again, various phrases will also perform the same task. Examples are *due to the fact that . . . , in light of the fact that . . . ,* and *for the following reasons . . . .* Again, you may be able to think of many more.

Now, premise and conclusion indicators can be very helpful when you are trying to follow a line of argumentation. Do not, however, rely mindlessly on them. The English language does not function strictly mechanically, so that a particular word or phrase always has the same meaning or purpose wherever it occurs. As we know, the context of the expression—where it occurs in a sentence or paragraph, the words around it, and even the occasion and circumstances of the communication—helps us to understand how the expression is being used in each case. This insight applies to premise and conclusion indicators in that many expressions that commonly introduce premises and conclusions sometimes serve other purposes.

Consider, for example, the word *so*. In the sentence "I was so angry," the word indicates intensity, and in the sentence "So far from home was the pup that he had to run for two hours before seeing the familiar front gate of the farm," the word indicates extent. In neither case does the word *so* serve as a conclusion indicator. Similarly, in the sentence "Thus far we have encountered no difficulty," the word *thus* does not function as a conclusion indicator. In the sentence "I've been lonely since you've been gone," the word *since* does not function as a premise indicator.

You must ultimately rely on your own good sense of the intention of the reasoner when you listen or read. Premise and conclusion indicators are a great help, but you must still be able to think through the reasoning. Finally, be aware that sometimes the line of reasoning cannot be clearly detected simply because it was not clear in the mind of the reasoner in the first place.

Multiple Conclusions

Is it possible for an argument to have more than one conclusion? Yes. As you know, a person sometimes has more than one point to make about a topic that is under discussion. If, in the course of a discussion, evidence is offered for more than one point, then we have multiple conclusions. The person is arguing for more than one point.

There are two kinds of arguments in which we might find multiple conclusions. First, we have the arguments in which more than one conclusion is presented as following from the same premises. Here is an example.

The defendant can be shown to have been out of the state at the time. Thus, he could not have been the man who robbed the bank. Nor could he have been the driver of the getaway vehicle.

In this argument, there is only one premise. From that one premise we draw two conclusions: the defendant could not have robbed the bank and he could not have driven the getaway vehicle. It is also possible, of course, to draw multiple conclusions from a *set* of premises.

Secondly, we have the "stepladder" arguments in which a conclusion is offered as a premise in support of a further conclusion. Consider the following conversational passage.

> You ask if I'm *certain* that the younger Harrell boy is too young to be served alcohol legally? I surely am. I remember that two years ago he was still too young to vote. The voting age is eighteen. Now, that means that he can't be more than nineteen years old. And the drinking age is twenty-one. Obviously, then, the boy is too young to be served alcohol—at least legally.

In this passage, the **ultimate conclusion,** stated both at the beginning and at the end, is that the Harrell boy is too young to be served alcohol legally. But the statement "he can't be more than nineteen years old" can also be called a conclusion because evidence is offered to support this claim. It is not, however, the ultimate conclusion to be drawn. It is, instead, a **transitional conclusion** that, once supported, is presented as a premise in another phase of the reasoning.

The argument can now be reconstructed and understood like this:

Premise: He could not vote legally two years ago.

Premise: The voting age is eighteen

Conclusion: He can't be more than nineteen.

Premise: He can't be more than nineteen.

Premise: The drinking age is twenty-one.

Conclusion: He cannot be served alcohol legally.

It's as if there were two arguments, with the conclusion of one being identical with a premise in the other. Be aware, however, that the ultimate conclusion need not be presented last. It can be presented at the beginning or elsewhere. An ultimate conclusion, then, is a statement that in a particular argument serves only as a conclusion; it is not a premise in support of any further point. A transitional conclusion is a statement that serves as both a premise and a conclusion in the same argument. In other words, the transitional conclusion is a statement that is offered as evidence for another statement *and* has one or more statements offered as evidence for *it.* Statements that serve as premises but not as conclusions of either type may simply be called **basic premises.**

To save ourselves the repetitious writing of *premise* and *conclusion* when we reconstruct arguments, we can write out the premises without the label, then draw a line under them as if we were going to see "what they add up to," and write the conclusion under that line. A "therefore" sign (∴) may precede the conclusion.

Now, if we write out the transitional conclusion only once, the preceding argument can be sketched like this:

$$
\left\{
\begin{array}{l}
\left\{
\begin{array}{l}
\text{He could not legally vote two years ago.} \\
\text{The voting age is eighteen.} \\
\hline
\therefore \text{ He can't be more than nineteen.}
\end{array}
\right. \\
\\
\text{The drinking age is twenty-one.} \\
\hline
\therefore \text{ He cannot be served alcohol legally.}
\end{array}
\right.
$$

The braces that frame the two subarguments may be omitted.

Unstated Conclusions and Premises

Sometimes, even when the point of an argument is quite obvious, no sentence in the passage actually states this conclusion. You may listen or look as carefully as you can, but the statement that presents the conclusion is nowhere to be found.

An unstated conclusion may still be implied or suggested by the premises. In the following example, the conclusion is implied but not actually presented in words.

> The murder weapon was found in Cain's possession, and only his fingerprints were on it. He had one of the strongest of motives—revenge. Finally, only he had an opportunity to be alone with the victim. Need I say more?

The conclusion that a listener is intended to draw from these observations is obviously that Cain is guilty of the murder. The unstated conclusion is signalled by the statement "Need I say more?" This tells us that there *is* something more that has not been said and suggests that the listener should easily identify the unstated conclusion. Various other phrases might be used to signal the unstated conclusion in this way. For example, consider that the statement "The conclusion, my friend, is obvious" also suggests both that there is an unstated conclusion and that it is obvious.

Often, although the conclusion is unstated, no signalling phrase is offered.

Only three people knew where the map was hidden—Varley, Garth, and Smythe. Now the map is gone, but it had been hidden so well that no one could have found it by mistake. And two of the men—Varley and Garth—have perfect alibis.

If this were from the dialogue of a movie script, we could imagine the speaker and his listener exchanging knowing looks at this point, both having drawn the same conclusion. What clearly follows from these statements, which serve as premises, is that *Smythe took the map.* Although there is no signalling phrase to suggest that we identify the missing conclusion, the point of the speaker's observations is nevertheless obvious.

Premises, as well as conclusions, are sometimes unstated but implied. The unstated premise can be considered to be an *assumption*—it is taken to be true but is not actually offered as part of the argument.

In some cases, the premise is left unstated simply because it is too obvious to mention. This is the case in the following example.

Of course the United States is larger than England. Why, Oklahoma itself is larger than England!

The conclusion is that the United States is larger than England. The single premise states that Oklahoma is larger than England. That premise alone, however, does not establish the conclusion that the United States is larger than England unless we also recognize that Oklahoma is not as large as the United States. The speaker has not, however, offered this as a premise. Should she have done so? Certainly there is no need if she knows that the listener is aware of the fact already. Almost without exception, we can consider this premise to be known if the listener is an American.

One advantage of discourse between persons who have a common culture is that many things go unsaid. We can assume, in most cases, that a fellow American will know that Oklahoma is one of the fifty states in the Union. This is only one example of the information-sharing characteristic of a culture that allows people to reasonably make certain assumptions. We can usually assume also that when we refer to the Super Bowl, most Americans will know already that this is a football game and that football games are played with a somewhat oblong ball. We do not need to supply this information in the form of premises. (The likelihood that this information can be safely assumed goes up or down depending, of course, on which Americans we are addressing.) We can also generally assume that when we refer to the President of the United States, Americans will know that the office of the President is an elective one.

A culture, however, need not be a national group. As the word is being used here, any grouping of people who share significant similarities and information comprises a culture. When one physician, for example, addresses another, certain assumptions about the other's knowledge of technical terms are normally made. The physician need not explain such terms to another physician, although the absence of such an explanation might be foolish when addressing most nonphysicians. If the physician is arguing for a certain stand on a health-care issue, certain premises that would be presented in the argument to the nonphysician could be omitted in the argument to the physician.

Of course, there are many such subcultures—information-sharing, often value-sharing communities within a larger culture. They are based on professional groupings, youth movements, and many other commonalities.

Missing premises are notably important when they are contentious—possibly but not obviously true, and thus subject to contention. Such premises are often value judgments or questionable generalizations. It is especially important that we recognize these unstated but essential premises in our own or in another's reasoning. The questionable assumption may be that your own nation must be in the right in a particular international conflict, or that members of a certain minority group or social group will hold a particular position on a certain issue. With unstated assumptions like this, it is necessary to be very aware of our points of logical vulnerability.

Parenthetical Statements and Tangents

Not every statement offered as part of an argument has a role as conclusion or premise. Some of the statements offered might actually be not at all essential to the success of the argument. In looking for the conclusion, we need to recognize such nonessential statements so we can more easily follow the reasoning.

Sometimes statements within an argument are made only parenthetically. In written material, parenthetical remarks may be marked off with parentheses—( ). The sign (marks the beginning of the statement and the sign) marks the end of the statement. In a spoken argument, we do not have the visual help of these signs. Sometimes in written material, a statement may function parenthetically but still not be signalled by parentheses. We must recognize that such statements are neither conclusions nor premises. The following short argument includes such a statement.

> There's no reason to worry about the party. John has taken care of the refreshments. Ann will have the whole house decorated and ready. And Phil will have party games arranged. Uncle Ed did that last year. Do you remember?

The conclusion is that there is no need to worry about the party. The reasons for believing this rest on the arrangements being made by John, Ann, and

Phil. The statement "Uncle Ed did that last year" is only a parenthetical remark. Likewise, the "Do you remember?" is not an essential part of the argument.

When we follow up a parenthetical remark with continued discussion of that or another insufficiently relevant point, we find ourselves pursuing a tangent. In this case, the entire topic of discussion shifts, at least for a while. In the example above, the speaker may go on to talk about Uncle Ed. Such remarks would be neither premises nor conclusions. Similarly, in an effort to prove that American military strength should be increased, the arguer may condemn a lack of moral fiber in the country. A single remark or two of this sort, if insufficiently relevant to the conclusion, may be considered parenthetical. If the remarks continue so that the focus of discussion shifts, then we would consider the speaker to have embarked on the pursuit of a tangent. In either case, such irrelevant remarks should not be considered as part of the argument unless they are really intended as evidence for the conclusion. In that case, the statements would simply fail to present adequate support for the conclusion, thus detracting from the strength of the overall argument.

Advice on Where to Place Your Conclusion

If you want your own argument to be understood easily, consider stating your conclusion at the beginning of your argument. By stating the conclusion at the beginning, you allow the listener or reader to evaluate the relevance and strength of each premise as it is presented. If a person knows the point the premise is intended to support while that premise is being presented, then evaluating the argument may not require a mental *reconstruction* of the argument. By stating the conclusion late in the argument, you do require the other person to think back through each premise after the point the premises are meant to prove is revealed. (Would you want to bet on the accuracy of the reconstruction?) There will, of course, be exceptions to this general advice.

■

EXERCISES

2.1 Basic

In each of the following arguments, find the conclusion. There are no multiple conclusions, and there are no unstated conclusions or premises to watch for.

Each argument includes at least one premise or conclusion indicator that can help as you try to find the conclusion.

1. That house is too expensive for you, because once you would have paid the loan you'd have only $250 a month to live on. You have at least that much in monthly bills now. On top of this, your job is not very secure.

2. All Italians are Roman Catholics, and some Roman Catholics are dishonest. Therefore, some Italians are dishonest.

3. The other contending teams in the National League West will not be much improved next year, so the Astros are likely to win the division again, since they are likely to be even stronger than they were this year. And this year they won the division easily.

4. I don't like math, so I'm sure there's no way I could pass that math course even if I did register for it. It's supposed to be a very difficult course, and from what I hear, the instructor is just about no help at all!

5. My roommate is moving out. Consequently, I will have to move out as well. I can barely pay my present portion of the rent.

6. No priests are dishonest, but many of them are intelligent. Therefore, there are at least some intelligent people who aren't dishonest.

7. Mr. Allison must be in charge today because whenever Ms. Wilkinson is out of the office, Mr. Allison is in charge. And she *is* out of the office today.

8. Mike has to take either algebra or statistics next year. Since Mike always takes the course with the shortest textbook and the algebra textbook is shorter, it's clear that he'll be taking the algebra course when next year rolls around.

9. If I pass at least one of my two math courses, Math 12 or Math 15, I will be able to graduate this year. It is certain that I will at least pass Math 12. Thus I will undoubtedly be graduating this year.

10. That bird has a swooping flight pattern so it couldn't be a finch, because finches don't have flight patterns like that.

2.2 Moderately Difficult

In each of the following arguments, find the conclusion. There are no multiple conclusions, and there are no unstated conclusions or premises to watch for. These arguments, however, have no easily recognizable conclusion or premise indicators.

1. Your talent at commercial art is among the best in the country. The company knows that. Everyone involved in making the hiring decision already likes you. Of course you'll get the job. No one else who is remotely qualified has even applied for it.

2. This will be a good Christmas. Aunt Ann will be visiting us this year, and she's always fun. Betty will be home for Christmas this year. And for once we have enough money to buy everyone a decent present. Besides, the first Christmas in a new house is always exciting.

3. I need a computer. My business accounts are now too complicated to keep organized without a computer. It would help with the kids' homework. And Susan could use it for word processing in her college classwork.

4. Anger is not productive. Neither are the other hostile emotions such as jealousy and envy. Any nonproductive emotion is to be avoided. Clearly, then, we should try to maintain a sense of serenity and emotional balance in our lives.

5. The YMCA deserves the support of our community. It offers programs for senior citizens. Most of the inexpensive physical education and crafts classes for children are available through the YMCA. It continually offers quality programs on a nonprofit basis.

2.3 Difficult

In each of the following arguments, find the conclusions. There may be more than one conclusion in an argument. If so, determine which conclusions are transitional and which are ultimate. Decide whether any important conclusions or premises are unstated.

1. Part of a letter from J. G. of Santa Cruz, California, to the editor of *Newsweek*, November 24, 1986:

   Since the International Court in The Hague has condemned U.S. harassment of Nicaragua, it seems to me that our government's covert and overt support of the contras is an act of international terrorism.

2. A foreign language is an important subject of study for college students. Through studying foreign languages, students learn about diverse cultures. They also learn about conceptualization by seeing how parallel words in different languages are not completely interchangeable. No college student's schedule should omit a foreign language, even if it is not required by the school.

3. A foreign language is an important subject of study for college students. Through studying foreign languages, students learn about diverse cultures. They also learn about conceptualization by seeing how parallel words in different languages are not completely interchangeable. No college student's schedule should omit a foreign language, even if it is not required by the school. You really ought to find a place in your college career for this subject, Steve.

4. From the *National Review*, November 7, 1986:

> President Reagan has shown again, politics aside, what a fine man he is. In his magnanimous speech at the opening of the Jimmy Carter Library, he toasted Carter's character while never diluting their differences. He did a similar thing five years ago when he presented Ethel Kennedy with a special Congressional medal for RFK that Carter had refused to issue during the bitter 1980 primaries. Ronald Reagan's gift for sentiment without sentimentality is rare in politics, and is appreciated as part of his special makeup.

5. We have to decide which movie to see tonight. We can go to either of the two movie theaters in town, the State or the Diamond. But the State isn't really a possibility, since you refuse to go into that part of town. It seems, then, that we'll be out of the theater in time for dinner, because the show at the Diamond is an early one.

6. You should invest that extra money in IBM, Tom. I read that a *Fortune* magazine survey determined IBM to be the company most admired by corporate executives and financial experts. That must mean that IBM is the best stock investment a person can make.

7. The third witness must have been bribed. If he had been telling the truth, he would have met my gaze as I stared at him. But he didn't meet my gaze at all. The only motive for him to lie in this situation is bribery.

8. From a letter written by L.W. and P.W. of Danville, California, to the editor of *Newsweek*, November 24, 1986:

> The Contadora group, a coalition of governments in Central America founded in 1983 and dedicated to encouraging nonviolent, democratic solutions to regional problems, continues its search for multilateral solutions. Why don't we give our support to the Contadoras instead of the Contras? Every act of violence in our world brings us closer to the possibility of global nuclear war. We have the responsibility to move in the opposite direction.

9. From the *National Review,* November 7, 1986, in reference to the U.S.-Soviet summit meeting at Reykjavík, Iceland, which resulted in no major agreements:

> Reagan didn't sign anything, so the Summit was a "failure." And Yalta was a success.

10. From a magazine advertisement for independent insurance agents:

> An agent who works for one company can only offer you the policies that his company sells. An Independent Insurance Agent represents <u>several</u> companies. So your Independent Agent can help you select the right coverage at the right price because there are <u>more</u> policies from which to choose. The evidence is clear.

11. From *Home* magazine, January 1986:

> The relocation [of the family barn, which was to be converted to a residence] had to wait until a period when the ground was hard and stable enough to support the barn's weight. Thus, the dead of winter, when the soil was frozen solid, was the only appropriate time to tackle the challenge.

12. From George F. Will, "Immersed in a Sea of Silence," *Newsweek,* October 27, 1986:

> Which is worse, blindness or deafness? Most people might say blindness because of the fear of colliding with the sharp edges of the physical environment. But late in her life Helen Keller, deaf and blind from birth, said she wished she had done more to alleviate the plight of the deaf. Blindness is an environmental disability. Its primary effect is to separate the afflicted from things. Deafness is a communication difficulty that separates the deaf person from other people. ∎

CHAPTER HIGHLIGHTS

■ Sometimes, when we use language to speak or write, we intend only to inform. At other times we intend to persuade. In the persuasive effort, we can use good or bad reasoning. A basic skill, necessary for any fair evaluation of the merit of someone's reasoning, is that of identifying the point to be proven and the evidence offered in support of it.

- The conclusion of an argument is the statement that presents the point to be proven. The premises are the statements offered as reasons for believing that conclusion. *Conclusion indicators* and *premise indicators* help us to identify the conclusion and the premises.

- Sometimes the same premises lead directly to two or more conclusions. At other times, "stepladder" arguments are offered. Here, *transitional conclusions* serve both as premise and conclusion in the same argument, and *ultimate conclusions* serve only as conclusions. Statements that serve only as premises may be called *basic premises*.

- Premises that are unstated but implied may be contentious, requiring identification and evaluation. Conclusions may also be unstated.

- Some of the statements that occur throughout an argument may be neither premises nor conclusions. These *parenthetical statements* are not essential to the argument.

For Further Reading

Cederblom, Jerry, and David W. Paulson. *Critical Reasoning.* Belmont, CA: Wadsworth, 1986.

A textbook in which chapters 2 and 3 give a good, easy-to-read introduction to premises, conclusions, and argument structure.

Churchill, Robert Paul. *Becoming Logical.* New York: St. Martin's Press, 1986.

Another textbook with a good introduction to premises and conclusions.

C H A P T E R

THREE

Deductive Validity

S ometimes, when we say that a person is reasoning well, we mean that the conclusion follows from the premises, that the premises are adequate to establish the conclusion *apart from the question of whether the premises are true.* Thus, although the argument would be unacceptable, the reasoning itself might be said to be good. More often, when we say that a person is reasoning well, we mean more than this. We mean not only that the evidence leads to the conclusion but also that the evidence is reliable. Obviously, the desirable arguments are of this latter kind.

We can think of arguments as having both form and content. An argument has good form if its premises offer adequate support for its conclusion. An argument has good content if its premises are justifiable. Our arguments should have both good form and good content. Looking at the same point from another perspective, we can observe that bad arguments can be expected to lack good form or good content—or both. By evaluating arguments in terms of form and content, we can locate their weak points. This is a worthwhile skill, whether the reasoning is our own or someone else's.

If the reasoning is someone else's, and if you intend to point out the error for that person, you will know whether to attack a point of fact or a point of logic. If that person has committed errors of each type, content and form, you can attack either. Consider, however, the following suggestion. When errors of both form and content have been made, you will usually make your point more effectively if you focus on form rather than content—on the "logic" rather than the "facts." Why? The questionable premise will quite possibly express a belief that has been long and deeply held. It may concern a point of logical vulnerability for that person. Your contention of that premise may generate more heat than light, because it may be a point on which that person is *unwilling* to change. Besides, if it is a social, political, or religious issue, clear-cut proof of your view may be elusive. On the other hand, if you focus on form, suggesting that "even if everything you say is true, that still doesn't seem to prove your point," the other person may back off, admitting that at least some revision in the argument is required. This is a start. The person is reconsidering his or her argument.

VALIDITY AND SOUNDNESS

In some arguments, the premises lead with certainty to the conclusion. This is to say that they *prove* the conclusion. It is *not* to say whether the premises are true or false. Such arguments are deductively valid. In other words, a deductively valid argument has good—in fact, perfect—form. Other arguments in which the premises fall short of proving the conclusion beyond any possible doubt are not deductively valid, even if their premises are true. Again, a judgment about the validity of an argument is made independently of a judgment about the truth or falsity of the premises. Of course, not all arguments that are correctly persuasive establish the conclusion beyond any possible doubt. Arguments that have an acceptable form even though they are not deductively valid will be discussed in Chapter 4.

Clearly, your concerns as a thinker go beyond the issue of good form. You know that any acceptable argument will have good content as well: the premises will be true. In a sound argument, the premises lead with certainty to the conclusion *and* the premises are true. The argument is unsound if either of these two conditions is not met. In other words, a sound argument has both good form and good content. Its conclusion can be accepted as true. Turn your attention now to the skill box on page 38 before you go on.

To decide whether the reasoning in an argument is valid* (whether the evidence proves the conclusion), it is not necessary to concern yourself with the question of whether the premises are true. You can ignore the truth or falsity of the premises and still determine whether the argument is valid. *In a valid argument, if the premises were true, then the conclusion would have to be true.* This means that although the premises may or may not actually be true, you should *imagine* that they are, then ask if that shows beyond any possibility of doubt that the conclusion must be true. In other words, to determine whether an argument is valid, you ask, "If the premises were true, would the conclusion then have to be true?" A "yes" answer to this question indicates that the argument is valid. An answer of "no" or "maybe," or even "probably" indicates that the argument is not valid, a condition logicians describe by saying the argument is invalid.

---

*The terms valid *and* invalid *will be used in this chapter to refer to deductively valid and deductively invalid arguments. In the next chapter, deductive validity will be contrasted with inductive "strength." In an inductively strong argument, the premises render the conclusion probable but not certain.*

SKILL

Skill 3. Recognizing validity and soundness

Distinguish correctly between deductively valid and invalid arguments and between sound and unsound arguments.

Why this skill is important

We can separate good from bad "proofs" in this way. If a "proof" is inadequate, we can determine whether it is the form or the content that requires revision. ∎

Consider two more definitions of validity. They present the preceding point in different words.

1. An argument is valid when it is inconceivable for the premises to be true while the conclusion is false.

2. An argument is valid if, by accepting the evidence, we must also (to avoid contradicting ourselves) accept the conclusion.

The reasoning in the following argument would be valid, and the argument itself will be called a valid one, even though one of the premises is false.

Earth must be the fourth planet from the sun because there are nine known planets in our solar system, only five are farther from the sun, and no planet is the same distance from the sun as we are.

The conclusion, "Earth is the fourth planet from the sun," is stated at the beginning of the argument. The argument is valid because *if* the premises were true, then the conclusion would have to be true. The argument has good form; its premises establish its conclusion with certainty. However, since one premise, "only five [planets] are farther from the sun," is false, the argument does not have good content. This is not an acceptable argument, even though the reasoning is valid.

The following argument is also valid.

> Since all corporate executives are over fifty, and anyone over fifty has at least minor health problems, absolutely anyone who is a corporate executive will have health problems—at least minor ones.

The conclusion is stated last. Both premises in this argument are false, but the argument is valid because *if* it were true that all corporate executives were over fifty and *if* it were true that anyone over fifty had at least minor health problems, *then* it would necessarily be true that any corporate executive would have at least minor health problems.

Consider another argument.

> Neil Simon must have a vivid imagination because he's a dramatist and it's very common for dramatists to have vivid imaginations.

This argument is invalid because *even if* Neil Simon is a dramatist and *even if* it is very common for dramatists to have vivid imaginations (in other words, many of them have vivid imaginations), this would not prove that Simon is one of those with such an imagination. Notice that you might believe—or even *know* on other evidence—that the conclusion is true; you still would have to admit that the argument presented here is invalid.

To decide whether an argument is sound (and thus whether the conclusion should be accepted), you must determine whether it passes both of the following tests.

1. The argument must be valid.

2. All premises must be true.

Test 1 requires that the evidence actually prove the conclusion. Test 2 requires that the evidence be *good* evidence. Obviously, when good evidence proves the conclusion, that conclusion should be accepted as true. The argument has both good form (it has passed the first test) and good content (it has passed the second test). If the argument fails either test, it is unsound.

Call to mind the first two arguments used in the explanation of validity.

> Earth must be the fourth planet from the sun because there are nine known planets in our solar system, only five are farther from the sun, and no planet is the same distance from the sun as we are.

> Since all corporate executives are over fifty, and anyone over fifty has at least minor health problems, absolutely anyone who is a corporate executive will have health problems—at least minor ones.

Both arguments were valid; the conclusion followed from the premises. Thus, they pass the first test for soundness. But one premise in the first argument and both premises in the second argument are false. Thus, each argument fails the second test for soundness. Although these arguments have good form, they do not have good content.

The following argument is sound.

> Earth must be the third planet from the sun because there are nine known planets in our solar system, only six are farther from the sun, and no planet is the same distance from the sun as we are.

To check its validity, we ask, "*If* there were nine planets in our solar system, and if only six were farther from the sun, while no planet was the same distance from the sun as Earth, *then* would it have to be true that Earth was the third planet from the sun?" The answer is "yes," showing that the argument is valid. This argument clearly passes the first test for soundness. The other question to be asked is this: "Are all the premises true?" Again, the answer is "yes." Since the argument passes both tests, it is sound, and the conclusion must be true.

Notice that it is possible for an argument to be valid and sound, valid and unsound, or invalid and unsound. Only one combination is impossible. It is impossible for an argument to be invalid and sound since, in order to be a sound argument, it must pass test 1, which requires it to be a valid argument. By the definitions of the terms, then, no argument can be invalid and sound. If the argument is invalid, it is necessarily unsound—you don't even need to determine whether the premises are true or false.

Form	Content or Premises	Acceptability of Argument
Deductively valid	All true	Sound
	One or more false	Unsound
Deductively invalid	All true	Unsound
	One or more false	Unsound

Notice also that unsound arguments will not always have false conclusions. For that matter, invalid arguments will not always have false conclusions. Here we see an example of an argument that is invalid and therefore unsound. The conclusion, however, is true.

Coal production is a major industry in my home state of Pennsylvania, but Kentucky certainly produces even more coal than Pennsylvania. Why, when I spent a week in Kentucky last month, I saw coal mines and heard talk of coal almost everywhere. I was in Bell County, Harlan County, Letcher County, and Knott County. Coal seemed to be the major industry everywhere.

The conclusion of the person who is presenting this reasoning is that Kentucky produces more coal than Pennsylvania. While the conclusion is true and could be firmly established with the appropriate premises, this person has drawn the conclusion merely from casual observation on a week's trip to Kentucky. This is an invalid argument with a conclusion that happens to be true. (It can also be noted that Bell, Harlan, Letcher, and Knott counties are all located in the same part of the state; they are contiguous. They lie in the rich Appalachian Plateau mining area. Elsewhere in Kentucky, our rash thinker may not have made similar observations.)

Finally, bear in mind that an argument is not to be considered unsound merely because *you do not know* whether a premise is true. If the argument is valid, then it is sound if the premises are true but unsound if the premises are not true. If you are not certain about whether a premise is true or false, the argument's soundness is undetermined until you look into the matter sufficiently to establish whether it is sound. Further, if you incorrectly judge a valid argument's premises to be true or false, then you will be wrong when you assess its soundness. The soundness of deductive arguments does not depend on personal perspectives.

Checking Subarguments for Validity and Soundness

Look back to the section on multiple conclusions in the previous chapter. It was shown there that, in an argument, a statement may serve both as a conclusion and as a premise. Such a statement would be called a transitional conclusion. We saw that when there is a transitional conclusion, it's as if there were two or more arguments within one larger argument. These smaller arguments can be thought of as "subarguments."

Subarguments can be analyzed for deductive validity and soundness without reference to other subarguments. We can look for a time only at the premises and conclusion of that particular subargument, and we can ask (1) whether the conclusion follows necessarily and (2) whether the premises are true. We may find, after considering each subargument, that part of the larger argument is acceptable and part isn't. We may find errors in each part. We may find that the whole argument is acceptable and that the conclusion should be accepted.

The following passage contains two subarguments.

> Contrary to what some people say, there *are* warm-blooded animals that have no sense of taste. I can establish this point easily enough. First, observe that all whales are warm blooded. To see that this is true, just remember that all whales are mammals and that every mammal is a warm-blooded animal. Second, observe that it is true—check your encyclopedia—that most whales have no sense of taste.

The ultimate conclusion is stated at the beginning. The statement "I can establish this point easily enough" indicates that the evidence follows. The two premises are introduced with the words *first* and *second*. The second premise is unsupported, but the first premise is seen to be a transitional conclusion when we notice that two statements are offered as reasons for believing it. The final argument looks like this.

All whales are mammals.

Every mammal is a warm-blooded animal.
_____

∴ All whales are warm blooded.

Most whales have no sense of taste.
_____

∴ There *are* warm-blooded animals that have no sense of taste.

Looking at the subarguments, we find that each is valid, and research (this topic is examined in Chapter 9) will show that each is sound. Now, what if only one subargument within a larger argument were invalid, while the other subargument(s) were valid? Would the whole argument be useless? Not necessarily.

Although the premises that were intended to support a transitional conclusion may fail to provide adequate support, that transitional conclusion might still be true. If the listener or reader knows on other grounds that this poorly supported statement is actually true, he or she can accept it as a premise in the remaining argument, thus salvaging some insight from the original argument.

Three Patterns of Valid Reasoning

While the content of an argument—the bold or controversial or exciting or disgusting or simply interesting claims made through the premises—receives much attention, the form generally should receive more attention than it gets. You should learn to recognize basic patterns of good reasoning. This is best done through careful attention to the form of the reasoning you encounter in daily affairs. What follows is just a hint of the patterns to be discovered.

Hypothetical Syllogism   The following argument is valid though not sound:

> *If* you like the art of Jackson Pollock, *then* you really know your art.
>
> *If* you really know your art, *then* you will like the sculpture of Rodin.
> _____
> ∴ *If* you like the art of Jackson Pollock, *then* you will like the sculpture of Rodin.

By accepting the premises, we bind ourselves logically to an acceptance of the conclusion. Thus, the argument is valid.*

Make up your own example of this pattern of reasoning. Here is the pattern:

> If A, then B
>
> If B, then C
> _____
> ∴ If A, then C

Your example will be valid, too! This can be predicted because *any* argument with this form is necessarily valid. Such arguments are called **hypothetical syllogisms.**

Some arguments with "if" premises and an "if" conclusion are not valid, however. If the repeated expressions occur in the wrong location, the form is not a standard hypothetical syllogism. These two forms of argument are invalid:

> If A, then B   If A, then B
>
> If C, then B   If A, then C
> _____   _____
> ∴ If A, then C   ∴ If B, then C

_____

*Recognizing that the phrase "really know your art" is a casual expression suggesting your overall sophistication in the art world, we see that the first premise is false. It is certainly possible for a person who is ignorant of art styles and traditions to like any artist's work. Thus, the argument is unsound. The second premise is almost certainly false as well.

A chain of valid hypothetical syllogisms produces a valid overall argument. This form displays valid reasoning:

If A, then B

If B, then C

If C, then D

If D, then E

∴ If A, then E

The premises might not have been presented in this order in the actual argument. As long as the reordered chain displays linked premises (*then B* followed by *if B, then C* followed by *if C*) and the appropriately structured conclusion, the argument is valid. The principle of the basic hypothetical syllogism applies whether the argument has two premises or twenty.

Disjunctive Syllogism   The following argument is valid and sound:

The flag of China shows white stars on a red background *or* it shows yellow stars on a red background.

The stars on China's flag are not white.

∴ The stars on China's flag are yellow.

By accepting the premises, both of which happen to be true, we bind ourselves logically to an acceptance of the conclusion.

Make up your own example of this pattern of reasoning. Here is the pattern:

A or B

Not-A

∴ B

Your example will be valid, too. Even if one or both of the premises you choose is false, the argument will be valid because of its form. Such arguments are called **disjunctive syllogisms.**

There are acceptable variations from the preceding form of disjunctive syllogism, but in each the basic structure is the same: if an "or" statement is accepted as true, and the statement on one side of the *or* is denied, the statement on the other side must be accepted. Consider the variations:

A or B   Not-A or B   Not-A or B

Not-B   A   Not-B

∴ A   ∴ B   ∴ Not-A

A or Not-B   A or Not-B

Not-A   B

∴ Not-B   ∴ A

Not-A or Not-B   Not-A or Not-B

A   B

∴ Not-B   ∴ Not-A

Universal Syllogism   The following argument is valid but unsound:

All religious fundamentalists are political conservatives.

All political conservatives are Republicans.

∴ All religious fundamentalists are Republicans.

By accepting these (false) premises, we bind ourselves logically to an acceptance of the conclusion.

Make up your own example of this pattern of reasoning. Here is the pattern:

All A is B (or: All A's are B's)

All B is C (or: All B's are C's)

∴ All A is C (or: All A's are C's)

If you choose obviously false premises, your argument will be a silly one. Still, it will be valid.

This **universal syllogism** is a common pattern of reasoning, and to many people its validity will be simply obvious. However, that obvious validity can itself be a problem. Being familiar with this useful pattern, *a person may mistake a similar but invalid pattern for the valid one.* Consider another argument form in which two premises and the conclusion begin with *all.*

All A is B

All A is C

∴ All B is C

This is the form of one kind of invalid reasoning. Here is an argument with that form:

All religious fundamentalists are political conservatives.

All religious fundamentalists are Republicans.

∴ All political conservatives are Republicans.

If you are at all tempted to say that this argument is valid, you can understand how careful you must be to distinguish between these two patterns of reasoning. If, however, you easily recognize its invalidity, consider whether either different argument content or the occurrence of these premises in a casual conversational setting (with parenthetical comments) might not invite error. Finally, even if you would not offer such reasoning yourself, don't be amazed if someone else does.

There is one more invalid look-alike that might be mistaken for the valid universal premise. Here is the form:

All A is B

All C is B

∴ All A is C

Try to create a valid argument that has this form. You can't.

■
EXERCISES

3.1 Basic

For each of the following arguments, indicate whether it is valid or invalid and whether it is sound or unsound.

1. Angelo is an Italian, and he's intelligent. Vasco is an Italian, and he's intelligent. In fact, Vasco's whole family is intelligent. I know five other Italians. Each of them is intelligent. Obviously, then, Italians are all very intelligent people.

2. Stalin was a dictator and he was ruthless. Hitler was a dictator and he was ruthless. Castro is a dictator. So he must be a ruthless leader, too.

3. It is clear that Harcourt is the one who murdered Fleisch. After all, he had hated Fleisch for years, he needed the money to pay off a gambling debt, and his fingerprints were found on the murder weapon.

4. Mesa College must have courses in anthropology, since it is a community college and most community colleges have courses in anthropology.

5. All Americans are materialistic, and anyone who is materialistic misses the true meaning of life. Consequently, Americans all miss the true meaning of life.

6. At least one nation in the Western Hemisphere is headed by someone over the age of seventy. After all, Reagan is over seventy and he heads the United States, which is certainly in the Western Hemisphere.

7. Joan's next baby will be a girl because girl babies always follow boy babies when the mother is in her later childbearing years. Joan *is* in her later childbearing years and her last baby was a boy.

8. Kohlrabi must be nutritious because it's a vegetable and most vegetables are nutritious.

9. Nixon was undoubtedly guilty of serious political crimes. So many people think he was guilty—he must have been.

10. No one under the age of eighteen can vote legally in our nation, so a child of twelve would not be able to vote legally in our nation.

3.2 Moderately Difficult

For each of the following arguments, indicate whether it is valid or invalid and whether it is sound or unsound.

1. California must be a desert, because it never rains in California, and anywhere that it never rains has to be a desert.

2. Some Coast Guard personnel must have top-secret clearances, since all Coast Guard personnel are government employees and some government employees have top-secret clearances.

3. Some Republicans are politically conservative, and some Republicans advocate liberal abortion policies. So some political conservatives apparently advocate liberal abortion policies.

4. All Italians are Roman Catholics, and some Roman Catholics are dishonest. Therefore, some Italians must be dishonest.

5. Psychology is not worth studying, since none of the behavioral sciences is worth studying, and psychology is one of the behavioral sciences.

3.3 Difficult

For each of the following arguments, discard the parenthetical statements and determine whether each subargument is valid or invalid and whether it is sound or unsound.

1. Career military officers are all neurotic, and some of the people we classify as neurotic are actually dangerous to society. As you can see, then, at least some career military officers are actually dangerous to society. Furthermore, of those people who are a danger to society, many have had sexual problems as adolescents. What you see now is that the problem with at least some career military officers is rooted in their adolescent sexuality.

2. No one who tries to be a good Christian would consider letting the helpless suffer. This should be recognized merely by noting that every American is a good Christian—or at least tries to be—but no American would even think of letting the helpless suffer. Torrey is a good Christian. That much is clear. So we know without a doubt that helpless people will not suffer if he can help them.

3. You say that women are always deeply religious. This generalization of yours is, not surprisingly, false. In fact, I can logically demonstrate that at least some women are atheists. First, all serious scholars are atheists. That's common knowledge. Second, some women are serious scholars. This clearly proves my point. And if you doubt that there are women who are serious scholars, think about the facts that all serious scholars are college educated and that some college-educated people are women. Logic alone proves my point. There's no denying it! ∎

CONDITIONAL ARGUMENTS

It is important for us to take a special look at the question of validity in one particular kind of argument—the conditional argument. The reason is simple: although conditional arguments are used continually in everyday reasoning, people consistently make mistakes when deciding whether the conclusion follows from the premises. Now go ahead and read Skill 4.

How many times do you say the word *if* in an average day? Since this

---

| **SKILL** |

Skill 4. Evaluating conditional arguments

Be able to determine when a conditional argument is valid and when one is invalid.

Why this skill is important

Conditional arguments are very common in everyday reasoning, yet sometimes invalid forms appear to be valid. ∎

---

little word is so familiar, we do not become especially alert to the logic involved in its use. We should. *If* is the traditional sign of a conditional statement, and conditional statements are often presented within deceptive conditional arguments.

An if-then statement such as "If your candidate is elected, then our country is doomed" is called a **conditional statement.** Part of the statement is offered as a *condition* for the other part. In the example just mentioned, the speaker is claiming that the existence of the condition ("your candidate is elected") guarantees the existence of a certain result ("our country is doomed").

In a conditional statement, the phrase that follows the word *if* is called the **antecedent.** The phrase that follows the word *then* is called the **consequent** of the conditional statement. In the example, the antecedent is "your candidate is elected" (the condition); the consequent is "our country is doomed."

Conditional statements sometimes vary from the regular if-then form. Here are three variations:

1. The *then* may be omitted.

   The meaning of the statement is not changed when we say, "If your candidate is elected, our country is doomed."

2. The *if* may be presented in the middle of the sentence instead of at the beginning.

   When we say, "Our country is doomed if your candidate is elected," the antecedent "your candidate is elected" comes after the consequent "our country is doomed."

3. Words such as *when* or *whenever* sometimes introduce the antecedent instead of *if*.

The meaning of the statement "If I drink too much alcohol I get sick" is basically the same as the meaning of the statements "When I drink too much alcohol I get sick" and "Whenever I drink too much alcohol I get sick."

Conditional arguments, by definition, involve conditional statements. Here is an example of a conditional argument.

Whenever Aunt Mary visits us during the summer, I have a miserable time. But I won't have a miserable time *this* summer because Aunt Mary is fortunately not going to visit.

The first premise is a conditional statement. Then the conclusion is stated and another premise is stated. Is the argument valid? No. Certainly other factors may cause the speaker's summer to be miserable. So even if the premises were true, the conclusion might not be true. This argument does not have good form, even if it appears to at first sight.

Here is another conditional argument.

Kim must not have known the material for this test, because if a person really knows the material, then that person will get an A, but Kim wasn't one of the students who got an A.

Here the conclusion is stated first. Then comes a conditional premise and another premise. Is this argument valid? Yes. If the premises were true, the conclusion would have to be true. So the argument passes the test for validity. Perhaps, however, this sounds like bad reasoning to you, and perhaps the previous argument sounded as if it were good reasoning. You should indeed sense something wrong with the argument, but the problem is not one of validity—it is not a lack of good form. The problem is that the argument is not sound. The problem you may sense is that the conditional premise is false. There are good grounds to doubt the truth of the statement "If a person really knows the material, then that person will get an A." Almost all of us remember situations in which someone "really knew" the material, yet did not receive an A. One possibility is that the person was nervous or very tired or distracted during the test and did not perform well for that reason. The reasoning is valid; our argument is not sound because the conditional premise is false.

Validity is the thorny problem in conditional arguments, however, because even short and simple conditional arguments are regularly evaluated incorrectly in this regard. Think of how very often we use conditional arguments in everyday reasoning: "If I take that course, then . . . ," "If the car could be fixed by tomorrow morning, then . . . ," "If you had changed your approach, then . . . ." Let's consider how mistakes are made in such reasoning and how they can be avoided. After all, if the conditional argument you judge wrongly has a conclusion that is important to you or to someone else, the price for that mistake might be high.*

Examine the following four arguments. They are similar in that each has the same conditional premise, but they are not identical. Each is different from the others. In each of the four cases, decide whether the argument is valid or invalid.

1. If Mr. Sager is the instructor for that course, then the students are enjoying themselves and learning a lot.

   (And) Mr. Sager *is* the instructor for that course.

   (Therefore) the students are enjoying themselves and learning a lot.

2. If Mr. Sager is the instructor for that course, then the students are enjoying themselves and learning a lot.

   The students *are* enjoying themselves and learning a lot.

   (Therefore) Mr. Sager is the instructor for that course.

3. If Mr. Sager is the instructor for that course, then the students are enjoying themselves and learning a lot.

   (But) the students are not enjoying themselves and learning a lot.

   (Therefore) Mr. Sager is not the instructor for that course.

4. If Mr. Sager is the instructor for that course, then the students are enjoying themselves and learning a lot.

   (But) Mr. Sager is not the instructor for that course.

   (Therefore) the students are not enjoying themselves and learning a lot.

Notice that the conditional arguments with which we are concerned in this section have one premise that is a conditional statement and one premise that affirms or denies the antecedent or consequent of the conditional premise. The conclusion then affirms (if the nonconditional premise affirms) or denies (if the nonconditional premise denies) the other part of the conditional premise (antecedent or consequent).

Stop here. Do not read the next paragraph unless you have already determined, to your own satisfaction, whether each of the preceding arguments is valid or invalid.

The argument in the top box is valid. When we accept as true the statement "If Mr. Sager is the instructor for that course, then the students are enjoying themselves and learning a lot," and when we also accept as true the statement that "Mr. Sager is the instructor for that course," we must, to avoid contradicting ourselves, accept the statement "the students are enjoying themselves and learning a lot." If the premises were true, the conclusion would have to be true. This, of course, does not show that the argument is sound. Still, the argument *is* valid.

The argument in the second box is invalid. Even if the premises were true, the conclusion might not be true because of the possibility that other instructors might also provide enjoyable courses in which the students learn as much. This argument is actually a counterfeit of the argument above it on the chart. It is a counterfeit because, while it is similar to the "real thing" (the form of the reasoning appears enough like the first version to be mistaken for it), it is unacceptable (it is invalid). In conversation, the invalid form may be mistaken for the similar-sounding valid form. Having the premises and conclusion occurring in different locations from argument to argument makes this error even easier to commit.

The argument in the third box is valid. When we accept as true the statement "If Mr. Sager is the instructor for that course, then the students are enjoying themselves and learning a lot," and when we also accept as true the statement that "the students are not enjoying themselves and learning a lot," we must, to avoid contradicting ourselves, accept the statement "Mr. Sager is not the instructor for that course." If the premises were true, the conclusion would have to be true.

The argument in the fourth box is invalid. As in the second argument, the premises do not prove the conclusion, since there may be other instructors who could provide enjoyable courses in which the students learned as much. Furthermore, as in the second argument, this argument is actually a counterfeit of the argument above it on the chart. It may be mistaken for that valid argument form because it is similar, but this last argument is definitely invalid.

There is one short word that, if added to the arguments in the second and fourth boxes, would transform them into valid arguments. The word is *only*. People sometimes think that when they say "only if," they are merely being emphatic about their "if" statement. Actually, however, that phrase can change the whole argument. These two alternate versions (with *only if*) of the two previously invalid arguments can be seen now to be valid.

Only if Mr. Sager is the instructor for that course will the students enjoy themselves and learn a lot.

(Or: The students will enjoy themselves and learn a lot only if Mr. Sager is the instructor.)

The students *are* enjoying themselves and learning a lot.

∴ Mr. Sager is the instructor for that course.

Only if Mr. Sager is the instructor for that course will the students enjoy themselves and learn a lot.

(But) Mr. Sager is not the instructor for that course.

∴ The students are not enjoying themselves and learning a lot.

Now, going back to the original four sample arguments, we need a way to determine when a conditional argument is valid because, although you may have seen clearly whether each of the four arguments in the boxes was valid, this is not always such an easy matter. Conditional arguments invite confusion when we fail to distinguish between form and content.

The following chart parallels the chart on page 51 and shows the form of each argument.

1.	If A then C A ___ C
2.	If A then C C ___ A
3.	If A then C Not C ___ Not A
4.	If A then C Not A ___ Not C

Each of the four arguments from the first chart—the one on page 51—is valid or invalid because of its form. By looking at the structure of the argument rather than the content, we can tell whether a conditional argument is valid. The chart on page 53 shows the form of each of the original arguments. The letter A stands for the antecedent of the conditional premise and the letter C stands for the consequent of that premise.

Compare this chart with the preceding one. Each box here corresponds with the appropriate box on that chart. To understand this second chart, note the following:

1. The phrase that follows the *if* of the conditional premise is represented on this chart by the letter *A* wherever it occurs in the argument. The phrase that follows the *then* of the conditional premise is represented on this chart by the letter *C* wherever it occurs in the argument.

2. *Not A* represents the denial of whichever statement is represented by the letter *A; Not C* represents the denial of whichever statement is represented by the letter *C*. If, for example, *A* represents the statement "Mathematics is an exact science," then *Not A* represents the statement "Mathematics is not an exact science." If *A* represents the statement "Physics is not an exact science," then its denial, "Physics is an exact science," is represented by *Not A*.

If you look from this second chart back to the first, you will notice that, since the antecedent of the conditional premise is "Mr. Sager is the instructor for that course," this statement can be represented by the letter *A*. Since this statement is also the nonconditional premise, we can use the letter *A* to represent that entire premise. Since the statement that is the consequent of the conditional premise is also the conclusion, we can use C to represent the entire conclusion.

Any argument with the form shown in the top box of the second chart will be a valid one, regardless of the content.

The counterfeit version of that form may be seen in the second box, where the nonconditional premise and the conclusion are reversed. Any argument with this form will be an invalid one, regardless of the content. When we think of the premises as coming before the conclusion as in the order displayed in the example, the error in constructing the argument occurs with the nonconditional premise. With this premise, instead of affirming the antecedent of the conditional statement to produce a valid argument, we *affirm the consequent* and produce an invalid argument. The logical error that we make is called **affirming the consequent.** It is a *formal* fallacy. In other words, it is a common error that is due to the form independently of the content of the argument.

Any argument with the form shown in the third box of the second chart will be a valid one, regardless of the content.

The counterfeit version of that form may be seen in the fourth box, where the nonconditional premise and the conclusion are reversed. Any argument with this form will be an invalid one, regardless of the content. When we think of the premises as coming before the conclusion (in the order displayed in the example), the error in reconstructing the argument occurs with the nonconditional premise. With this premise, instead of denying the consequent of the conditional statement to produce a valid argument, we *deny the antecedent* and produce an invalid argument. The logical error that we make is called **denying the antecedent.** Like affirming the consequent, it is a formal fallacy.

Two formal fallacies, then, are sometimes committed in conditional arguments: affirming the consequent and denying the antecedent. You should be able to recognize these when considering someone else's reasoning and when you are reasoning on your own.

Finally, here are the answers to four reasonable questions about conditional arguments.

1. *Are these formal fallacies common in everyday reasoning?*

Yes.

Reasoning from if-then premises is a common and casual part of everyday thinking. This makes quite notable the research suggesting that people *more often than not*, given certain common patterns of conditional reasoning, identify as valid arguments ones that exhibit the formal fallacies of affirming the consequent or denying the antecedent.*

2. *Do the two valid forms of conditional reasoning also have names?*

Yes.

Certainly we could name them by referring to what happens in the nonconditional premise, as we do with the invalid forms. They would then be called affirming the antecedent and denying the consequent. However, they are more often known by their Latin names, *modus ponens* (first box) and *modus tollens* (third box).

3. *Do I need to memorize the second chart?*

No.

The chart should have helped you understand the form of conditional arguments. You do not, however, need to keep a mental picture of it in order to distinguish between valid and invalid conditional arguments.

---

*In his article "Selective Processes in Reasoning," Jonathan St. B. T. Evans refers to a 1981 Evans and Beck study that found 54 percent of the respondents accepting the reasoning of the fallacious denial of the antecedent and 53 percent accepting the affirmation of the consequent. He also refers to a 1977 Evans study that yielded 38 and 67 percent results, respectively. From Jonathan St. B. T. Evans, Thinking and Reasoning: Psychological Approaches (London: Routledge & Kegan Paul, 1983), pp. 135–63.

If you encounter a conditional argument of the sort that we have been examining, you need only identify the conditional premise, the nonconditional premise, and the conclusion. Then, looking at the nonconditional premise (not the conclusion!), determine first whether it is similar to the antecedent or the consequent of the conditional premise, and then whether it affirms or denies that part of the conditional premise. Then you will know whether, in the crucial nonconditional premise, the argument involves affirming the antecedent, affirming the consequent, denying the antecedent, or denying the consequent. Since the two errors to watch for are affirming the consequent and denying the antecedent, these are the two names you must remember.

4. *Are there exceptions to these rules of logic?*

The only apparent exception occurs when a speaker or writer casually words an "only if" statement as if it were simply an if-then statement. Consider this example. A person wistfully observes, "If we had some money, we could go out to eat at a restaurant tonight." Perhaps this is the simple if-then statement it appears to be. In this case, by denying the antecedent, we create an invalid argument because there may be ways of eating out that do not require cash in hand; credit cards are one possibility, for example. Perhaps, however, we can envision the possibility that the speaker is really (and correctly) suggesting that *only if* they had money could they go to a restaurant. Here he or she is implying that there are no other ways to manage to dine out. If this is what is intended—and sometimes we do word the "only if" statement with a simple *if*, then by denying the antecedent through claiming that "we don't have any money," we *validly* produce the conclusion that "we can't go out to eat at a restaurant tonight."

■

EXERCISES

3.4 Basic

Determine whether each of the following arguments is valid or invalid. If it is invalid, name the formal fallacy.

1. If a person is rich, then he or she is certain to be well dressed. The fellow I met last night was certainly well dressed. Therefore, he must be rich.

2. If you had had a good logic course, you would not have been misled by my "argument from ignorance" fallacy. But you *were* misled by my use of that fallacy. Thus, you cannot possibly have had a good logic course.

3. When the person viewing an artwork understands the personal and cultural influences on the artist, that viewer can find meaning in the artwork. But you don't know anything about the personal and cultural influences on Picasso. Therefore, you will be unable to find meaning in his painting *Guernica*.

4. When the person viewing an artwork understands the personal and cultural influences on the artist, that viewer can find meaning in the artwork. And you are finding meaning in Picasso's *Guernica*. I conclude that you understand the personal and cultural influences that affected Picasso.

5. If a person is very deeply moved by the victims of famine in Africa, then that person will contribute to the effort to alleviate the suffering. You have contributed to that cause. I know, therefore, that you have been deeply moved by this tragedy.

3.5 Moderately Difficult

Determine whether each of the following arguments is valid or invalid. Notice that the premises and the conclusion are not always in the same order. Notice also that the antecedent does not always precede the consequent in the conditional premise. Supply any unstated but implied premise or conclusion.

1. There is no God. There would be no evil in the world if God existed. Yet, alas, there is indeed evil in this world!

2. God must exist because there is an intricate pattern of interdependent designs in this world. Certainly, if such a pattern exists, then God must also.

3. Jennifer is broke again. She must have been to the racetrack yesterday because she's always broke whenever she's spent the previous day at the track.

4. He would understand things like this if he had really been raised on a farm. So we can safely assert that he was, after all, raised on a farm since he *does* obviously understand these things.

5. Yes, I did hear that the boss gets violent when he feels threatened. But don't worry. He won't get violent with you, since I'm sure he won't feel threatened by you in any way.

6. A quote from G. Gordon Liddy that appeared in *Newsweek*, November 10, 1986:

   Obviously crime pays, or there'd be no crime.

7. Lettering on a T-shirt:

   Dull Women Have Immaculate Homes

3.6 Difficult

Determine how many conditional arguments, obvious or subtle, are in each of the following passages. Then determine whether each conditional argument is valid or invalid. For each invalid conditional argument, name the formal fallacy that is committed.

1. *Terry:* Where's Dad? It's time to leave for the ball game.

   Chris: I don't know. Maybe he went into the bedroom to lie down. He said he felt dizzy.

   Terry: Oh, no! He must have taken his twice-a-week medicine this morning. Doctor Herndon said that he would feel dizzy for hours whenever he took that medicine.

   Chris: Well, if he took it just this morning, then he's not going to be alert enough to go to the game at eleven thirty. Dad didn't get out of bed until nine. He must have just taken it.

   Terry: You're right. Dad won't be alert enough to go to the game. But who can we sell his tickets to?

2. At a meeting of the Administrative Council of the National Veterans Organization, the officers of the NVO are discussing the Presidential Awards Banquet. Their organization must select someone to represent them when the president presents them with the American Service Award. Part of the discussion follows:

   Sanders: You say that this McReynolds fellow would be a fitting representative for the NVO?

   Jameson: Yes, we think so. He has seen combat action and earned the Purple Heart award for his war injuries.

   Sanders: Well, someone who has earned the Purple Heart would certainly be a good representative for our group.

Harrell: Wait a minute, fellows. You've made a mistake, Jamie. McReynolds *is* the man we've recommended, but he never earned a Purple Heart. That was Tarantino, the other man we were considering seriously. So I guess, Colonel Sanders, from what you said about the Purple Heart, you don't now think that McReynolds is a fitting representative. Do you want us to look at the list of candidates again?

3. A letter to the editor:

Editor:

The letter from Mr. Springer (dated August 8, 1987) shows his lack of appreciation for the small farmer.

For the past two years, small and medium-sized family farms have been going bankrupt at an alarming rate. Unless a broader program of aid to such farms is enacted, this rate will not only continue but actually increase. This is a matter of personal tragedy for thousands of our hardest-working, traditional-valued Americans. Mr. Springer's cold reference to "the necessary displacement of persons during social change" reflects his low regard for farmers and for people in general.

It is now clear—listen to so many politicians backing off from their long-standing support for farmers—that no further programs of significance will be initiated. My sad conclusion is that the rate of defaults will continue to rise. Still, although I have no illusions, I have nothing but contempt for the Mr. Springers of this nation.

Signed,

A sad but angry soul ∎

LOGICAL ANALOGIES

Sometimes a person will make only one error in a long line of reasoning, and to notice it you must be alert. At other times, the errors and questionable moves are unbelievably numerous. When there is more than one weak point in an argument, and you have decided to question that argument, you need to determine which point or points to address. It is tedious and usually inadvisable to attack every one of an arguer's many errors. Besides, in conversation at least, we normally want to allow the other person to preserve the self-esteem necessary for him or her to eventually change positions. Crucial to the issue of which point to address is the question of whether you want to focus on bad form or bad content. Obviously, there is sometimes no choice. When there is, keep this general rule—as mentioned earlier—in mind: *It is usually advisable to question form rather than content.*

When the form is bad, remember, the evidence does not adequately support or "prove" the conclusion; when the content is questionable or bad, there is reason to doubt the truth of one premise—or more than one. Questioning the premises themselves often leads to a face-off with the other person. Since the premise is so strongly maintained, progress toward seeing its weaknesses is not easily made. People will more readily admit that their reasoning in a particular case was hasty than that an old and dearly held premise is false.

Sometimes you realize that another person's argument is invalid and you want to communicate this insight to that person. To demonstrate that an argument is invalid, you can sometimes make up another argument—one that has the same structure as the original argument but has obviously true premises and an obviously false conclusion. This second argument is called a **logical analogy.** Please take a good look, before you go on, at the skill box below.

Let's consider the "Italians" argument that we've seen in the exercises following skills 2 and 3. Some people have difficulty seeing that this argument is invalid. To refresh your memory, here is the argument.

All Italians are Roman Catholics.

(and) Some Roman Catholics are dishonest.

∴ Some Italians must be dishonest.

SKILL

Skill 5. Creating logical analogies

Produce effective logical analogies to demonstrate the invalidity of particular arguments.

Why this skill is important

The person who reasons invalidly may find it difficult to see that the conclusion does not follow from the premises offered, even when this is pointed out by another person. Logical analogies can illuminate an argument's invalidity so clearly that even the arguer must admit that something has gone wrong. ∎

This argument can be shown to be invalid by stating the argument clearly and then suggesting that "that's like saying . . . ," then offering a parallel argument such as this one.

All popes are Roman Catholics.

(and) Some Roman Catholics are children.
_____

∴ Some popes must be children.

The arguments are parallel—they have the same structure—because each is constructed on this pattern:

All A is B

Some B is C
_____

∴ Some A is C

In each argument, then, we have the same kind of reasoning. Words like *all* and *some* cannot be changed, and the order of the terms *A, B,* and *C* must be preserved. In the logical analogy (the second argument), however, the premises are obviously true and the conclusion is obviously false. This shows that, *with this kind of reasoning, even the most reliable premises can produce an unacceptable conclusion.* There must, therefore, be something wrong with that original reasoning.

Let's review briefly. Presented with the "Italians" argument, someone who wants to communicate its invalidity says this: "You are saying that, since all Italians are Roman Catholics and some Roman Catholics are dishonest, some Italians must be dishonest. But that's like saying that, since all popes are Roman Catholics and some Roman Catholics are children, some popes must be children." Yes, the second argument sounds ridiculous, but it's *supposed* to. With your reasoning, the speaker is suggesting, true premises can lead to a false conclusion. Thus, you should reevaluate your reasoning.

In the preceding example, one of the terms, *Roman Catholics*, was kept when the logical analogy was constructed. This is not necessary; all the terms can be new ones. It is important, however, that the premises be uncontentious and beyond discussion (not even inviting a passing comment or joke) and that the conclusion be so obviously false, even ridiculous, that it could not be construed as true. The purpose in constructing the logical analogy is to direct attention to the form and away from the content. The person being addressed is sure to miss the point if attention is now inadvertently drawn to the *content* of the logical analogy. Consider an example.

What if the following argument had been offered as a logical analogy for the "Italians" argument?

(that's like saying . . .)

All colleges are schools.

Some schools are high schools.
_____

∴ Some colleges are high schools.

This argument has the same structure as the original argument. It has obviously true premises and an obviously false conclusion. However, if a person who was attending, or knew of, a college that he or she considered to be academically weak, the conclusion of the logical analogy may draw a sarcastic comment. "Well, some colleges *are* high schools!" If this happens, attention has been drawn away from the form of the arguments. The point of your logical analogy will almost certainly be missed.

Let's examine one more invalid argument for which a logical analogy could be useful.

Original argument: Some teachers are Democrats and most Democrats are political liberals. So some teachers must be political liberals.

This argument is invalid. In fact, it's "like saying . . ."

Logical analogy: Some children are professional actors and most professional actors are adults. So some children must be adults.

The premises of the logical analogy are true and uncontentious. The structure or form of the arguments is identical. We are showing that with reasoning like this, even good evidence can lead to an unreliable conclusion.

Logical analogies can be used to show another person that his or her reasoning is invalid—that the conclusion being offered does not follow from the premises. There are both advantages and limitations to a reliance on logical analogies to do this job.

Advantages of Logical Analogies

1. We can avoid a discussion of sensitive premises by focusing completely on the form of the argument.

2. No technical terms such as *invalid* or *premise* are necessary to make your point.

3. Successful logical analogies present their point with great psychological power.

Limitations of Logical Analogies

1. While the preparation of written responses to an argument allows time to create logical analogies, for immediate spoken responses the ability to think on your feet is crucial. Some people are better than others at creating logical analogies, and sometimes you simply can't think of one.

2. Having a good logical analogy is not enough. If the person or persons you are addressing do not, for whatever reason, see the similarity in the structure of the two arguments, you have failed to convey the intended message. Note also the following advice on this matter: Use the same voice inflection and body movement when articulating each of the two arguments. If you raise the tone of your voice, for example, or wave your hand in a certain way at the end of each premise of the first argument, do the same when you give the second argument. Use any such tools that may help the listener to sense the similarity.

Remember, finally, that in actual conversation—or in writing, for that matter—the conclusion may be stated first, last, or elsewhere, and that many parenthetical statements may separate the premises from each other and from the conclusion. When you use a logical analogy, however, you should first offer a clear reconstruction of the other person's argument by eliminating all parenthetical statements and by placing the conclusion last.

■

EXERCISES

3.7 Basic

For each of the following invalid arguments, create a logical analogy to demonstrate its invalidity.

1. Some Republicans are politically conservative and some Republicans advocate liberal abortion policies. So some political conservatives apparently advocate liberal abortion policies.

2. All scientists are college educated and some college-educated people have artistic talents, so there must be some scientists who have artistic talents.

3. Since some teachers are scholars and many scholars are humanists, some teachers must be humanists.

4. There aren't any priests who are dishonest (or: "No priests are dishonest"), but some priests aren't intelligent. Therefore, some intelligent people must be dishonest.

5. Since all socialists are political leftists and all communists are also (or: "All communists are political leftists"), anyone who is a socialist is also a communist (or: "All socialists are communists").

3.8 Moderately Difficult

For each of the following invalid arguments, create a logical analogy to demonstrate its invalidity. The conclusion is not necessarily stated last, and in some cases you will encounter parenthetical statements that you may omit in reconstructing the argument.

1. Physicians are all quite wealthy, so some of them must not be compassionate people, since many wealthy people are not compassionate.

2. Some people with good memories must be interpreters, since all interpreters are bilingual and some bilingual people have good memories.

3. In college, different types of students are drawn to different subjects. Take psychology majors, for example. With them, however, it's more complex. Here you see multiple characteristics. Some very intelligent people are psychology majors. This is easily documented. Observation will tell you something else: some very disturbed people are psychology majors. One interesting side conclusion here is that some very intelligent people are also very disturbed.

4. It's not possible that any Italians are atheists. Think of it. The Vatican is right there in Rome. Most Italians, as you might guess, are Roman Catholics. Certainly, whoever is a Roman Catholic is not an atheist.

5. In all schools, there are some discipline problems. What kind of student poses such a problem? Observe, first, that some children with behavior problems are kids who are abnormally active. The clinical term is *hyperactive*. Now, many hyperactive children are quite intelligent. This proves what many educators have known for years: many children with behavior problems are really quite intelligent children. ∎

∎

CHAPTER HIGHLIGHTS

■ An argument is *deductively valid* when, apart from the question of the truth of the premises, the conclusion is so well supported by those premises that if the premises were true, then the conclusion would have to be true. If the premises fall short of establishing such certainty, the argument is deductively invalid. The "proof" fails to establish the certainty of the conclusion. An argument is sound if it meets both of the following requirements: (a) it is deductively valid, and (b) all of its premises are true. Subarguments can be assessed separately when making judgments of validity and soundness; a single inadequate subargument does not necessarily render the overall argument useless. Certain patterns of reasoning (such as the *hypothetical syllogism*, the *deductive syllogism*, and the *universal syllogism*) can be recognized as necessarily valid.

- We can easily misjudge the validity of conditional arguments if we do not pay attention to their form. The modus ponens and modus tollens forms always yield valid arguments. The forms known as *affirming the consequent* and *denying the antecedent* (by reference to the nonconditional premise) are formal fallacies that always yield invalid arguments.

- An error in the form of someone's argument can sometimes be illuminated through the creation of a *logical analogy*. To demonstrate that the argument is invalid, compare it with another argument. This second argument, called a logical analogy, is one you make up on your own. It must have the same structure as the original argument, as well as obviously true premises and an obviously false conclusion.

For Further Reading

Lambert, Karel, and William Ulrich. *The Nature of Argument.* New York: Macmillan, 1980.

A study in deductive validity that explores the application of symbolic logic to practical argument.

C H A P T E R

FOUR

Inductive Strength

E ither the available evidence proves the point being considered or it doesn't. If the evidence, once accepted, establishes the conclusion with certainty, the reasoning is deductively valid. If the reasoning falls short—even by a bit—the reasoning is deductively invalid. It's as simple as that. Isn't it?

Yes, it is. If we are concerned only with unqualified proof, we can reject as invalid any argument that falls short. Deductive certainty was the topic for Chapter 3. Skill at this kind of argument evaluation is useful. Among those arguments that do fall short of unqualified proof, however, many are "good arguments" in the sense that they move reasonable people *closer* to an acceptance of the conclusion, and in some cases they are all that we can reasonably expect.

EVALUATING INDUCTIVE STRENGTH

Although many arguments must be judged to be deductively invalid, some can still be judged worthwhile because of the *inductive strength* that they may have in varying degrees.

An inductively strong argument is one in which the evidence, once accepted, establishes a firm probability that the conclusion is true. This is one example:

Judge Burnet has dismissed the charges against every one of the hundreds of graffiti defendants he has seen over the past eight years.

The charge against me is the same, and there seem to be no special circumstances in my case.

∴ Judge Burnet will dismiss the charge against me.

If Judge Burnet does not dismiss the charge in this case, we cannot say, "That's impossible." We did not have deductive certainty. We can only say,

Skill 6. Evaluating inductive strength

Assess the inductive strength of arguments that do not qualify as deductively valid.

Why this skill is important

In everyday life much can rest on the reliability of the reasoning we accept, and our premises more typically establish probability than certainty. The assessment of inductive strength is thus a continual task for us. ∎

"That's very surprising." It was simply unlikely, based on previous experience. Here is another example of an inductively strong argument:

Coyotes are almost never found in this part of the country.

You have never seen a real coyote before.

∴ The animal you saw in the field was not a coyote.

It *could have been* a coyote, but it probably wasn't one. If the conclusion to this argument were "The animal you saw was a dog," the argument would not be as strong, since the animal may have been a fox or another kind of animal. Since coyotes do look much like dogs, and since dogs are probably more common in the area, the chances are reasonably good that it *was* a dog. The argument with this conclusion has some strength, but not as much as the original argument we considered.

If the conclusion to this argument were "You must have dreamed it," the argument would have very little inductive strength. In fact, we would have to say that the argument was inductively weak. Unless the person reporting the sighting has a habit of confusing dreams with reality, the evidence does not establish a *probability* that the conclusion is true. It does, of course, allow for such a *possibility*, but the chances are very good that this conclusion is false. Please turn now to Skill 6 above.

A distinction between an argument's form and its content was discussed in Chapter 3. There, in the discussion of deductive certainty, an argument was considered to have good form if the premises were of the right sort to establish the truth of the conclusion beyond any possible doubt, logically speaking; an argument was considered to have good content if all of its premises were true.

A form/content distinction can also be used in assessing inductive strength. However, since the separation of good and bad form is not so clear here, the tidy concepts of validity and soundness are not used. When judging inductive strength rather than deductive certainty, an argument can be considered to have *good form* if the level of probability established for the conclusion is high. Such an argument can be considered to have *good content* if its premises are true or are likely to be true. Since we are not using deductive certainty as a standard of acceptable reasoning now, both form and content can allow for some possibility of error.

Assessing the Forms of Arguments*

Deductive Certainty	Inductive Probability
Valid *Acceptable because certainty has been established.*	*There is no inductive correlate to deductive validity.*

Invalid
 	
Not deductively valid. Certainty has not been established, although the argument may have a high or low degree of inductive strength.
	Very strong support/almost certain
	
	Almost always acceptable because the conclusion has been established as very probable.
	
	Strong support
	Almost always acceptable.
	
	                    Stronger
	Moderate ————
	strength, with
	various levels ————
	of probability ————
	
	————
	                    Weaker
	
	Very weak support; does not establish a probability
	
	Worthless/no support
	Unacceptable.

When we assess an argument for deductive certainty, there are two categories: valid and invalid. However, many arguments that do not establish deductive certainty still have acceptable form because they have sufficient inductive strength to make them useful.

The R-E-T Method of Evaluating Inductive Strength and Acceptability

The form and content of an argument can be checked for inductive strength and acceptability by the R-E-T method, which is simple and easy to remember. Essentially, it involves merely the steps you take whenever you think out a matter thoroughly.

There is certainly no way to avoid having to identify the conclusion and the evidence before assessing an argument. Once you have identified them, however, the R-E-T method involves simply asking yourself three questions:

1. Are these reasons the Right kind for supporting such a conclusion?

2. Are they Enough to warrant accepting the conclusion?

3. Are they True?

In short, we ask: Are the reasons . . . the *Right kind? Enough? True?* The letters *R-E-T* signal the three questions to be asked when assessing your own or another's reasoning (R: Right kind; E: Enough; T: True). Let's briefly discuss each of the three questions.

R: *Are the reasons the right kind?*

In other words, is the evidence offered relevant to the conclusion drawn? Sometimes, the problem with an argument is that the very sort of evidence offered is not the sort required to establish the point at issue. As with most errors, this is more easily recognized in others' arguments than in our own. If the R question receives a "Yes," go on to the E question.

E: *Are the reasons enough?*

Sometimes the evidence, being the Right kind, or relevant, is also clearly sufficient for reasonable people to accept the argument. In other arguments, the evidence, even though it may be relevant, is clearly insufficient to make a good case for the conclusion. In dealing with inductive strength rather than deductive certainty, there are subtle and innumerable distinctions to be made between these extremes. What seems sufficient to one person will fall short for a person who is more cautious on the issue being considered. However, the question must be asked. There is seldom, if ever, a clear dividing line between inductively strong and weak arguments. If you honestly judge the case for the conclusion to be too weak, you must reject the argument—but not necessarily the conclusion. If the E question receives a "yes," go on to the T question.

T: *Are the reasons true?*

The inductively strong argument, like the deductively valid and sound argument, must have reliable premises. In both cases, we must ask if the evidence presented is to be accepted as true. Since inductive strength requires probability rather than absolute proof, however, the *likelihood* that the evidence is true will generally be adequate. As with the E question, the reasoner's judgment must be based on the circumstances and the particular argument.

If all three questions receive a "yes," the argument is acceptable. The conclusion can be considered well supported.

Consider two examples of how the R-E-T method of evaluating reasoning may be used in practical contexts.

EXAMPLE

Practical context: Andrew has done poorly in his two previous philosophy courses. On this basis, he concludes that he will do poorly in the Introduction to Logic course, which is another philosophy course.

Application of R-E-T: Andrew's past performance in philosophy classes is not irrelevant. It is not at all obvious that he is considering the *wrong kind* of evidence for his conclusion. Still, while his concern about his previous performance is legitimate (it is, in this sense, "the right kind"), it is not alone sufficient ("enough") to lead persuasively to his conclusion. Although this additional philosophy class may involve some difficult abstractions like those in his other two courses, perhaps a "process-oriented" logic course will be significantly different from those "content-oriented" courses. If Andrew applies R-E-T, and does just a bit of casual research, might he not see that he doesn't have *Enough* evidence to justify his disturbing conclusion? Note again that it is usually easier to see the fault in another's reasoning than in one's own; it is easier to imagine Robert, let's say, who has already been exposed to the R-E-T method, helping Andrew reason this out. Also, perhaps this particular instructor will teach in a way that makes it easier for Andrew to learn. Here again, in applying R-E-T, we identify the problem as we find that the E question yields a "no." We need more evidence than we have if we are to make a really strong case for Andrew's conclusion, although his concern is not wholly without foundation. ∎

EXAMPLE

Practical context: Daniel, age fifty-eight, works in a factory, attending college at night. Simon, his working partner for thirty years, has just retired. Upon hearing that his new workmate will be someone who is "hardly more than a youngster," Daniel is tempted to declare his refusal to work with the boy, whom he expects—although he doesn't know him—will not do the job well.

Application of R-E-T: Put in terms of logic, Daniel's reasoning runs thus:

Premise: He is young.

Conclusion: He won't do his job well.

First, we ask (we can imagine Daniel assessing his own reasoning or having it assessed by a family member or a fellow worker) whether the reason given for accepting Daniel's conclusion is the *Right kind.* Our answer is probably "no."

However, what if, on further information, Daniel considers a different reason for coming to that conclusion?

Premise: He is forgetful.

Conclusion: He won't do his job well.

This is perhaps the *Right kind* of reason to consider. If Daniel had heard this about his new workmate, and especially if their job is dangerous, he might quite justifiably want to know more. This information alone, however, is not *Enough* to show that his conclusion is warranted. Perhaps the new worker is forgetful "only about certain things," but never about job-related matters. This is certainly not inconceivable. To satisfy the E requirement in the R-E-T test, Daniel must have additional evidence before accepting his conclusion. This would do it:

Premise: He is often forgetful about important aspects of his job.

Conclusion: He won't do his job well.

Is the reason the *Right kind*—is it relevant? Yes. Is it *Enough*? Yes (unless the boy can change his ways). Is it *True*? Daniel would certainly have to substantiate any such rumor before justifiably accepting his conclusion. If the information is reliable, if the new person indeed "is often forgetful about important aspects of his job," the conclusion is warranted. If the information is determined to be very probably true, Daniel has at least good grounds for concern.   ∎

The R-E-T method can also be used to assess deductive certainty. The E and T questions would simply be answered according to stricter standards.

■

EXERCISES

4.1 Basic

Evaluate the reasoning in each of the following situations. Write down your reasons for giving either a "yes" or a "no" for each of the three questions to be asked in the R-E-T method. Stop at the first "no." Then assess the overall inductive strength of the reasoning.

1. "Arnie, you would be a *great* teacher," concluded his sister Gail. "You're smart and you always think of a good way to get your point across."

2. Lonnie regularly shies away from difficult courses. Today he decided not to register for the abnormal psychology course that he had earlier planned on taking. "I found out that the professor for that course has two Ph.D.'s! There's no way I could ever pass a course as difficult as that one is bound to be."

3. Stalin was a dictator and he was ruthless. Hitler was a dictator and he was ruthless. Castro is a dictator. So he must be ruthless, too.

4. "But I need a top-notch architect who knows his stuff," snorted the company president. "And what do you send me? A woman barely into her thirties. This is obviously not someone who will do the best possible job for our company."

5. The old Imperial Theater on the west end of town often shows older classic films. Tonight, *Singin' in the Rain*, starring Gene Kelly, is playing. Jenny's friends plan to go to the Imperial tonight, and although Jenny would like to spend an evening out with them, she is considering staying home. She is sure that she wouldn't like the film. "I've seen Gene Kelly in films before," Jenny reasons. "Twice, in fact. I didn't like his style." ■

EVIDENCE AND COUNTEREVIDENCE

Most of us would like to be certain about more things than we can justifiably claim certainty about. There's so often more to be considered, including evidence that conflicts with what we *want* to believe. The problems we typically deal with in our daily lives as consumers, workers, family mem-

---

SKILL

Skill 7. Considering evidence and counterevidence

Identify, through creative inquiry, worthy arguments against a proposed belief and additional arguments for it.

Why this skill is important

Our beliefs—important ones included—can become firmly entrenched as we forget or ignore the fact that we never actually sought out and seriously considered all the evidence.   ■

---

bers, and citizens call for an assessment of the inductive strength of our reasoning. Rarely can we justify the deductive certainty we might desire. It is important for us, as the skill box above points out, to continue to be open to—and to actively seek—the additional information that can either secure or challenge our present opinions and beliefs. Sometimes there is a high price for being wrong.

As careful as we may be to consider fairly each aspect of certain issues, we sometimes get lazy or fall victim to one of our points of logical vulnerability on *other* issues.

A person needs to see more than one side of an issue in order to weigh the evidence, in any meaningful sense, and to arrive at fair conclusions. If a person, after noting which evidence he or she judges to be relevant and important, finds that it all supports the same position, the chances are good that there is counterevidence (evidence against that position) that has not been considered seriously enough. This is especially true on social issues, which are so often complex and elusive. You probably know people who believe that there is basically "nothing to be said for" an opposing view on abortion, labor-management disputes, the national defense budget, or price supports for farmers. Check your own points of logical vulnerability. Admitting that there is *some* relevant support for a conflicting claim does not require you to remain skeptically indecisive. You can judge what it is reasonable to believe while acknowledging that the issue has other sides that you honestly and carefully (that's the trick!) judge to be less compelling. (At this point, it may be helpful to reread the sections on points of logical vulnerability, winning and losing, and fairmindedness in Chapter 1.)

Psychological research confirms a blindness to the power of evidence that supports personally distasteful conclusions. The phenomenon of being more alert to evidence that supports a welcomed conclusion and less receptive to the presence and power of counterevidence has been described by psychologists as "the fallacy of positive instances." Indeed, sometimes the very existence of counterevidence never comes to mind. When it does, psychologists agree, it may not be well received. In a study performed in 1979,* three psychologists presented Stanford University students with two supposed research studies on whether capital punishment deterred crime.

The two studies had opposing conclusions. After students read both studies, there was stronger disagreement than ever between those students who had favored capital punishment on grounds of crime-deterrence and those who opposed capital punishment. The people on each side readily accepted the study that confirmed their preconceptions and were very critical of the evidence that supposedly counted against them.

These findings are neither exceptional nor surprising. We have all seen how people weigh evidence when a point of logical vulnerability is involved. Besides, there is resistance to the simple acknowledgment that "the view I've been holding until now is wrong."

Two problems exist, then. First, when analyzing an issue on our own, we need to be able to think up evidence that does not readily occur to us— evidence on different sides of the issue. Second, when evaluating arguments produced by us or another in support of conclusions we resist, we need to be receptive to the actual force of the evidence.

While there is no simple and sure way to acquire either of these skills, consider one suggestion concerning each. First, when trying to think up evidence that is relevant to the issue, you can start by asking the general question "What *kinds of evidence* could bear on this issue?" Essentially, the same search is initiated by asking "Which *sources of information* could help to build insight in this matter?" Just list the kinds/sources. Don't concern yourself with the question of whether any evidence is available from each category. After making the list (more items for the list may occur throughout the process), enumerate the evidence that *is* available from each category. The disciplined use of this method lessens the chance of overlooking (1) entire types of evidence, as well as (2) unfavorable evidence within categories. It is simply a more deliberate, less haphazard search for evidence.

Second, when trying to consider fairly the weight of "unfriendly" evidence, you can make a serious effort to "put yourself in the other's shoes" or in the other's *position*. To take on the other person's perspective, you might start by focusing on the other's feelings as if they were yours. Each

*C. G. Lord, L. Ross, and M. Lepper, "Biased Assimilation and Attitude Polarization: The Effects of Prior Theories on Subsequently Considered Evidence," Journal of Personality and Social Psychology 37 (1979): 2098–2109.

of us knows the feelings of pride, resentment, concern for the plight of others, and, generally, all the feelings that are common to human beings. If you then associate the other's feelings with the same objects and beliefs as that other person does, you may be in a position to produce respectable arguments for this view that might have previously eluded you.

The person who opposes all social welfare programs might temporarily put aside her own perspective in favor of a focus on the other person's feeling of sadness for those who have been "caught in the system" despite an industrious nature. Sadness and concern for the undeserved misfortune of others are familiar feelings. The situation of Pennsylvania steelworkers who have worked hard to support families and who are suddenly "unemployable" at age fifty or fifty-five because of the closing of the steel mills provides a focus for those feelings. Now, if such a change of perspective is genuinely accomplished, the result is likely to be a greater appreciation for the other's arguments. A further possible result is the capacity to generate additional evidence and argument on this "other side" of the issue. Similarly, another person, someone with sympathy for the less fortunate, may view *any* attack on welfare programs as a reflection of a lack of concern, or even meanness. This person might temporarily put aside his perspective in favor of a focus on the other person's feelings of anger about widespread abuses of welfare programs or fear for the nation's financial solvency in consideration of the great expense of the programs. In either case, allowing oneself to feel the emotion(s) the other person experiences, and tying this emotion to specific instances that seem to justify such emotion, should bring about appreciation of that other perspective and perhaps the discovery of yet new evidence to consider on "that side" of the issue.

■

EXERCISES

4.2 Basic

For each of the following claims, think up as much relevant evidence for differing perspectives as you can. First list the kinds *of evidence that would be relevant; then see if you can offer specific evidence that you know to be true. In other words, first ask, "What kinds of evidence would we need" to support or reject this claim? Then ask, "What evidence do I have?"*

1. Harvard University offers the best general education in the United States.

2. People's actions are basically self-serving.

3. Chrysler makes the best-built American cars.

4. Republicans are more inclined towards military solutions to international political problems than are Democrats.

5. All college students should have a course in logic or critical thinking.

6. The United States uses military force too often to resolve international problems.

7. Men are more aggressive by nature than women are.

8. There have been actual instances of ESP (extrasensory perception).

9. People who have played team sports are more successful in their careers than are those who haven't.

10. Children at age fourteen generally would not make decisions as well as adults would if they were allowed to vote in national elections.

11. A person's character is determined more by environmental than by biological—including genetic—factors.

4.3 Difficult

A. *For each of the following claims, think up as much relevant evidence for differing perspectives as you can. First list the* kinds *of evidence that would be relevant, then see if you can offer specific evidence that you know to be true. In other words, first ask, "What kinds of evidence would we need" to support or reject this claim? Then ask, "What evidence do I have?"*

B. *Identify typical emotions of people on different sides of the issue. Attempt to feel these emotions and associate them with specific objects and beliefs. Write down the additional evidence that comes to mind in each case.**

1. Capitalistic economic systems contribute to the development of intelligence in people more than communistic economic systems do. (Note: If you don't know the difference between a capitalistic and a communistic economic system, look up the information or skip to the next statement.)

2. Given time for development, computers will be able to perform every kind of thinking function that humans can perform.

3. Prayer should be required in public schools.

4. A period for silent meditation should be required in public schools.

5. Religion is a subject that should be taught in high school.

*You don't have to work at these exercises in the order presented here.

6. The quality of American cars has been decreasing in recent years.

7. Sex education in the schools leads to increased promiscuity.　　■

GENERALIZATIONS

We often generalize. Much of the reasoning that produces generalizations is inductively strong and compels us to consider seriously, and sometimes act on, the general conclusion. We have learned, however, that we are supposed to be very cautious when accepting generalizations. What is the basis for such a special caution? The answer is that, while generalizations are not objectionable in themselves, problems arise when we fail to distinguish between generalizations and universal statements. Now, to clarify your sense of the skill to be mastered here, take a moment to read the next skill box carefully.

"Don't generalize!" Most of us have given, received, or heard this warning. Most often the warning is meant to discourage stereotyping and similar grouping of all people of a certain sort. Generalizing, it would seem, is one of the greatest sins a thinker can commit. **Generalization** is not, however, primarily an enemy of rational thought. It is an ability without which there would be no rational thought. We generalize each time we make observations of a particular kind, then expect that such observations could readily be applied to wider experience. The ability to categorize on the basis

---

SKILL

Skill 8. Dealing with generalizations

Recognize clear cases of, and confusions between, generalizations and universal statements.

Why this skill is important

The grammar of generalizations and universal statements is often identical. This invites confusion about the intent of a speaker or writer. It also invites sloppiness in one's own thinking.　　■

of similarities is part of what makes us intelligent beings. How is it, then, that the words *generalize* and *generalization* have taken on such negative connotations?

Statements that we call generalizations present claims that are intended to be *generally* true. That is, the claim is expected to be true in most cases of that kind. These generalizations are usually based on experience. "Summer is warmer than winter" is a generalization that holds true on most days. "Behaviors that are rewarded get repeated," psychologists tell us. Does this mean that there are no exceptions to this claim? No. The claim is intended only as a *general* claim. If you were to approach a psychologist who had made such a remark, deriding her because you knew of a case in which a rewarded behavior was not repeated, she would tell you that there was no intention to suggest that the generalization held in all cases. You simply misunderstood, you would be told.

Universal statements are statements that are general in the sense that they refer to many individual cases. However, universal statements are *intended* to apply in all cases. "Three-month-old babies cannot walk." There are no exceptions to this general claim, and this was recognized when the claim was made. It is a universal statement. A practical difficulty arises because the grammar of generalizations and of universal statements is often identical. You can't always tell the difference between them merely by hearing or reading them. Thus, when we say, "Rewarded behavior gets repeated," the generalization can be mistaken for a universal statement.

Generalizations are so often perceived as dangerous because they are easily mistaken for universal statements. In fact, when we condemn "generalizations," we are usually rejecting unwarranted universal statements. We actually find ourselves calling universal statements generalizations. Hence we warn people not to generalize. After all, one simple counterexample (a case in which the general claim is not true) is sufficient to disprove the claim.

Sometimes, indeed, we really can't tell whether a particular statement was intended as a generalization that allows for exceptions or as a universal statement that doesn't. Think about the following statement. "Social revolutions—uprisings of the people against their rulers—do not come when conditions of oppression are actually at their worst; they come after conditions have begun to improve. It is then that the people finally see the possibility of something better." Upon hearing or reading that claim, having in mind a historical instance in which this was not true, you may be tempted to disagree with the statement. Whether you have grounds for objection will depend, for one thing, on the statement's intended function as either a generalization or a universal statement. The same wording can be used in both cases.

Dicto simpliciter is a Latin name (meaning "simple saying") for the mistake we make when we apply a true generalization inappropriately in a particular case. In other words, we treat the generalization as if it were a universal statement (or at least as if it were intended to have too extensive a range of application). If, despite Uncle Harry's serious heart condition and the physician's warning to engage in no strenuous exercise, we insist that Uncle Harry should jog "because jogging is good, healthy exercise," our error is that of *dicto simpliciter*. The true generalization is here applied to an exception, an instance in which it does not hold true. Similarly, if five-year-old Andrea says, when asked by her aunt what she will do this weekend, "I'm going to the surprise birthday party for you," her confusion between a generalization and a universal statement may explain why she gave away the secret. "Children are supposed to tell the truth when their aunt asks something, aren't they, Mom?"

In argumentation, universal statements or generalizations that can be mistaken for universal statements must be used with caution. Remember that premises that are universal statements can be disproven with a single counterexample. If a premise is intended as a generalization but might be mistaken for a universal statement, unnecessary and distracting attention to that premise is invited. Evidence that *should* be accepted might not be. Even if you settle the issue after some discussion, getting back on track with the entire original argument may be difficult. On the other hand, if a premise is intended as a universal statement but might be mistaken for a generalization, it is possible for it to be accepted when it should be challenged. Further, this confusion could weaken the overall strength of the argument, because the generalization would probably not offer as much evidence for the conclusions.

■

EXERCISES

4.4 Basic

Which of the following claims are clearly intended as generalizations rather than as universal statements? Which of the following claims are clearly intended as universal claims rather than as generalizations? Which of the following claims could be read in both ways? For this last group, try to determine which way was intended and which is justified.

1. A quote by George F. Will from *Newsweek*, August 18, 1986:

   No nation's security has ever been guaranteed or even significantly enhanced by arms control.

2. From Karl Marx and Friedrich Engels's *Manifesto of the Communist Party*, January 1848:

   The history of all hitherto existing society is the history of class struggles.

3. From Thomas S. Kuhn's *The Structure of Scientific Revolutions*:

   Normal science . . . often suppresses fundamental novelties because they are necessarily subversive of its basic commitments.

4. From M. I. Finley's *The Ancient Greeks*:

   Barring exceptions, temples are chiefly distinguished by "order," Doric or Ionic.

5. From Wanda Shipman's "The Practical Country House" in *Country Journal*, September 1986:

   Most house plans . . . lock the owner into a single method of frame construction—the architect's.

6. From Frederick Turner's "Design for a New Academy" in *Harper's*, September 1986:

   Every great advance, every profound insight in the sciences and other intellectual disciplines, has torn down the barriers and distinctions between those disciplines.

7. From Frederick Turner's "Design for a New Academy" in *Harper's*, September 1986:

   . . . it is precisely *values* that our education system lacks.

8. From Sigmund Freud's *Civilization and Its Discontents*, 1930:

   It is impossible to escape the impression that people commonly use false standards of measurement—that they seek power, success and wealth for themselves and admire them in others, and that they underestimate what is of true value in life.

9. From John Taylor's *Backyard Poultry Keeping*, 1976:

   Generally speaking, all breeds and varieties of poultry that are raised as a hobby, wholly for their ornamental or aesthetic value, fall into this ["Fancy"] group.   ■

ANALOGY

Sometimes you can best make your point by comparing the situation being discussed with something quite different. Comparison with something else—

something simpler, more familiar, or less controversial—can free up a mind that is struggling with or resisting the original argument. The issue can be seen in a new light. Occasionally, an analogy is even used as the *initial* way to convey a point.

You have learned about logical analogies. These show the similarity between the *structures* of two arguments. Analogies generally—not the special argumentative device called the logical analogy—focus instead on the *content* of an argument. One situation is claimed to be similar to another. Since the one situation typically illuminates the other but does not provide uncontestable proof, the objective should be to establish inductive strength rather than deductive certainty.

An **analogy** is a comparison of two generally dissimilar things that are similar in one way, with the inference that they must be similar in a second way. It is often true that two generally dissimilar things have something in common. This is, of course, not sufficient proof that some *other* characteristic that one has is shared by the other. Thus, analogies can be misleading. Before you go on, consider the skill box below on evaluating analogies.

This is the general structure of an analogy.

Item X	Item Y
Premise:	Premise:
. . . has characteristic #1	. . . has characteristic #1
Premise:	Conclusion:
. . . has characteristic #2	. . . has characteristic #2

SKILL

Skill 9. Evaluating analogies

Recognize, create, and evaluate the strength of argumentative analogies.

Why this skill is important

Analogies can convey a point with persuasive power, but sometimes they are less well founded than they initially appear. ∎

The suggestion is that these two things (for example, people, situations, organizations) that are alike in one respect will also be alike in a second specific respect. Here is an example of an analogy.

A conscientious and indignant employee, wagging a finger, scolds his lazy fellow-worker, saying, "Anyone who wastes time on the job, just loafing around like you do, should be fired . . . or, for that matter, arrested! It's the same as stealing money from the company." ∎

Wasting time on the job and stealing from the company are different sorts of activities. They are the same in the sense that in each case the lazy employee ends up with the company's money, through wages or stealth, and does not give anything in return. The speaker concludes, then, that since dismissal or arrest is appropriate in one instance (actually stealing the money), dismissal or arrest will also be appropriate in the second instance (wasting time on the job).

The indignant worker uses an analogy to deliver his condemnation clearly and powerfully. How good is his reasoning? Specifically, the question is, "Is this a fair analogy?" Up to a certain point, this is not an unreasonable analogy. If we ignore the reference to arrest, the reasoning in the analogy has this structure.

Stealing	Wasting Time on the Job
Premise:	Premise:
Money is taken but no appropriate services are returned.	Money is taken but no appropriate services are returned.
Premise:	Conclusion:
The offender should be fired.	The offender should be fired.

Although we might first want to know, in the case of wasting time on the job, whether this problem is chronic and whether management has warned the worker, the reasoning is worth consideration. The manner in which the two situations are similar may well suggest the appropriateness of the same management response.

The worker who issues the scolding does not, however, limit himself to the endorsement of a dismissal. He adds that such an offender should be arrested. This is a second conclusion. The reasoning in the analogy now has this structure as well.

Stealing	**Wasting Time on the Job**
Premise:	Premise:
Money is taken but no appropriate services are returned.	Money is taken but no appropriate services are returned.
Premise:	Conclusion:
The offender should be arrested.	The offender should be arrested.

When carried this far, the analogy breaks down. This conclusion does not follow plausibly from the premises. While the two situations—stealing and wasting time on the job—are similar in the first way, they are not similar in the second. The evidence clearly should not lead us to believe that a person should be arrested for wasting time. Perhaps there is *no* evidence that would establish this. In fact, we can be more specific about the *disanalogy*—the crucial difference—between the two arguments. The "stealing argument" has an unstated second premise: "This way of taking money is prohibited by law." This second premise is not true for the "wasting time argument." Thus, a point that is essential to establishing the conclusion in one case is simply absent in the other.

Here is another example of an analogy.

EXAMPLE

Jacob is criticizing his younger brother, Greg, for spending "every minute" of his free time playing video games. Jacob claims that Greg will grow up to be a narrow-minded person if he doesn't investigate more aspects of life around him and listen to other people's views. Greg, especially annoyed by criticism from his older brother, gets personal, responding angrily, "What about *you*? You spend all *your* time in the library. That's just like spending time in the video arcade. You spend all your time doing one thing: studying in the library. That must lead to just as narrow a mind as anything else that a person gives so much time to." ∎

Like many analogies, including the one in which wasting time was compared with stealing money, this analogy is good only up to a point. Greg's analogy has the following structure.

Video Games	Library Study
Premise:	Premise:
A person's spare time can be spent entirely on this activity.	A person's spare time can be spent entirely on this activity.
Premise:	Conclusion:
Narrow-mindedness would be the result.	Narrow-mindedness would be the result.

Greg is using this analogy in an interesting way. He is trying to show that Jacob, by using his own premises, would have to admit that his dedication to library study shows the same narrowness with which he is charging his brother. Greg intends for Jacob to withdraw his objections to his younger brother's fun in order to avoid that conclusion.

The analogy itself suggests that complete dedication of free time to library study will produce the same narrow person who does not investigate different aspects of life and does not expose himself or herself to other persons' views. There is only a bit of merit in the analogy and its conclusion. The person who spends *all* of his or her free time in the library certainly may miss out on some worthwhile experiences in life. Generally, it seems wise to moderate even a passion for scholarship. However, this analogy is a weak one because, far from being "just like spending time in the video arcade," library work—if it is sufficiently varied—will actually yield the knowledge of many aspects of life and many points of view on issues. The narrowness that Jacob warned against can be defined as an ignorance of such perspectives. Greg's conclusion that Jacob would end up "just as narrow" is not well supported. Note that to evaluate the reasoning thoroughly, we would consider the truth of Jacob's crucial premise concerning the kind of person Greg would become.

Few analogies will provide perfect matches between the dissimilar elements or prove the conclusion with deductive certainty. Fair analogies are effective up to a reasonable point of comparison. In these cases, the premise claims are true or probable and the conclusion is a reasonable product of the comparison. Unfair (often called "bad") analogies are those that do not provide reasonable grounds for strengthening a person's belief in the conclusion or those that present only an illusory parallel.

Guidelines for Evaluating Analogies

Analogies can be subtle, enlightening, and ingenious. They can also be elusive, misleading, and frustrating. No set of rules for the analysis of analogies can replace the need for thoughtful attention to the unique character of each analogy. Still, general advice on the evaluation of analogies may be helpful.

When you are deciding whether an analogy is good, bad, or acceptable up to a point, you can ask yourself these questions.

1. *Are* the two items similar in the first stated way?

2. Does this similarity increase the probability that the two items will be similar in the second way? (This is usually difficult to answer. Asking the question, however, may lessen our gullibility by encouraging careful evaluation of the *relation* between the two stated similarities.)

3. Even if the answer to the second question is "no," is there a parallel between the two items that strengthens the conclusion?

Finally, remind yourself that, ultimately, all analogies appear faulty if the comparison is carried too far. The two items will certainly be different in some ways. You must determine only whether they are similar in the ways that are relevant to the reasoning.

Analogical Explanation

Our focus has been on the analysis of argumentative analogies, which have a premise/conclusion structure. Analogical comparisons can also have an explanatory function. Sometimes we want to *explain* an idea or set of facts rather than to *convince* someone of a conclusion. Here, mere understanding rather than persuasion is the object. Occasionally an analogy may fall somewhere between these two categories.

Here are some examples of how analogical reasoning can be used in explanation. Certain computer processes might be explained through comparison with common functions of the human mind. Certain functions of the human body might be explained through comparison with the workings of a machine. Methods for detecting bad study habits might be explained through comparison with a mechanic's assessment of a car engine that is performing poorly. In cases like these, the comparison is intended to clarify a process or relationship rather than to lead a person to accept a specific belief.

An excerpt from Edward Bellamy's classic book, *Looking Backward*, provides a detailed example of analogical explanation. In the novel, a gentleman from nineteenth-century Boston has awakened in that same city in the year 2000. The advanced society he encounters knows no strife or poverty. In the following passage, the gentleman is describing the nineteenth-century society he has left behind.

By way of attempting to give the reader some general impression of the way people lived together in those days, and especially of the relations of the rich and poor to one another, perhaps I cannot do better than to compare society as it then was to a prodigious coach which the masses of humanity were harnessed to and dragged toilsomely along a very hilly and sandy road. The driver was hunger, and permitted no lagging, though the pace was necessarily very slow. Despite the difficulty of drawing the coach at all along so hard a road, the top was covered with passengers who never got down, even at the steepest ascents. These seats on top were very breezy and comfortable. Well up out of the dust, their occupants could enjoy the scenery at their leisure, or critically discuss the merits of the straining team. Naturally such places were in great demand and the competition for them was keen, every one seeking as the first end in life to secure a seat on the coach for himself and to leave it to his child after him. By the rule of the coach a man could leave his seat to whom he wished, but on the other hand there were so many accidents by which it might at any time be wholly lost. For all that they were so easy, the seats were very insecure, and at every sudden jolt of the coach persons were slipping out of them and falling to the ground, where they were instantly compelled to take hold of the rope and help to drag the coach on which they had before ridden so pleasantly. It was naturally regarded as a terrible misfortune to lose one's seat, and the apprehension that this might happen to them or their friends was a constant cloud upon the happiness of those who rode.

But did they think of themselves? you ask. Was not their very luxury rendered intolerable to them by comparison with the lot of their brothers and sisters in the harness, and the knowledge that their own weight added to the toil? Had they no compassion for fellow beings from whom fortune only distinguished them? Oh, yes, commiseration was frequently expressed by those who rode for those who had to pull the coach, especially when the vehicle came to a bad place in the road, as it was constantly doing, or to a particularly steep hill. At such times, the desperate straining of the team, their agonized leaping and plunging under the pitiless lashing of hunger, the many who fainted at the rope and were trampled in the mire, made a very distressing spectacle, which often called forth highly creditable displays of feeling on top of the coach. At such times the passengers would call down encouragingly to the toilers of the rope, exhorting them to patience, and holding out hopes of possible compensation in another world for the hardness of their lot, while others contributed to buy salves and liniments for the crippled and injured. It was agreed that it was a great pity that the coach should be so hard to pull, and there was a sense of general relief when the specially bad piece of road was gotten over. This relief was not, indeed, wholly on account of the team, for there was always some danger at these bad places of a general overturn in which all would lose their seats.

It must in truth be admitted that the main effect of the spectacle of the misery of the toilers at the rope was to enhance the passengers' sense of the value of their seats upon the coach, and to cause them to hold on to them more desperately than before. If the passengers could only have felt assured that neither they nor their friends would ever fall from the top, it is probable that, beyond contributing to the funds for liniments and bandages, they would have troubled themselves extremely little about those who dragged the coach.*

The author is not presenting argumentation. He is *describing* in order to *inform* with clarity and power. His efforts to leave us with the impression of injustice are obvious, but the passage is still primarily explanatory. We are being told what society was like.[†]

■

EXERCISES

4.5 Basic

Evaluate the following analogies by indicating the ways in which the two items are being claimed to be similar, then by assessing the accuracy of those comparisons.

1. It's amazing that the human race is allowing the world to be increasingly polluted. Birds don't foul their own nests. People don't dispose of their garbage on the living-room floor. The consequences in each case threaten healthy survival. It doesn't make sense to ruin your own habitat.

2. On the new proposals for science education in California schools (from *The San Diego Union*, November 16, 1985):

> While a majority of local educators say they are excited about teaching the new curriculum, a few are concerned that the rigorous subject matter will force some students who are weak in the sciences out of academia.
>
> "Our drop-out rate in the schools already is very high," said Richard Robinson, head of textbook selection for the Oceanside Unified School District. "I have a great concern for the non-academic student, and we have a great many of them. We need to

---

*Edward Bellamy, Looking Backward: Two Thousand to Eighteen Eighty-Seven, *1888. Reprinted with permission of Hendricks House, Inc. from their 1960 edition.*

[†]*Explanatory analogies sometimes also are used to relate why an event has taken place in a certain way. For example, a chemistry teacher might explain the reaction between two substances through analogical comparison with something quite different.*

have more regional occupation classes for those students who just can't cut it in the classroom.

"The curriculum next year is going to be a lot tougher, and for the kids who are just barely making it, it might mean they'll drop out. I hope we learned a long time ago that we can't cut one suit and have it fit everybody."

3. Attributed to Carl Sandburg:

You can't go tramping around from church to church and fulfill yourself. You've got to settle on one church and throw your life into it and build it up. Who would want to go on a picnic all the time and eat out of other people's baskets? You've got to feel the importance of your own individual participation in its life.

4. A Seattle man whose cancerous spleen was removed by UCLA specialists is suing the University of California system, which could make millions of dollars off cells cloned from his tissue. His attorney's comment on the issue was reported in *The San Diego Union*, August 23, 1985:

Our position is that Mr. Moore provided the work of art and [the medical researchers] simply put a frame around it.

5. It is praiseworthy to force people to accept the gospel for their own good, just as force must be used to prevent a delirious person from throwing himself over the edge of a steep cliff.

6. In a campaign advertisement in *The Vista Press*, November 3, 1986, voters were urged to vote out an incumbent candidate for the Tri-City Hospital Board of Directors:

She has brought public infighting and distrust to the Board of Directors severely impairing its ability to compete and progress in today's complex world of hospital management. As a supervisor of a competing hospital, she has a clear conflict of interest. Certainly other multi-million dollar public corporations would not tolerate such activity, or obvious lack of business acumen on their Board! (Does G.M. place on its Board an employee from Ford?)

7. From Christina Hoff Sommers's "Once a Soldier, Always a Dependent," *Hastings Center Report*, August 1986:

Why are [armed service] veterans entitled to special benefits, such as free medical care? Not because such a benefit is an inducement to military service, or because a soldier accepts risk. Rather, the relationship of the Army, to use one service as an example, to a soldier is like that of a parent to a child. The right to health care, even carried beyond the term of service, is an extension of this quasi-familial relationship.

8. From a letter to the editor, *Rutgers Alumni Magazine,* September 1985:

   With regard to [M.C.R.'s] question: do I "need a Ph.D. to perform" my work? Would she let a good nurse with many years of experience perform an operation on her? Or would she require an M.D. to do it? My position in the College of Urban Affairs at Cleveland State University requires that I demonstrate research skills. Without a Ph.D., with just a Master of Library Science degree, I doubt I could prove such skills to my present employers. And I certainly doubt they would let me write the "Graduate Student Research Guide" with which they hope to train their doctoral candidates in Urban Affairs.

9. In November of 1985, the Associated Press reported that the State Education Assessment Center plans to develop new state-by-state comparisons of public school achievement. Here is one reported reaction to these plans:

   Florida's Ralph D. Turlington, whose state was a pioneer in competency testing, said the move "will significantly impact upon achievement in our schools."
   "What would happen if you took down from our athletic fields the scoreboards?" he asked. "If you do not keep score, it is not important."

10. President Reagan reportedly did not remember whether he had approved the 1985 Israeli arms shipment to Iran. On December 10, 1986, *USA Today* reported the following defense of the Reagan claim:

    Do you recall what you had for lunch on the first day of September 1985?

11. From a letter to the editor of *Newsweek,* August 18, 1986 (responding to a National Affairs article in the July 28 issue):

    It's sad that the seven fundamentalist families in Tennessee are so insecure about their own beliefs that they feel obliged to shield their children from the incredible richness of science and human history. They are like totalitarian governments, which seek to control their populations by limiting the information allowed in from the outside world.

4.6 Moderately Difficult

Evaluate the following analogies by indicating the ways in which the two items are being claimed to be similar, then assessing the accuracy of those comparisons.

1. From "Coping with Anxiety," by Carol Tavris, cover story in *Science Digest*, February 1986:

   > All this research suggests to many that a medical model of anxiety is more appropriate than a psychological model, a view that has been picked up by the media. . . .
   >
   > Ultimately, though, the medical-psychological argument is like a debate on whether eggs or flour is more important in baking a cake. Stewart Agras, director of behavioral medicine at Stanford University, observes that within the brain cell, learning and biological processes are joined. Biology influences behavior, but behavior affects biology. Even in a simple organism such as the sea snail, Agras reports, "learning changes the genetic structure of cells within the central nervous system."

2. In William Shakespeare's play *Julius Caesar*, Brutus is attempting to convince Cassius that they must immediately engage in combat with the opposing armies of Octavius and Antony. Brutus says the following:

   > There comes a tide in the affairs of men
   > Which, taken at the flood, leads on to fortune;
   > Omitted, all the voyage of their life
   > Is bound in shallows and miseries.
   > On such a full sea are we now afloat,
   > And we must take the current when it serves,
   > Or lose our ventures. ∎

CHAPTER HIGHLIGHTS

- Many arguments that are not deductively valid are still "good" arguments in the sense that they move reasonable people closer to an acceptance of the conclusion. In such cases, the evidence does not prove the conclusion, but it still offers rational support for the conclusion. The degree of support determines the *inductive strength* of the argument.

- The R-E-T method of evaluating inductive strength requires us to answer three questions.

R: Are the reasons the RIGHT KIND to support the conclusion?

E: Are they ENOUGH to warrant accepting the conclusion?

T: Are they TRUE?

- For a fair consideration of different sides of an issue, we need to be aware of the existence and strength of evidence that conflicts with conclusions we *want* to accept. One recommendation in this chapter was to list the kinds of possible evidence, then to review the list in order to record the available evidence within each category. Another recommendation was to focus on the other person's feelings, then to associate these feelings with specific aspects of the issue.

- *Generalizations* present claims that are intended as generally true. *Universal statements* present claims that are thought to have no exceptions. Since the grammatical form of generalizations and universal statements can be identical, we sometimes can't tell whether a particular statement was intended as a general or a universal claim. Awareness of this important distinction helps us avoid misinterpretation of an argument.

- *Analogies* suggest that since two things are similar in one way they can be expected to be similar in another way. A particular analogy will be specific about the ways in which the items are supposedly similar. In good analogies, the premise claims are true or probable and the conclusion is a reasonable product of the comparison. Unfair or "bad" analogies do not provide reasonable grounds for strengthening a person's belief in the conclusion, or they present only an illusory parallel. Analogy can be used in explanation as well as in argumentation.

For Further Reading

Govier, Trudy. *A Practical Study of Argument*. Belmont, CA: Wadsworth, 1985.

    A study of reasoning that includes an excellent section on analogies.

Scriven, Michael. *Reasoning*. New York: McGraw-Hill, 1976.

    A classic discussion of the practical evaluation of reasoning.

Skyrms, Brian. *Choice and Chance*. Belmont, CA: Wadsworth, 1986.

    An exploration of inductive logic. The deductive-inductive distinction in *Logic in Everyday Life* is consistent with that distinction in *Choice and Chance*.

C H A P T E R

FIVE

Fallacies

Whether your objective is the certainty of a deductively sound argument or the probability established by an inductively strong argument, you undoubtedly make errors in your reasoning from time to time. We all do. Sometimes we even make the same error repeatedly. Such repetition of a single pattern of bad reasoning can be avoided in many cases by learning to recognize the most common logical fallacies.

A **fallacy** is an incorrect pattern of reasoning. There are many such patterns. Each fallacy is given a name that, in some way, describes the error. The same fallacy can be committed on different occasions and in reference to different topics. It would be the *same* fallacy (with the same name) in the sense that the same erroneous pattern of moving from evidence to conclusion was present in each case.

IDENTIFYING FALLACIES

Finding a fallacy in your own or someone else's reasoning does not show that the conclusion is false. It shows only that the conclusion has not been adequately supported by the evidence. In most cases, the fallacy identifies a particular kind of inadequate evidence.

The type of fallacy that we are now discussing is technically called an *informal* fallacy. It is to be distinguished from *formal* fallacies, such as those we examined in Chapter 3 when we considered conditional arguments. (In this book, the word *fallacy* will refer to informal fallacies unless otherwise indicated.) An important difference between formal and informal fallacies is that their persuasive power has a different basis. The formal fallacies persuade us because they so closely resemble arguments whose form is deductively valid. The informal fallacies—the subject of Skill 10—persuade us because the evidence offered can be mistaken as having more bearing on the issue than it really does.

SKILL

Skill 10. Identifying fallacies

Locate and correctly identify informal fallacies when they occur in speech or in written passages.

Why this skill is important

Many erroneous patterns of reasoning, especially when presented in familiar phrases, are not readily recognized as faulty. They often convince when they should not. ∎

FREQUENTLY COMMITTED FALLACIES

Many fallacious patterns of reasoning exist, and names have been given to dozens of them. The eleven fallacies that are defined, explained, and illustrated through examples in this chapter are among the most frequently committed ones.

Attacking the Person

The fallacy of **attacking the person** is committed when we reject a person's reasoning or position by criticizing the arguer instead of the argument.

Premise: An attack on the person's character or circumstances.

We conclude that: That person's reasoning or position is wrong.

In Chapter 1, we observed that people sometimes get off the original track in their thinking and reasoning by "getting personal"—that is, by making critical comments that shift attention from the line of reasoning to the person who is presenting it. It is best to avoid calling this a fallacy, because questionable *reasoning* is not necessarily involved. However, if it is carried one step further, a fallacy is indeed committed, since a questionable conclusion is drawn.

If, on the basis of an irrelevant personal comment, we draw the conclusion that the person's reasoning is flawed or that the person's position is incorrect, we commit the fallacy of attacking the person. Here is an example.

EXAMPLE

After her exercise class, Kim found herself discussing the coming local elections with several of her classmates. Kim confessed, with some embarrassment, that she hadn't thoroughly researched the candidates. In fact, she reported, there was one candidate for the city council about whom she knew nothing: Al Kaplan.

"Oh, he's the one to vote for," Helen, the teacher, called from across the room. She had overheard Kim's last comment and now hurried over to the small group that Kim was in. "Kaplan has more political experience by far than any of the other candidates. He is very intelligent and he's always fair, looking at all sides of an issue. Once I heard him . . ." Helen detailed Kaplan's experience and fairness, then went on to mention a few more of the candidate's strong points. Kim was impressed with the report she received. In fact, while thanking Helen for the information, she commented that she believed she now had a candidate to vote for.

Kim then looked for her friend Marie, and the two of them left the building. As they walked down the sidewalk toward the bus stop, Marie asked what the conversation with Helen had been about. "Oh, Helen was just giving me some reasons for voting for Kaplan for city council," Kim explained.

"What?!" Marie stopped in her tracks and stared at her friend with wide-eyed amazement. "*Helen* was giving you reasons for voting for *Kaplan?*"

"Yes. Why?" asked Kim, physically backing off from her still wide-eyed companion.

A knowing smile came to Marie's face as she relaxed a bit. "Didn't you know? Helen is Kaplan's *sister-in-law*! You would expect her to be in favor of Kaplan in the election."

Kim felt foolish. In the classroom, she had been embarrassed that she hadn't thoroughly researched the candidates. That was nothing when compared with the embarrassment she felt now. "How stupid I was," she confessed. "There I was, nodding my head and taking it all in. I was actually convinced. I had no idea that she had such a personal investment in how I voted. Now I have to forget everything she said. One thing is certain—I'm not going to vote for Kaplan." ∎

Kim's reaction is perhaps understandable. She felt that Helen had taken advantage of her ignorance. Nevertheless, Kim commits the fallacy of attacking the person because she draws the conclusion that Helen's conclusion about Kaplan is unreliable solely on the grounds that Helen's circumstances suggest that she would *want* Kim to believe it. Notice that Kim is not, at this point, considering the evidence that Helen has presented. Kim's rejection of the conclusion that Kaplan would be the best choice for the city council is based on a fact about the arguer; it should be based on an examination of the arguer's premises.

Consider the possibility that the same reasons Helen had presented were now presented by Marie, who has no personal interest in the outcome of the election. Would the reasons that were insufficient to establish the conclusion now become sufficient? Would Helen's reasoning now become good reasoning? Does the soundness of an argument vary, depending on who produces the argument? Certainly logic is more objective than this. To justifiably reject someone's reasoning or position, you must examine the reasons themselves, not the characteristics of the person who is presenting the reasoning.

Sometimes there *is* a reason to doubt someone's word, and Kim may be justified in questioning the reliability of Helen's premises. However, there is usually a possibility of checking those claims through other sources. It is still fallacious to reject the reasoning or position on personal grounds.

Let's look at one brief additional example of the fallacy of attacking the person.

EXAMPLE

Watching a videotape of a convict in a federal prison arguing for certain changes of policy for all American penal institutions, your friend elbows you and comments, "Don't listen to that criminal argue for his point. You know that anything he says will be self-serving." ∎

Your friend commits the fallacy of attacking the person because he is encouraging you to dismiss the convict's entire argument without looking at it. He apparently presumes that nothing the convict says—regardless of what it is—will have any merit. What if the same argument about penal institutions were presented by a noted law-enforcement official or your friend's favorite politician? That same argument might look more credible. Again, to evaluate the merit of an argument, we must at least consider the argument.

The fallacy of attacking the person has also been known as the genetic fallacy (referring to the source or "genesis" of the argument), the fallacy of poisoning the well (fouling the source of the water or argument), and the *ad hominem* fallacy (Latin for "against the man").

Argument from Ignorance

The fallacy of **argument from ignorance** is committed when we suggest that our position is proven by a lack of conclusive evidence against it.

Premise: A claim that a certain position has not been disproven.

We conclude that: That position must be correct.

Sometimes, instead of presenting actual evidence for our own position, we focus on the opposition's inability to *disprove* our point. We may do this by discrediting their arguments to an opposing position or by simply observing that they have no evidence at all to offer. In either case, we commit the fallacy of argument from ignorance if we conclude that this lack of counterevidence is itself proof of our position.

Observe how the fallacy of argument from ignorance is committed in the following example.

EXAMPLE

David and his wife, Nara, have much in common. On the topic of psychic phenomena, however, they are worlds apart. Usually, they avoid the topic for the sake of peace in the family. Today, however, they have slid into heated debate. "Denying that a belief in psychic phenomena has some basis in fact is just closed minded," David charges. "Despite all the many efforts of skeptics around the world, no one has ever been able to show that all of these sincerely reported experiences have other possible explanations or that the realm of the psychic is an impossibility. Doesn't that tell you something?" David is becoming sarcastic and believes that with his last statement, Nara must concede that he is right, or she will indeed settle for being "closed minded." ∎

Perhaps it does not occur to David that conclusive evidence is elusive on *both* sides of the issue. While a belief in psychic phenomena is not easily disproven, neither is the opposite belief easily disproven. Considering the nature of the topic, the kind of proof that would establish a deductively sound argument appears, at the present time, simply unavailable.

Nara could now show David that his reasoning is inadequate by using **parity of reasoning** (the same kind of reasoning) to "prove" the opposing position. After all, a person could argue like this: "Insisting on a belief in fairy tales about super powers of the mind is just irrational. In spite of all the experimentation, no consistent verification of psychic powers has ever been provided through laboratory experiments. Doesn't *that* tell you something?" By at least pointing out how, with the same kind of reasoning, we could produce the opposite conclusion, Nara could show David that his argument is definitely fallacious.

It is often the case, when a person commits the fallacy of argument from ignorance, that this person has a notably limited range of specific evidence to support the original position. The argument-from-ignorance fallacy may be used simply because nothing better comes to mind. It is not surprising that we often see this fallacy committed in discussions and articles on issues for which conclusive evidence is difficult to come by: the existence of spirits, life on other planets, the existence of God, and pseudosciences like astrology.

The elusiveness of evidence should not suggest, however, that in such cases one belief is as reasonable as its opposite. The "burden of proof"— the primary obligation to justify one's claim—often rests more with one side than another. For example, when the existence of something (such as psychic phenomena, extraterrestrial life, or leprechauns) is being claimed, the burden of proof rests more heavily with the person who is making the claim than with the skeptic. Ultimately, of course, both believer and skeptic should remain receptive to new evidence.

The fallacy of argument from ignorance is not completely limited to such mysterious topics. Here is an example of the fallacy in a quite down-to-earth matter.

EXAMPLE

The boss's wallet, which had been lying in the top drawer of his desk, is missing. He is certain that the secretary, whom he has come to dislike, is the thief. "*Of course* I'm sure he did it," the boss proclaims. "I've already questioned him about it, and there's no way that he can prove that, as he claims, he never came into my office while I was out." ∎

This is perhaps a more obvious example of the fallacy of argument from ignorance. The boss's thinking is certainly muddled. Still, whether anyone in the office wants to venture to show the boss, by parity of reasoning, that the opposite ("The secretary did not steal the wallet") could also be shown to be true, remains to be seen. One would hope that *someone* would choose to point out to the boss that the burden of proof rests with him.

Questionable Cause

The fallacy of **questionable cause** is committed when, on insufficient evidence, we identify a cause for an occurrence that has taken place or a fact that is true.

Premise: A statement of fact or an observation that an event has taken place. (This is generally an uncontentious claim.)

We conclude . . . by naming a cause. (This is a contentious claim because there are other possible causes.)

Quick judgments are sometimes necessary. They are often made, however, even when they are unnecessary, and quick judgments can involve oversights.

In naming the cause for something, people sometimes latch on to the first possibility that comes to mind and never give serious consideration to other possible causes. At other times, the problem is not that what has been named as a cause is not one at all; the problem is that the person is seeing only one of several contributing causes. In judgments of either kind, the fallacy of questionable cause is committed.

The fallacy of questionable cause is committed in the following example.

EXAMPLE

Brad recently rented a new apartment that was one of six in a small apartment building near the store where he worked. One morning, about a month after Brad moved in, he was locking his door from the outside. He had to be on the job in fifteen minutes. Suddenly he heard someone shouting. He turned and saw his new landlord running towards him, waving some paper overhead. The landlord, as he approached Brad, slapped his right hand against the papers he held in his left and demanded to know why the water bill (which was not itemized by apartment) was so high. "Every month, it's within ten bucks of the same figure. Now you move in, and the bill almost doubles! What do you do—leave the water running day and night?" The landlord was seething and threatened to add the excess amount to Brad's rent next month.

Brad didn't say anything. He didn't know how to respond. He climbed into his car and drove away.   ■

You don't know Brad. Maybe the landlord was right about him. Maybe he *does*, for some reason, leave the water running "day and night." Still, the landlord, even if he happens to be right, reasons dangerously and fallaciously if he fails even to consider alternate possible causes.

What could explain the sudden rise in the water bill? Could it be that the landlord didn't notice that the rate the Municipal Water District charged had increased sharply? Could it be that there is a serious leak in apartment #6, while the tenant there is on vacation? Could it be that the landlord forgot about the sprinkler system that was on every day now that the weather was hot, or about some extensive tree plantings that were being watered heavily? If the landlord did not give sufficient consideration to other possible causes, he committed the fallacy of questionable cause.

Here is another example.

EXAMPLE

Jonathan was in his second year of college, and he had earned all A's and B's up to this point in his college career. He lived at home with his parents. One morning during breakfast, Jonathan mentioned—as casually as he could—that he would be moving out of his parents' home at the end of the semester. He had found an apartment near the college.

His parents conceded that he was old enough to move out. They were concerned, however, that the many household activities that Jonathan would now have to perform—shopping, cooking, washing clothes, and more—would take too much time from his studying.

Jonathan moved out, but his parents insisted on keeping track of his grades. At the end of the following semester, Jonathan's grade report showed a C and a D. When his parents saw this, they exclaimed, almost in unison, "We told you so!" Jonathan's parents insisted that he return home. The evidence showed that he could not handle both his studies and independent living.   ■

Considering only the information given here, Jonathan's parents may have been right. However, like Brad's landlord, they reason dangerously and fallaciously if they do not ask Jonathan about, or otherwise consider, different possible causes for the drop in grades.

What could account for the lower grades? There are many possibilities. This may have been the semester that Jonathan enrolled in the difficult chemistry course that so few students even pass. Perhaps, as bad luck would have it, this was also the semester when Jonathan began studying a foreign language. Foreign languages can be difficult, even for many bright students. To some, they come easily; to others, it seems as if the thousands of bits of information are just challenging them to be memorized. If Jonathan's parents have not given sufficient consideration to—if they have not even asked about—other possible causes, they commit the fallacy of questionable cause.

The fallacy of questionable cause is common in everyday life. We rashly determine a person's motivation when she makes a comment or acts in a certain way. We attribute to the distrusted politician the worst intentions when he votes against the bill we favor; we attribute to the trusted politician the best intentions when his actions could as easily be conceived differently. We draw hasty conclusions concerning why a job was lost, why the media reported in a certain way, why we succeeded, why we failed, why crime is increasing, why a particular Third-World nation seems determined to humiliate the United States. We are sometimes more enamored of opinions than of the careful rational processes that bring about insight and true beliefs.

Begging the Question

The fallacy of **begging the question** is committed when we assume the truth of our conclusion in a premise.

Premise: A statement that, in order to be true, requires that the conclusion be true.

We conclude . . . what we have already assumed to be true.

We occasionally hear a person make the charge that someone else is "arguing in a circle." One form of arguing in a circle is the fallacy of begging the question. By assuming, in the evidence offered, the very point we wish to prove, we end up proving nothing at all.

Follow the argumentation in this conversation.

EXAMPLE

Ben casually mentions God in his conversation with Theresa. "Wait a minute," Theresa interrupts. "You seem to think that it's just obvious that God exists."

"Well, it's true," Ben responds with surprise. "God certainly *does* exist."

The conversation continues:

Theresa: What makes you so sure of that?

Ben: It's right there in the Bible.

Theresa: And just how does that prove that it's true?

Ben: The Bible is infallible—it has no errors.

Theresa: And what makes you think that the Bible is perfect? Do you believe everything you read in *Reader's Digest*? Or *Newsweek*? Or the morning newspaper? What makes the Bible so different?

Ben: The difference is that the Bible is the Word of God.   ■

What is Ben's point? His point—the conclusion that "God exists"—is stated at the beginning of the argument. Actually, this statement was originally just a claim—not a conclusion—since no evidence was being presented to support it. When his statement was challenged, however, Ben began to give reasons in support of his position. As soon as he offered the first premise ("It's right there in the Bible"), the statement that "God exists" became a conclusion.

Let's reconstruct Ben's argument. Since his last statement is offered as evidence for his previous one, the statement "The Bible is infallible" is a transitional conclusion and not just a premise.

Premise: The Bible is the Word of God.

Transitional Conclusion: The Bible is infallible.

Premise: The Bible says that God exists.

Conclusion: God exists.

Has Ben proven his point? His argument does seem to be valid: *if* its premises were true, the conclusion would follow and be true as well. There is a problem with this attempt to persuade, however. The conclusion is already *assumed* to be true in one of the premises. The conclusion that "God exists" must be accepted as true *before* the premise that "the Bible is the Word of God" is accepted. This makes the argument useless. If Ben were addressing someone who already accepted the existence of God, the argument would be unnecessary. He or she would need no argument. If, however, he addresses someone who does not already accept the existence of God, he should be unable to persuade that person: if he or she cannot accept the conclusion that "God exists," then neither will that person be able to accept the premise that "the Bible is the Word of God."

Ben's argument requires a certain type of circular reasoning. The premises are intended as evidence to establish the conclusion but, in order to accept one premise, the conclusion must already be established. The preceding example does not show that reference to the Bible is irrelevant to a belief in God, but it *does* show that, worded as it is here, this argument should be unconvincing to the unbeliever.

Another version of the fallacy of begging the question can be shown through the following example.

EXAMPLE

Sam and Jed are discussing the National Football League's next season.

Sam: Seattle will be the strongest team at running the football next year—at least in the American Conference.

Jed: What makes you think so?

Sam: It's just that all of the other teams—however good they may be—will be unable to produce the same effectiveness at running the ball that we'll see with Seattle. ∎

In this case, the single premise is merely a rewording of the conclusion. The conclusion is that "Seattle will be the strongest team at running the football next year (in the American Conference)." The premise states that the other teams will not be as effective at running the ball. The premise not only assumes the truth of the conclusion; it echoes the very same statement in different terms.

In each kind of example, the truth of the conclusion is assumed in a premise. We believe we have proven a point that we have merely *assumed* to be true. This is the fallacy of begging the question.

Two Wrongs Make a Right

The fallacy of **two wrongs make a right** is committed when we suggest that an act is morally permissible, offering as evidence the claim that someone else has done something similar.

Premise: A claim that someone has performed an act that is similar to this one.

We conclude that: This act is not morally wrong.

The scene is classic. Little Timmy is perched on a kitchen stool. On his tiptoes, he can just manage to reach the cookie jar. He is elbow-deep in the cookie jar when . . . Who walks into the kitchen? Yes. It's Mommy. Knowing quite well that cookies before dinner are not allowed, Timmy can only come up with the defense that "Johnny did it first!"

The desperation in little Timmy's voice is enough to show that even *he* knows that this response will not get him out of trouble completely. Pointing the finger of blame will, at the most, allow Timmy to share the spotlight of guilt with someone else. *The fact that another person—in this case, Johnny—has done the same thing does not prove that the act is proper.*

Timmy does not use fallacious reasoning—he does not commit a fallacy. It is not clear that he misunderstands or reasons incorrectly. Sometimes, however, people draw unjustified conclusions using Timmy's approach; they commit the fallacy of *two wrongs make a right*. On the grounds that someone else has done something similar, they conclude that a particular act is not morally wrong. Here is an example of *two wrongs make a right*.

EXAMPLE

Charged with campaign improprieties, the politician huffily responds with the following defense: "I've done nothing wrong. Why, look at my opponent. He's done the very same thing for years!" ■

The speaker's conclusion is that he's "done nothing wrong." His only premise is his claim that his opponent has behaved in the same way. This kind of evidence does not establish the conclusion.

What kind of evidence does establish such a conclusion? This is certainly difficult to say. People do not always agree on what kind of evidence it takes to establish a *value claim* such as the conclusion in the preceding example. Still, despite such disagreement, we would be rather universal in our agreement that a particular act is not right simply because it has been done before. The fact that a president of the United States has used public funds for private purposes, for example, does not justify the same behavior by a subsequent president. It may have been morally wrong in the first place and, as the common saying puts it, "two wrongs don't make a right." The logical error, then, is made in offering the wrong kind of evidence to establish the conclusion.

Two wrongs do not make a right. Nor do *many* wrongs make a right. Sometimes, in attempting to justify an act, we may offer as evidence the claim that many people have done something similar. Examine this example.

EXAMPLE

A wife and her husband are driving through the parking lot at the Food Basket market, looking for a parking space. At first they see none. Suddenly, the wife, who is driving, spies a space that is conveniently located near the sliding-glass entry doors of the market. She quickly pulls into the parking space and turns off the ignition. She feels the burning gaze of her husband. Perturbed by his apparent disapproval, she turns to him and snaps, "Don't look at me as if I've done something terrible by parking in a 'Handicapped Only' space. People do it all the time!" ∎

The wife commits the fallacy of *two wrongs make a right* because her suggested conclusion that parking in a "handicapped only" space is acceptable is supported only by her claim that "people do it all the time." She means, of course, that it is done *very often*. This evidence is, by any common standard, insufficient to establish that the act is morally permissible.

Although there are more than just two "wrongs" in cases like this, the reasoning is similar, whether the argument refers to one or to many other instances, and we can say that the same fallacy is committed: *two wrongs make a right*—or, for brevity, "two wrongs."

Division

The fallacy of **division** is committed when we conclude that any part of a particular whole must have a certain characteristic, using as evidence the claim that the whole has that characteristic.

Premise: The claim that a whole has a certain characteristic. (This is generally an uncontentious claim.)

We conclude that: Any part of that whole must have the same characteristic. (This is generally a false conclusion.)

A basketball team is nothing more than all of its players. A committee is nothing more than all of its members. A stamp collection is nothing more than all of the stamps *in* that collection.

Certainly, in one sense, each of these statements is true. In each case, the whole (the team, the committee, and the collection) is being considered as the sum of its parts (the players on the team, the members of the committee, and the stamps in the collection). In each case, we have a *part-whole relationship*; the similar parts completely constitute the whole, which usually has a name of its own. The fallacy of division is committed only when reasoning about part-whole relationships. Consider other examples of part-whole relationships.

Whole	**Part**
Encyclopedia set	Its volumes
News article	Its paragraphs
Family	The members
Pack	The wolves
Orchestra	The musicians
Deck of cards	The individual cards

When we reason that whatever is true of the whole must therefore be true of each of the parts, we commit the fallacy of division. Consider this example.

EXAMPLE

The army sergeant was walking through the lounge of the Officers' Club to deliver a message when he was seen by several officers at one of the tables. "Hey, sergeant!" a young lieutenant at the table called out, "I see from your organizational patch that you're from the Fighting Fourth Division, the bravest combat unit in this country. Sit down and have a drink and some conversation with us. We're always glad to share our table with a brave soldier." ■

Do you see how the fallacy of division is involved in the lieutenant's thinking? The lieutenant knows or accepts the perhaps common belief that the Fighting Fourth Division is the bravest fighting unit in the country and concludes that the sergeant must be brave since, for a unit to perform bravely, its soldiers must. The characteristic of being brave is attributed to this *part* simply because of its membership in the *whole*. This shows that the lieutenant would expect the same of any—and therefore all—of the "parts." His reasoning is faulty, however, because it is not necessary for every soldier in the unit to have acted bravely in order to justify the unit's label of "bravest."

Consider another example of the fallacy of division.

EXAMPLE

The young man was clearly perturbed. "I've heard that the BBC's dramatic series 'Great Lives' was one of the most notable productions for television in the past twenty years," he complained. "Well, last night I took the time to see one of the programs in that series. It was good but it wasn't great. 'One of the most notable productions in twenty years'! These critics sure get carried away with their rhetoric sometimes." ∎

While it may be true that the series is one of the most notable productions for television in the past twenty years, a reasonable expectation is that some of the programs in that series will be better than others. It is even possible that particular programs in the series are, considered alone, not especially noteworthy at all. Thus, while the whole—the series—may be a very notable production, not each program will necessarily be so notable. The characteristic of being "one of the most notable productions for television in the past twenty years" may be true of the whole but not be at all appropriate to a particular part of that whole (even though the series is nothing more than the sum of the programs).

False Dilemma

The fallacy of **false dilemma** is committed when we consider too few of the available alternatives and assess all but one as impossible or unacceptable.

Premise: A statement of available alternatives (omitting at least one that is worthy of consideration).

Premise (often unstated or indirectly stated): A suggestion that all but one of these stated alternatives are impossible or unacceptable.

We conclude that: The remaining alternative must be accepted. (The conclusion is often unstated also.)

We sometimes hear people complain that they are "in a dilemma." They often seem to mean that they must make a choice between two or more alternatives, none of which is wholly desirable. Literally, a person faces a dilemma whenever there are multiple alternatives to choose from, whether desirable or not.

You are being presented with a dilemma when you are told, "There are only two routes you can take to get to the top of Mount Rennen—Archer's Road, which is winding and treacherous, or Route 74, which is a very steep climb." This is a true dilemma—the statement that there are only two alternatives is true—if, indeed, there is no other route to the top. However, if there is another route, the dilemma is a false one. Your alternatives have been incorrectly limited to two.

Let's examine an obvious example of the fallacy of false dilemma.

EXAMPLE

The father, thinking that a college education is essential to his son's, or any child's, success in life, demands an answer to his question: "Are you going to go to college and make something of yourself or are you going to end up being an unemployable bum like me?" ▪

The father is presenting his son with a false dilemma. The dilemma is his son's supposed choice between college, on the one hand, and personal failure, on the other. The dilemma is a false one because it is quite possible to "make something of yourself" without a college education. The father has suggested that his son has two alternatives: "go to college" or be an "unemployable bum." An alternative not considered is that of being employable—indeed, even being quite successful financially—but not going to college. Tens of thousands of real-life cases in business and industry confirm this possibility.

People may set the trap of a false dilemma (also called the *either/or fallacy*) for themselves by their tendencies to adopt extreme views and to distort others' views into extremes. Consider the following comment.

EXAMPLE

"Look, the choice is simple. It's either capitalism pure and simple, as it was meant to be, without any government interference through regulation . . . or else you have the government having complete control over not only business, but also political and private affairs." To the speaker, a businesswoman, the choice did, indeed, seem to be simple.   ■

Each alternative, as presented here, is an extreme. There are certainly alternatives between these extremes. You need look no farther than the American economic and political system to find an example of limited government control over business. While there is government regulation of American businesses, such regulation falls short of "complete control" of business or of "political and private affairs." The speaker in the preceding example, along with many other businesswomen and men, may believe that government control over business is too extensive, but they should admit that it is not without limit.

Colloquially, a person sometimes writes or says that another person has gone "between the horns" of a dilemma. A person goes "between the horns" when he or she recognizes the dilemma as a false one by identifying a position that is *between* the extremes of the stated dilemma. It's as if you were backed to a wall with a mad bull racing toward you. With the bull just five feet away, you seem to have only two alternatives: lunge to your right and be gored by the left horn or lunge to your left and be gored by the right horn. It seems that you will be caught on one horn or the other. Perhaps, however, by turning sideways or positioning yourself just right, you may avoid both horns. To avoid being caught on one of the "horns of a dilemma," we should consider whether each "horn" is an opposing and extreme position and whether there is, indeed, any position between those horns.

Contrary-to-Fact Hypothesis

The fallacy of **contrary-to-fact hypothesis** is committed when we state with an unreasonable degree of certainty the results of events that might have occurred but did not.

Premise (often unstated): A belief that hypothetical event A could have resulted in event B.

Premise (often unstated): A belief that A could have had no other result. (This is a false premise.)

We conclude that: If A had occurred, then B would have resulted.

It is not unlikely that all people at times speculate about how things *would have been* if a particular event in the past had occurred differently. Sometimes, through the process of such speculation, a person comes to an unjustified conclusion about what the results of that change in history would have been. Here is an example of such speculation.

EXAMPLE

She felt sad because of her neighbor's family problems. "If only she hadn't got married at such a young age, she would be a happier woman today." ∎

Perhaps the woman would be happier. Perhaps she wouldn't. We can't know what her extended single life would have been like; it could have been, for whatever reasons, as miserable as her married life. We also can't know what her married life would have been like if she had married later or chosen another person to marry. Certainly it may be reasonable, depending on the circumstances, to think of the woman's marriage as a *contributing influence* on her state of mind, but the preceding claim about what "would have been" is unknowable. Too many variables remain.

The armchair sports fan commits this fallacy when she claims that "if Flannery had pinch-hit in the eighth instead of Brown, when the bases were loaded, we would have won the game." This kind of claim may sound foolish, but it's also common. For another example, however, let's consider a more serious situation.

EXAMPLE

Terrorists and hostages have achieved an unwelcome but regular presence in the news of the modern world. So many people seem to know how a particular situation should have been handled. Recently, Presidents Carter and Reagan have had to make important decisions without complete knowledge of the consequences of various courses of action and without the benefit of hindsight. One person swears that "if the president had shown a readiness to use military force from the very beginning, the crisis would not have gone on so long." Another person insists, "Had the President admitted that those people had a legitimate complaint in the first place, a negotiated settlement would have followed." There are, of course, still more views on which actions would have produced which results. Many of them are voiced with indignation. ∎

In at least one of the hostage crises, one of the two opinions mentioned may have been more well founded than other opinions. Still, we are unjustified in claiming with deductive certainty that we know the necessary results of actions that produce consequences that rely on so many uncontrollable and unpredictable factors. Sometimes, in fact, we are even unjustified in claiming that a result is *probable*.

A statement in which the fallacy of contrary-to-fact hypothesis is committed will not always start with the word *if*. Notice in the preceding example the comment that begins, "Had the president admitted . . ." There are many other ways in which this fallacy might be worded. Sometimes there is no key phrase at the beginning. With the sentence "We would not be alive today were it not for the quick thinking of this young man," a conditional statement about the results of a change in the past is made. The fallacy of contrary-to-fact hypothesis is committed if other circumstances might have resulted in the rescue as well.

A claim to know the results of an event that might have taken place is not always unjustified. When someone says, for example, "If I had spent the day at home studying as my brother said I should, I would not have broken my leg in that motorcycle accident," the fallacy is not committed. The definition of this fallacy does not include such a statement; there is no *unreasonable certainty* about the results. Of course, pondering such might-have-been circumstances usually serves no good purpose.

When we can learn from the past, and thus serve our future, reflection on what might have been is worthwhile. It may be worthwhile to speculate on the results of having gone to a different school, having accepted a different job offer, or having responded differently in a personal crisis. It is also worthwhile to avoid hasty judgments about those results—in other words, to avoid the fallacy of contrary-to-fact hypothesis.

Common Belief

The fallacy of **common belief** is committed when we accept a statement as true and offer as evidence the claim that many other people believe it.

Premise: The claim that many people accept a certain statement.

We conclude that: That statement is true.

We know that other people can be wrong even when they are absolutely convinced that they are right. We also know that *many* people can be wrong about the same belief. The fact that a certain belief is held by dozens or hundreds or thousands of people is not sufficient to prove that the belief is a true one. Nevertheless, people occasionally suggest that we accept this kind of evidence in particular cases. Often, when such reasoning is offered, the arguer had been inclined to accept that conclusion in the first place.

How would such clearly fallacious reasoning ever be effective when discoursing with another person? The following example suggests an answer to this question.

EXAMPLE

She knew about President Nixon's 1974 resignation from hearing her parents talk and from her high-school history class. Willa knew that the impeachment process had never begun. Perhaps, she thought, Richard Nixon was not guilty of all the charges that had been informally made against him. When she ventures this comment to two friends at school, however, one of them scoffs, "Of course Nixon was guilty. Everyone knows that!"

Willa hesitates. "Well, I guess he *was* guilty . . . actually. I just think it would be interesting to know more about political scandals like that." ∎

The friend who insists on Nixon's guilt offers only one reason to get Willa to agree with his position. He says, "Everyone knows that." Certainly he doesn't mean that, literally, *no one* thinks otherwise. He does mean that since so many people believe Nixon was guilty, it must be true. At this point, Willa's friend commits the fallacy of common belief.

Why does Willa back off from her suggestion, immediately conceding that she was wrong? She quickly admits, "Well, I guess he *was* guilty," despite a glaring lack of evidence in this conversation for either position. She probably backs off for reasons of esteem rather than logic. When someone says, "Everyone knows that!" an implication seems to be that any person who doesn't possess this common information must be especially dense or poorly informed. In the company of peers or those who are perceived as superiors, many people will relinquish even the most secure positions. In this instance Willa's was not particularly secure.

Have you ever been the only person in a crowded room who didn't agree on a particular emotional issue? In this kind of situation, most of us would be uncomfortable about raising a hand and actually voicing our dissent. On some topics and in some situations, many of us simply would not do it. Research done by Solomon Asch shows that a person who draws a conclusion based on *personal observation* can come to reject that conclusion after hearing that others have drawn a different conclusion.* Asch brought the person to be examined, along with seven others, into a room. Each of the eight was shown three lines of easily distinguished length. The person who was to be examined was placed last when all were lined up. This person did not know that the others were part of the study and had been previously instructed on how to respond to questions. When subsequently shown a single line to determine whether it matched previous line A, B, or C, the eighth person often answered incorrectly *when the first seven did not answer correctly*. In fact, this happened in one-third of all such cases. However, when studied individually, without the distorting influence of the others, those examined responded correctly in 98 percent of their judgments. If the pressure of conflicting conclusions is so great when people are reporting on the basis of personal observation, how much more readily will people relinquish their conclusions if they are based wholly or in part on less secure grounds?

Consider the following exchange as another example of the fallacy of common belief.

EXAMPLE

Jovine sits at the breakfast table, shuffling the morning newspaper much longer than on most mornings. It's a day off for her. It's Lincoln's Birthday. She looks up from her paper. Her roommate is at the stove. "You know, it's interesting that some presidents get immortalized and others don't."

"Immortalized?" Terry's voice reflects no great interest.

"Yes. We get a day off for Lincoln and Washington, but there are other presidents who lots of Americans have never heard of. I wonder if there's really such a big difference between them. For example, maybe old Honest Abe wasn't such a great man after all. . . ."

Terry is suddenly awake. "*Of course* Lincoln was a great man. Any schoolchild knows that!"   ∎

---

*S. E. Asch, *"Studies of Independence and Conformity: A Minority of One Against a Unanimous Majority,"* Psychological Monographs 70 (1956).

"Any schoolchild knows that." This single premise suggests that if Jovine is not aware of that which is common knowledge even to little children, she must be a sad case, indeed. Terry has given no actual evidence for the conclusion that Lincoln was a great man; instead, he commits the fallacy of common belief.

"Everyone knows that." "Any schoolchild knows that." Other familiar phrases are also called on in the commission of this fallacy: "No one seriously doubts that" or "No one in his right mind could doubt that" or "No educated person would doubt that." The latter two are especially intimidating. "It's just common knowledge." "That's obvious to anyone who gives it any thought." You can probably add to the list.

How does the fallacy of common belief differ from the fallacy of *two wrongs make a right*? They *are* different. Review the definitions. The *two wrongs* fallacy dealt with action; the fallacy of common belief deals with belief. *Two wrongs make a right* gave rise to the conclusion that something was right—morally permissible; common belief gives rise to the conclusion that something is true.

Past Belief

The fallacy of **past belief** is committed when we accept a statement as true and offer as evidence the claim that it has been believed in the past.

Premise: The claim that a certain statement has been believed in the past.

We conclude that: That statement is true.

The phrase *tried and true* reflects the common view that whatever stands the test of time must have some merit. Perhaps this common view is well based. When someone takes this to an extreme, however, the result can be fallacious reasoning. We do not actually hear people say, "It's been believed in the past, so it must be true." Still, we do hear something very close to that.

EXAMPLE

Luis does not believe in the immortality of the soul. In fact, Luis does not believe that anything like a soul exists at all. This bothers his brother, Leon, who is quite religious and pleads for Luis to try to see the issue differently. "Look," argues Leon, "human beings must have souls. This belief goes back for centuries and centuries!" ∎

Leon commits the fallacy of past belief. It is certainly possible for false beliefs to be held for long periods of time. Even if you insist that humans do have souls, you should recognize that the preceding argument is fallacious.

"People have accepted [or *believed* or *known*] that for centuries." Whenever such a statement is offered as a premise to support the conclusion that the belief at issue is true, the fallacy of past belief is committed. After all, some beliefs that had been popularly held for years turned out subsequently to be false. An example is the ancient belief that in humans, only the male contributes hereditary characteristics to an offspring. With this in mind, follow this example of faulty reasoning.

EXAMPLE

Mona is wondering whether The Holistic Clinic in St. Louis might provide successful therapy for her bad back. Her son is skeptical, insisting that holistic health is just a fad without any scientific basis. Mona disagrees, saying, "But there *must* be something to this holistic health business. Did you know that the ancient Greeks had a holistic conception of health?" ■

It may well be true that there is, as Mona puts it, "something to this holistic health business." However, the Greeks' possession of a similar view does not prove that this is so. The Greeks, after all, were wrong—from our present perspective, at least—about many other things. Might they not have been wrong about this as well? Mona needs evidence of a different kind if she is to avoid the fallacy of past belief in arguing for her present belief.

The modern Western world has revered the ancient Greeks. Our view of the history of civilization has endowed some groups of people with a halo of honor. Different characteristics are applied to different groups, and with some, such as the ancient Greeks and the ancient Egyptians, the aura is that of a special, though primitive, capacity for insight into the truth. However well or poorly founded such a view might be, our reverence for such cultures is excessive if it curtails our independent reasoning about particular topics.

The preceding example is correctly referred to as an example of the fallacy of past belief rather than the fallacy of common belief because, while many people may have believed this conclusion, it is the ancient Greeks' special place in history that seems to warrant their credibility. The earlier example of people "believing that for centuries" exhibits the fallacy of past belief because the notion of the longevity of the belief is a crucial element in the persuasive attempt.

False Authority

The fallacy of **false authority** is committed when we accept a statement as true and offer as evidence the claim that it was accepted by a particular person whose knowledge or reliability on this issue is questionable.

Premise: The claim that person X accepts this statement. (This person's knowledge or reliability is questionable.)

We conclude that: That statement is true.

If we were to rely only on information based on our personal experiences and not at all on reports of others' experiences, we could claim much less knowledge than we do. Those who did not have firsthand knowledge of the politics of the White House staff or the Vatican or the Kremlin would have to profess ignorance of the subject and leave the consideration of the matter to those who did have such knowledge. Those who hadn't been to the meetings of the U.S.-Soviet summit would have to do the same. Those without extensive experience in nuclear weaponry would forfeit the possibility of making intelligent comments on that topic.

Actually, we do rely on information provided by others when we think about both global and mundane matters. It seems silly to suggest that we do otherwise. We are fortunate to have books, newspapers, magazines, acquaintances, and other sources to expand our horizon of understanding.

Still, not everything that is reported to us is true, and it's not clear whether it's worse to believe too little or too much. As information users, we need to be able to distinguish between more and less credible sources. This is often difficult, since there is not always a clear line of distinction between the justified authority and the unqualified source. Nevertheless, we can make a beginning with the fallacy of false authority.

When the argument for the truth of a statement rests on the testimony of someone who is not in a position to know or, for some other reason, is likely to convey incorrect information, the fallacious reasoning may be branded as false authority. Let's examine an obvious example of the fallacy.

EXAMPLE

"I'll let you in on a hot financial tip," the bartender confides in his already glassy-eyed regular. "When you're deciding where to invest your money, keep in mind that the economy is going to take a sharp and long-term upswing in April."

The customer manages a question, but his gaze doesn't wander from the neon advertising lamp. "How do you know?"

"My neighbor told me." The bartender leans closer. "And he's been very involved in financial dealings for years—stocks and bonds and real estate and things like that."　　　　　　　　　　　　　　■

Initially, the bartender does not argue for his claim that the economy is going to take a sharp and long-term upswing in April. He offers no evidence. In response to his customer's question, however, he does offer a single premise: "My neighbor told me." At this point, it seems that we are dealing with a rumor. Having no reason to believe that the neighbor has any special insight, we should recognize the fallacy of false authority. The bartender does go on to describe the neighbor's credentials ("he's been very involved in financial dealings . . ."), but this is insufficient to eliminate the fallacious character of his reasoning. Many people "are very involved with financial dealings," and even within this group there is wide disagreement concerning economic forecasts. Contrary to the bartender's suggestion, the neighbor's claim is not sufficient to guarantee the truth of the conclusion. Notice, too, that the claim about the upswing was not qualified in any way. Economics is a social science that notoriously produces divergent predictions even from the experts. Even the word of an expert economist should not be taken as proof of such a conclusion.

It is true, then, that the fallacy of false authority can be committed even when an expert is speaking within his or her own area of competence. Examine this passage.

EXAMPLE

Mike is in a lazy sprawl across his favorite TV chair, watching a talk show on which an astrophysicist is being interviewed. "And what about the interesting question of intelligent life on other planets?" asks the host. "Dr. Wexler, being an astrophysicist, you must have considered the issue of this possibility. Tell us, *is there* intelligent life elsewhere in the universe?"

"Yes, I'm certain that there are creatures whose capacity for intelligence is at least equal to ours. . . ."

Mike presses the off button on his remote control box and walks out of the room. Talking to no one but himself, he says quietly, "How interesting. I guess she knows what she's talking about. She's an astrophysicist. I never thought there was life out there, but this isn't the first time I've been wrong." ∎

Dr. Wexler does not commit the fallacy of false authority. Even if she is wrong about extraterrestrial beings, she displays no fallacious argumentation in the preceding example. In fact, the television set is turned off so soon that we do not even know whether she offers any argumentation at all.

On the other hand, Mike *does* commit the fallacy of false authority in concluding that he has been wrong and that there is, after all, intelligent life in outer space. Although the issue does, at least partially, fall within the range of Dr. Wexler's expertise, no one, as far as we know, possesses any evidence that would establish a conclusion such as this with certainty. Therefore, despite Dr. Wexler's knowledge in the general area and on related topics, Mike should realize that unquestioned acceptance of this conclusion is unjustified. Unless it is a closely guarded secret, news like this would have lit up the pages of books, magazines, and newspapers, and provided seemingly endless hours of television coverage. Mike should certainly not just dismiss Dr. Wexler's comment, but he should pay close attention to the evidence before passing judgment. Perhaps Dr. Wexler holds this belief on religious or other grounds, rather than on the basis of scientific evidence. Perhaps she makes this point after Mike's television is off. Whatever the case, Mike has judged hastily.

Often there is no good reason to doubt that someone's testimony assures the truth of a certain conclusion. If the baseball coach says that his star pitcher has a sore arm, we should believe him unless there is a good reason to doubt it. If the psychology professor says that phobias have been reclassified, we should believe her unless there is a good reason to doubt it. We are not committing a fallacy every time we accept someone's word. Still, it is important to remember that there is a difference between knowing that something is true "on good authority" and knowing that something is true on the basis of personal observation and reasoning. The latter is almost always a firmer knowledge than the former.

In technical areas such as nuclear power, ecology, governmental budgets, health care, automobile safety, and urban design, we need to use information provided by people who have special knowledge. We should also listen carefully to their reasoned judgments concerning probabilities. Their expertise is valuable. When listening to the experts, however, remember the following:

1. *It is sometimes difficult to identify the most qualified authorities.* Some people who have much experience in one area or who have advanced university

degrees (M.A., Ph.D.) may nevertheless be barely competent in that area. The *quality* of a person's work in that field is relevant but often unknown to the casual inquirer. Persons who head organizations with impressive names sometimes gain unwarranted respect and credibility. For a nominal fee, however, a person can file for a "fictitious name." That person can then identify himself or herself as, for example, the president of the National Association of Taxpaying Americans. Such an "association" might have one or several members. We should thus avoid being impressed by mere "expert appearances."

2. *Experts can be biased.* Anyone, including scientists, priests, psychologists, historians, and statisticians, can have points of logical vulnerability that draw them towards or away from certain kinds of data or certain conclusions, even in their own specialties. Sometimes a person's previous positions in research publications incline him or her toward that same position or a similar one. Few people are willing to encourage the perception that their previous work is seriously flawed.

3. *The conclusions of even the best experts can conflict.* When the most credible authorities disagree, there is no reasonable alternative to weighing the evidence for yourself. Even if the issue is highly specialized, you will need to evaluate the strength of each position by examining the authorities' expressed reasons for settling on their positions. You should seek information that is in "layman's terms," or nontechnical language. At last, sometimes there is no choice but to make a provisional decision on the basis of partial information and that dangerous sensibility called intuition.

COMMENTS ON THE FALLACIES

Fallacies can occur in spoken or in written communications. In some instances they will be obvious; in some they will be hard to recognize. Although the pleasure of the successful recognition of another person's fallacious reasoning may incline you to bring it immediately to that person's attention, you should first consider the probable reaction to, and results of, your comment. If your comment undermines your intentions for your overall interaction with this person, you must exercise self-discipline by withholding or rewording it.

Who commits the fallacy—the person who presents it or the person who "falls for it"? Generally, both the person who originates and the person who accepts fallacious reasoning commit the fallacy. The first person *argues fallaciously* by presenting the reasoning, regardless of whether he or she is aware of the error. The second person *reasons fallaciously* (as does the first person, if the fallacy is committed unwittingly) by accepting the reasoning as adequate.

While most of the patterns of reasoning in these fallacies are erroneous when judged by the standard of deductive validity (begging the question is an exception), some arguments that are examples of these fallacies may have a degree of inductive strength. For example, the fallacy of division may yet allow inductive strength, especially if the whole has few parts.

FALLACY LOOK-ALIKES

Beware of look-alikes. By knowing the definitions of the fallacies, you can determine whether the fallacies are committed in particular cases. On occasion, a person's reasoning may resemble an actual example of a certain fallacy, but the resemblance will not be sufficient to qualify that reasoning as another example of that fallacy. In cases like this, either the similarity is incidental and does not fit the definition, or the reasoning conforms to part but not all of the definition. One logic textbook writer has actually named "False Charge of Fallacy" as a fallacy itself, committed when a person incorrectly charges that another has committed a specific fallacy.*

Consider some examples of how an overzealous fallacy-spotter might incorrectly label a comment or written passage as fallacious.

The fallacy of *attacking the person* might be incorrectly specified when a relevant claim about the person's background has been made and no questionable conclusion concerning the person's reasoning or position has been drawn. Example: "George will certainly know something about prison routine. He's an ex-convict who served eight years in the state prison."

The fallacy of *attacking the person* might be incorrectly specified when the person has sidetracked the matter by "getting personal," but has drawn no questionable conclusion concerning the person's reasoning or position. Example: "You just like to argue for the sake of argument, don't you? I hate it when you do that."

The fallacy of *argument from ignorance* might be incorrectly specified when a lack of evidence for an opposing view has been mentioned, but that position has not been rejected on this basis. Example: "We have found no evidence to support the claim that he acted in self-defense."

*Howard Kahane, in Logic and Contemporary Rhetoric *(Belmont, CA: Wadsworth, 1984), p. 121.*

The fallacy of *questionable cause* might be incorrectly specified when a well-justified claim has been made concerning the cause of something. Example: Extensive hair loss immediately following certain kinds of chemotherapy would quite reasonably be attributed to that therapy.

The fallacy of *begging the question* might be incorrectly specified when a second claim has repeated or assumed an earlier claim, but there is no premise-conclusion relation between the two claims. Example: "You'll get the raise you asked for. Your boss knows he can't replace you, and he thinks you'll quit if he turns you down. There's no doubt about it. He'll give you the raise."

The fallacy of *two wrongs make a right* might be incorrectly specified when claims concerning the success of past practices have been offered as reasons for adopting the practice, but no issues of right and wrong are concerned. Example: "My attorney, Mr. Carr, has served me well in the past. So I intend to use his services again this time, even if this area of law is not his specialty."

The fallacy of *division* might be incorrectly specified when a characteristic has been determined to be possessed by a member of a whole on the basis of the claim that this characteristic was possessed by "every one" of the members rather than by the whole considered collectively. Example: "*Of course* he's a brave soldier. *All* soldiers in the First Division are brave."

The fallacy of *false dilemma* might be incorrectly specified when the omitted alternative was not a workable or viable one. Example: A friend says, "You're not really limited to the alternatives of passing this final test or failing the course. Just get the teacher to let you do an extra-credit assignment." This teacher, however, does not accept extra-credit work.

The fallacy of *contrary-to-fact hypothesis* might be incorrectly specified when the result which has been named is actually a necessary result rather than a merely possible result. Example: "If you had joined the army last year, as I suggested, you wouldn't be out of work with no paycheck and no place to live, like you are now."

The fallacy of *common belief* might be incorrectly specified when, although widespread acceptance of a belief has been noted, this has not been offered as proof of its truth. Example: "Interest in extraterrestrial beings is greater than ever. Tens of thousands of people actually believe in UFOs."

The fallacy of *past belief* might be incorrectly specified when, although past acceptance of a belief has been noted, this has not been offered as proof of its truth. Example: "Many cultures of the past have believed in some form of karma."

The fallacy of *false authority* might be incorrectly specified when a person who is not in a position to be knowledgeable about a claim nevertheless makes such a claim, but there has been no third-party acceptance of the claim on the basis of that testimony. (Speaking without justification does not necessarily involve fallacious reasoning.) Example: Your brother describes the "secret war plans" of the Soviet Union.

These are by no means the only ways to mistake a look-alike for the actual fallacy. There are many ways for two comments or passages to "look alike." You must simply know the fallacies so well that you recognize the essential aspects of each one and seldom get "taken in" by a look-alike. While this is not easy, it is important.

Finally, there will be cases in which the line separating a fallacy and a look-alike is not clear, even to the competent fallacy-spotter. You must, in these cases, be able to analyze the comment or passage so well that you are at least *aware* of the ways in which the wording is similar to exact examples of the fallacy and the ways in which it is dissimilar.

■
___

EXERCISES

5.1 Basic

For each of the following examples of reasoning, name the fallacy that is committed. These are the possibilities: attacking the person, argument from ignorance, questionable cause, begging the question, two wrongs make a right, division, false dilemma, contrary-to-fact hypothesis, common belief, past belief, false authority. Then explain how that particular example of reasoning conforms to the definition of the fallacy that you have named.

Example: Since there's not a bit of objective evidence to show that spirits exist, we must conclude that they belong only to the realm of fantasy.

Correct answer: Argument from ignorance.

Explanation: A lack of proof for the belief that spirits exist is insufficient to prove the opposing belief that spirits do not exist.

The explanation can be worded differently, but you should show that you know the definition of the fallacy and that you know which elements of the example play a part in that definition.

1. A quote from R. Gregory Nokes, Associated Press diplomatic writer, July 1986:

   . . . administration officials, risking new controversy over their South African policy, are saying freedom for blacks might be possible without black majority rule or a system of one-man, one-vote.

   "There are a lot of different ways they can go about it that will work," Secretary of State George P. Shultz told Congress this week. He said one-man, one-vote isn't perfectly practiced in the United States and need not be a model for South Africa to follow.

2. Had it not been for Abraham Lincoln, black people would still be slaves today.

3. A passage by George F. Will that appeared in *Newsweek*, August 18, 1986:

   This summer the administration has agreed to subsidize grain sales to the Soviet Union. American taxpayers will pay to enable the invaders of Afghanistan to buy grain cheaper than Americans can. Why? Because 22 of the 34 seats contested this year are in farm states. Bob Dole, senator from the breadbasket of the Soviet Union, a.k.a. Kansas, rationalizes this blunder by recalling Eisenhower's statement that we should sell the Soviets anything they cannot shoot back at us. Alas, dumb thoughts, unlike wine, do not improve with age.

4. From a television commercial for Public Insurance Corporation:

   No one else can give you such low rates because no one else represents our company.

5. If John F. Kennedy had not been assassinated, he would not have been such a famous president.

6. From *The Washington Post* (National Weekly Edition), February 10, 1986:

   "I can tell you one thing about the difference between a liberal politician and a conservative one," Mr. Bush said recently at a Conservative Party dinner in New York. "Gov. Ronald Reagan kept cop killers in jail."

   The reference was not lost on the audience. New York's Gov. Mario Cuomo recently recommended parole for Gary McGivern,

a convict who has served 18 years for the felony murder of a prison guard. Among others, writer William F. Buckley, Jr., who has studied the case, believes parole should be granted. But the parole board denied it. All 56 Republicans in the New York Assembly oppose it. The White House is reported to have urged Republicans to attack Gov. Cuomo for his decision.

7. There's nothing wrong with misrepresentation on tax forms. You can be sure that most of the people holding government posts are doing the very same thing.

8. A financial advisor to a client:

   You can either invest as I suggest or you can lose your money to inflation.

9. Speaking in English in a tent at Tripoli's Al Fatah University, [Libyan leader] Qaddafi gave reporters the following statement that appeared in *The Tribune*, (AP), April 11, 1986:

   I don't worry about his [Reagan's] declarations, particularly what he said about me personally. He's an old man.

10. From *Good News, etc.*, April 1986:

    . . . most families [in this area] feel the need for two incomes in order to live comfortably. This creates an artificial choice of either loss of parental guidance or loss of added income.

11. I heard that the nation's educational community is opposing the new tax bill. George, you're a teacher. Just why do you think the bill is a bad one?

12. Despite constant criticism of the Electoral College system, it's clear that this is the best method for selecting a national leader. After all, it has been accepted as a fair and good method for a couple of centuries now.

13. From *The Plain Truth*, June 1985, back cover:

    Will the next 15 years bring human extinction—or the dawn of a new world of peace and incredible achievement?

14. What will *you* do? Will you give every penny you can afford for helping the pathetically starving people in Africa? Or will you clutch desperately to each dollar you earn, using all of your abundance of wealth for personal comfort and convenience?

15. I see nothing wrong with doing my civic duty and casting my vote in a local election even if I am uninformed on the issues. Why, I'll bet that half of the people who vote have done essentially no research prior to election day.

16. Just disregard Ralph Nader's latest list of reasons to require stricter safety standards on new cars. He has been critical of the United States auto industry for years. Why should we expect anything different now?

17. Were it not for a handful of brave colonists in the eighteenth century, we would still be paying taxes to the English crown!

18. A driver of a car to a companion:

    "That fellow up ahead is weaving. He must be drunk."

19. Sportswriter Jerry Magee questioned whether it was proper for television (through instant replays) to be used to help in the refereeing of games in the National Football League. His comment on the subject appeared in *The San Diego Union*, August 1, 1986:

    Should television, with a mission only to report, help police games?

20. You can't prove he was to blame for her misfortune, so it must actually have been someone else who was responsible.

21. *Bank officer:* You say, Dr. Selch, that you will repay this unsecured loan. How does my bank know that you are honest and trustworthy so we can take your word for that?

    Dr. Selch: You can ask my department chairperson, Dr. Velnoy.

    Bank officer: But how do we know we can rely on the word of Dr. Velnoy?

    Dr. Selch: Oh, don't worry about that. I can vouch for him without reservation!

22. A high-school teacher comments:

    My students don't seem to be doing as well on the tests I've been giving lately. Students are apparently not as smart as they used to be.

23. Altruism, the view that people do not always act out of self-interest, is clearly false. There is no proof that, when you consider ultimate motivations, any motive other than pure self-interest is at work.

24. Were it not for the Watergate scandal of the 1970s, the American people would never have discovered the extent to which corruption had gone on in our government.

25. From a letter to the editor of the *Morning Press*, October 8, 1985:

> I get so fed up with [Speaker of the House of Representatives] Tip O'Neill's prattle about Africa.
> Does he want the Commies to take over Africa and South America? He has lived off the taxpayer all his life. Take a look at the big pension he will receive.

26. *Of course* women are more emotional than men. Everybody knows that!

27. From *Time*, September 9, 1985:

> When a British Tory asked him about religious freedom in the U.S.S.R., [Soviet leader] Gorbachev testily replied, "You persecute entire communities. . . ."

28. Even the ancient Egyptians believed in a form of life after death. So there must be some truth in that idea.

29. You had better think twice about taking a logic course. They are, without exception, terribly difficult and demanding courses. That's a well-known fact.

30. In the movie *The Bishop's Wife*, the bishop (played by David Niven) asks the angel (played by Cary Grant) who he is. The angel replies, "I'm an angel." The bishop's challenge, "How do I know that?" meets with the following reply: "Surely you, of all people, know you can believe an angel."

5.2 Moderately Difficult

Using the list of fallacies from Exercise set 5.1, name the fallacy for which each of the following examples might be mistaken. Then explain, through reference to the definition, why this is not a good example of that fallacy. Each of these is a fallacy look-alike.

1. A columnist from the *San Marcos Courier* reported the following on August 8, 1985:

> Bradley says Justice [Rose] Bird is interpreting [the Constitution] to her own prejudice against the death sentence. If that is true, it has not been proved to me.

2. Dr. Stanley Weiss of the National Cancer Institute was quoted in *Newsweek*, November 10, 1986, with reference to AIDS:

   What happens in the next five years will depend on our success in changing people's attitudes and behaviors. If we don't succeed, the virus will continue to spread.

3. In the same issue of *Newsweek* as the previous example, there was an article on our ancestors of the late Ice Age. In this article, we read:

   . . . mammoth bones were stacked in precise ways. One hut was made primarily of long bones; in another, 95 jawbones are stacked above skulls in a herringbone pattern. [Olga] Soffer [of the University of Illinois] speculates that the architecture may have been the result of ritual. . . .

4. You wouldn't be in such misery defending yourself against charges of medical malpractice, Arlene, if you had gone into financial planning, as I had advised you, instead of medicine.

5. From *Time*, September 29, 1986:

   Augustine more than any other writer defined Roman Catholic teaching on the Trinity, conditions for waging a "just war" and the "original sin" of Adam and Eve that corrupts all humanity. With the latter teaching, complains French Philosopher Jean Guitton, "he weighed down Christianity with his pessimism."

6. From the article "Coping with Anxiety" by Carol Tavris, *Science Digest*, February 1986:

   "In spite of promising successes in treating some anxiety disorders with medications, there is a complete lack of evidence that drugs alone will do the job," says [David] Burns [founder of the Behavioral Sciences Research Foundation].

7. Arthur Schlesinger, Jr., after arguing his case in "Against a One-Term, Six-Year President" (*The New York Times*, January 10, 1986), observes at the end of his article:

   The Founding Fathers were everlastingly right when they turned down this well-intentioned but ill-considered proposal 200 years ago.

8. John is a liar and a cheater.

9. If I hadn't had a serious motorcycle accident when I was a teenager, I might have been a concert pianist.

10. You have two choices. You can either do military service or you can remain a civilian all your life. There might be advantages with each choice.

11. An increasing lack of public trust in, and political support for, former President Richard Nixon was the cause of his resignation.

12. You have lied on the application form for financial aid in college, just as thousands of others have. It's a very common practice; people are learning how to make themselves appear poorer than they are.

13. You cannot prove your claim that human souls are immortal. Nor can you prove your claim that God will ultimately save all of humankind. From this evidence, I conclude that you are more attracted to opinions than you are to rational investigation.

14. President Duarte of El Salvador is a heavy-handed dictator who is ruthless in his attempts to maintain power. I reject his approach to the political realities.

15. A mother to her daughter over breakfast:

    "You wouldn't have to deal with this problem of coming up with enough money to repair the car if you hadn't taken the car last night. I *told* you to stay home and leave the car in the garage. You got just what you deserved for not listening to me."

16. From *National Geographic*, December 1985 ("How We Found *Titanic*," by Robert D. Ballard):

    It was from [the crow's nest of the *Titanic*] that lookout Fred Fleet, who survived, first sighted the iceberg one-fourth of a mile dead ahead. Instinctively he gave three rings on the bell above the crow's nest. . . . Fleet warned the bridge [by telephone], "Iceberg right ahead!"

    Ironically, Fleet's words doomed *Titanic*. In response to the warning her officer-in-charge tried to reverse engines and turn hard to starboard. The reversal actually turned the ship slowly to port, and she suffered the fatal gash in her starboard side. Had she rammed the berg head-on, she would likely have flooded only two or three compartments and remained afloat.

17. From a letter to the editor of *The New York Times*, February 25, 1986:

    There is not an iota of evidence to suggest that Moslems in North Africa have been involved, directly or indirectly, in any terrorist activity.

18. From a letter to the editor of *The New York Times*, February 25, 1986:

> From this perspective, I believe that the national interest can ill afford the kind of contentious, anti-labor bias your article conveyed and which the Reagan Administration often incites. Confrontation must be replaced with cooperation. In achieving such a spirit of working together to restore our industrial competitiveness, we all have a responsibility: labor leaders, business executives, government representatives, and newspaper editors.
>
> > Stan Lundine
> > Member of Congress, 34th District,
> > New York

19. From an Associated Press release concerning political unrest in the Philippine Islands:

> "There has been widespread speculation that Mr. Salvatierra's death was politically motivated by pro-Marcos supporters. Our ongoing, thorough, and exhaustive investigation has discovered no evidence whatever to support that position," Thompson told a news conference at police headquarters.

5.3 Difficult

Which of the following involve fallacies? Explain why each is either an actual fallacy or merely a look-alike that might be mistaken for one.

1. Written by Susan Van Raalte, author of *Apply Yourself: Writing College Applications That Get Results*:

> Students frequently tune out their parents at [college] application time because they fear their parents' advice will be out-of-date, unrealistic or simply incorrect. One mother recounts how her daughter rejected her advice by exclaiming: "What do you know about college? You went to an all-girls school. No one goes to an all-girls school anymore!"

2. After the space shuttle *Challenger* exploded and fell into the sea, debris was found afloat in the Atlantic Ocean. One private citizen found a bone and tissue fragment with blue fabric attached. The following excerpt is from *The San Diego Union*:

NASA officials in Houston said the astronauts were issued blue flight suits, but the officials said no link to the shuttle explosion had been established.

3. *David:* But how do we know that he *meant* to kill the old man?

   Mark: It's a matter of intentions. It's clear that he intended from the outset to kill him. It was his purpose in the first place. That's how we know.

4. DRGs (Diagnosis Related Groups) are being instituted to limit health-care costs. These will limit Medicare's reimbursement to hospitals according to the type of health-care problem. I read an article in Sunday's *L.A. Times*. It was written by a physician and it opposed the DRGs as undesirable for the patient. But I'm not listening to a word of it. It's clear to me that physicians oppose the DRGs because they'll end up making less money themselves.

5. From an interview with Daniel Ellsberg that appeared in *The Progressive*, July 1985:

   Our Presidents have come close to using nuclear weapons—close in the sense that they passed the trigger to our opponents. Whether there would be an explosion was up to what our opponents did.

   They were *not* bluffing. If the Chinese had attacked Quemoy, or if the blockade had been fully effective, I think Eisenhower would have done what he told the Joint Chiefs of Staff he intended to do—he would have used nuclear weapons. That scares me, and I think it would scare a lot of people to know that we almost went to war over Quemoy, if the Chinese had not been mature enough, cautious enough, to back down. If the Chinese had been like Khomeini, let's say, we would have had a nuclear war.

6. From a promotional brochure for *The Plain Truth*:

   "What Next? Prosperity or Economic Depression? Peace or Another World War?"

7. From a columnist for the *San Marcos Courier*, August 15, 1985:

   The four-page election sheet that came from [Assemblyman] Ron Packard was obviously written by a Reagan propagandist who does not think the rest of us know much. No economist I ever read . . . could have made such a mindless, illogical mess of mishmash. If anyone falls for this pack of trash they are also mindless.

8. You are insisting vehemently that nuclear accidents are avoidable in a world in which nuclear power plants are common. I refuse to accept that unless I have proof of it. To date, I have seen none.

9. From Congressman Ron Packard's *Special Report on Tax Reform*, a mailer to voters in his district:

> President Reagan told us before the key vote that, if the bill as written by the House came to his desk, he would veto it. In good conscience, I could not support a bill that the President himself said he could not sign.

10. Yes, I cheated on the test, but so did a lot of other people. To be fair, you should punish all of the offenders equally.

11. The only life in the universe may be right here on this planet. On the other hand, there *may be* life elsewhere in the universe. Who knows which of these claims is true? Certainly one or the other is true.

12. Written by Henry Kissinger and quoted in *Harper's*, July 1985:

> If the United States had not suffered a tragic loss of executive authority in the early 1970s, which, in creating the oddest coalition of liberals who disliked President Nixon and conservatives who disliked the Russians, destroyed the political basis for further negotiations, the superpowers would surely have completed agreements on mutual restraints [on nuclear arms]—which might or might not have worked.

13. We know that Pope John XXIII was moved by compassion, since all popes have been moved by compassion.

14. Don't look to your physician for sympathy on medical costs, George. Dr. Diaz will undoubtedly be unsympathetic. The medical community has strongly opposed virtually all significant cost-containment efforts and shown no practical concern to limit the costs of health care to the public.

15. The Atlanta Braves are going to win the National League pennant this year. It's true! I heard Ted Turner, the owner of the team, say so himself.

16. I don't see how you can think you have a moral obligation to feed the starving masses overseas. No one else seems to feel that way.

17. How can you doubt that good and right will eventually triumph? This has been a basic assumption of Western thought for ages.

18. Reported in *The Sporting News: 1986 Pro Football Yearbook*:

Later someone asked [Miami Dolphins coach] Don [Shula] how he would have reacted if his son [playing for the opposing Baltimore Colts] had broken away on a long punt return.

"I would have chewed out my coverage team," he said. "It could have cost us the game."

19. There will be no World War III. A famous novelist has explained that the new and inevitable direction of the world community is toward cooperation among people, factions, and nations.

20. It's all just talk. The Schusters aren't going to sue the school district. The superintendent of schools just told me yesterday that no one would *dare* sue the district over such a small issue.

21. From the *Los Angeles Times*, Harry Bernstein on Labor, August 14, 1985:

> [Marvin] Miller scorns [Baseball Commissioner] Ueberroth's claim that he is not a tool of the owners. After all, Miller says, "they hired (Ueberroth), pay his salary, and can fire him. It is simply absurd for him to contend that he is the 'commissioner of baseball for the fans.'"

22. From *The San Diego Union*, April 21, 1985:

> With two outs in the bottom of the 10th, first base was open with Alan Wiggins, off to a 2-for-22 start, in the on-deck circle. [Los Angeles Dodgers manager Tommy] Lasorda could have walked [San Diego Padres player Kurt] Bevacqua.
>
> Instead he had reliever Ken Howell pitch to Bevacqua. [Bevacqua batted in the winning run.]
>
> "I didn't want to walk him," said Lasorda. When asked why, the Dodger manager tersely replied, "because I didn't want to." ∎

CHAPTER HIGHLIGHTS

- *Informal fallacies*, simply referred to as "fallacies" throughout this book, are incorrect patterns of reasoning.

  The fallacy of *attacking the person* is committed when we reject a person's reasoning or position by criticizing the arguer instead of the argument.

The fallacy of *argument from ignorance* is committed when we suggest that our position is proven by a lack of conclusive evidence against it.

The fallacy of *questionable cause* is committed when, on insufficient evidence, we identify a cause for an occurrence or fact.

The fallacy of *begging the question* is committed when we assume the truth of our conclusion in a premise.

The fallacy of *two wrongs make a right* is committed when we suggest that an act is morally permissible, offering as evidence the claim that someone else has done something similar.

The fallacy of *division* is committed when we conclude that any part of a particular whole must have a certain characteristic, using as evidence the claim that the whole has that characteristic.

The fallacy of *false dilemma* is committed when we consider too few of the available alternatives and assess all but one as impossible or unacceptable.

The fallacy of *contrary-to-fact hypothesis* is committed when we state with unreasonable certainty the results of events that might have occurred but did not.

The fallacy of *common belief* is committed when we accept a statement as true and offer as evidence the claim that many other people believe it.

The fallacy of *past belief* is committed when we accept a statement as true and offer as evidence the claim that it has been believed in the past.

The fallacy of *false authority* is committed when we accept a statement as true and offer as evidence the claim that it was accepted by a particular person whose knowledge or reliability on this issue is questionable.

- A *fallacy look-alike* resembles a specific fallacy but does not conform to the actual definition of the fallacy. It is important to be able to distinguish between fallacies and their look-alikes.

For Further Reading

Acock, Malcolm. *Informal Logic Examples and Exercises.* Belmont, CA: Wadsworth, 1985.

A collection of quotes and written passages which exemplify certain concepts in logic. Chapters 13, 14, 15, and 16 cover fallacies.

Damer, T. Edward. *Attacking Faulty Reasoning.* Belmont, CA: Wadsworth, 1987.

An extensive listing of fallacies, with examples and advice on attacking each fallacy.

Engel, S. Morris. *With Good Reason*. New York: St. Martin's Press, 1986.

An introduction to the fallacies.

Kahane, Howard. *Logic and Contemporary Rhetoric*. Belmont, CA: Wadsworth, 1988.

An introduction to persuasion in politics, advertising, and the public media. The three chapters on fallacies are illustrated with examples from these sources.

Building on Logical Foundations

C H A P T E R

SIX

Mapping
Arguments

Whenever someone asks, "Did you follow my reasoning?" do you often say, "No, I didn't"? If you do, you are an uncommonly honest person regarding this matter. People are often too embarrassed to make such an admission, thinking that this would reveal a lack of intelligence. Most of us know what it is like to nod our heads knowingly while we are sadly lost in tangles of language that sometimes even the speaker isn't really following.

PREMISES AND CONCLUSIONS

Often when we *think* we are following the reasoning, we aren't. We may believe ourselves to have followed the reasoning if we have noticed no outrageous claims or sudden shifts of focus. However, to have followed an argument is to have understood the relations between premises and the relations between those premises and their conclusions. If you cannot reconstruct the argument within a premise-and-conclusion structure, then you need to ask for repetition or clarification. Like other skills, your ability to reconstruct or "map" arguments improves with practice. Before you acquaint yourself with each step of the mapping process, however, read Skill 11.

THREE STEPS IN MAPPING ARGUMENTS

By mapping an argument, we structure that argument in a logically ordered way, evaluate the reasoning, and provide a format for *reevaluation* of the reasoning.

SKILL

Skill 11. Mapping arguments

Construct maps of arguments, showing the premise/conclusion structure, the reliability of the claims, and the strength of the inferences.

Why this skill is important

When we are not attentive to the actual structure of an argument, we may not really follow the line of reasoning. This invites hasty evaluations and error on our points of logical vulnerability. ■

Step One

Using Skill 2 to identify conclusions and premises, draw a diagram in which the most foundational premises are at the top and an ultimate conclusion is at the bottom. Use arrows to show each move from evidence to conclusion.

The maps of some arguments would show the following structure.

$$
\underbrace{1 \quad + \quad 2}
$$
$$
\downarrow
$$
$$
3
$$
$$
\downarrow
$$
$$
4
$$

In this case, statements 1 and 2 are offered as premises to be considered together in support of statement 3, which is a transitional conclusion. This transitional conclusion is offered as evidence for statement 4, the ultimate conclusion. Remember that this will not necessarily be the order in which the statements are presented in the original argument.

Instead of using numbers to represent statements, as in the preceding sample, you should use abbreviations of the actual statements. You might, for example, abbreviate the statement "Each year in the United States, more people go hungry" as "Hunger increasing in U.S." or even "Hunger incr. in U.S." Use any abbreviation that will allow you to scan the completed map and recall the argument without distortion. You should also feel free to delete parenthetical statements and to (carefully) combine sentences when this will simplify your map.

Examine the following map structure.

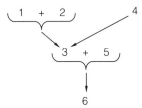

Notice that *two* arrows point to statement 3, which is a transitional conclusion. Since statements 1 and 2 are offered as joint support for statement 3 because they are meant to be considered together, they are bracketed and warrant just one arrow. Since statement 4 is offered as evidence for statement 3 but does not rely directly on the other two premises, it comprises a *separate case* that is to be made for statement 3. It thus warrants a separate arrow. Statement 5, being unsupported, functions as a premise but not as a conclusion. Statements 3 and 5, considered together, are offered as justification for accepting statement 6.

Innumerable possible maps exist, and sometimes the structure of an argument will be elusive. Sometimes the problem is a lack of grounds for judging whether a statement is meant as a premise, a conclusion, or a parenthetical statement. In other cases, the language of the argument does not clearly dictate whether the premises are to be joined or whether they are meant to function separately. In everyday life, the presentation of reasoning is sometimes sloppy. It is especially difficult to deal with such reasoning, but it is worth the effort of analysis to discover the specific ways in which the reasoning lacks clarity and allows different interpretations.

Step Two

Extend step 1 to include unstated premises and conclusions. Avoid adding unnecessary statements; much is assumed even in the most complete arguments. Add only those statements that demand inclusion because of their integral role in the argument. They are especially important if they embody contentious claims.

Placing the unstated premises or conclusions in parentheses, you can clearly distinguish, during argument evaluation in step 3, between the stated and unstated claims. The actual structure of the first argument from step 1, for example, might look like this:

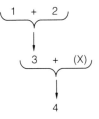

At this point, if you replaced the numbers and the X with the abbreviations of specific statements, you would have a conception of the logical order of that argument. In an argument like this, with an unstated (transitional) conclusion, step 2 must be done with step 1.

The actual structure of a different argument might look like this:

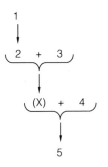

Step Three

As important as it may be to follow a line of reasoning, almost no one wants to stop at that. We also want to know *how good* the reasoning is.

After completing steps 1 and 2, consider the reliability of each premise. If you know the premise to be true, or if its truth is so likely that the matter is not reasonably worth considering further, write a circled *T* above the premise. If you know the premise to be false, or if its falsity is so likely that the matter is not reasonably worth considering further, write a circled *F* above the premise. If the truth of the premise is open to question, write a circled question mark above the premise. You may use a *T?* or *F?* sign when you are fairly certain but lack evidence to justify a simple *T* or *F* sign. You do not need to use such signs for transitional conclusions. The argument itself should be used to justify these claims. Still, if you know on independent grounds (be wary of opinion in contentious matters!) that a transitional conclusion is true or false, you may indicate this on the map. You should almost always use a question mark after a *T* or *F* for transitional conclusions. At this point, your map will look similar to this one except that, instead of numbers, you will have statement abbreviations.

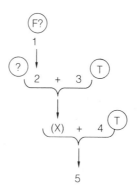

Now make a note, just to the right of each arrow, concerning the reliability of that logical move. Write "OK" if the move is acceptable *apart* from the adequacy of the premises; write "NO" if the move is not acceptable *apart* from the adequacy of the premises. If it's not clear whether sufficient support for the conclusion has been provided, then write a "?" there. Now, whenever possible, indicate why the move is or is not reasonable. See the list of possible notations on the next page.

Do not restrict yourself to this list. You may want notations that detail your rejection, reservations, or even acceptance of the logical moves. You may want to indicate that an inductively weak move was rejected because the *E* question of the R-E-T test failed (Skill 6) or that unstated counterevidence weakens the argument (Skill 7). Be creative in detecting strengths and weaknesses in arguments. The skills discussed in this book cannot alert you to the whole range of specific challenges you will encounter in everyday reasoning, so don't go to the chart to discover whether an argument is good. First determine the legitimacy of the argument; then decide on your notation. There's often a wonderful subtlety to human reasoning, a subtlety that continually breaks through the patterns we previously noticed. You will detect more kinds of errors than you have learned about in this book.

Kind of Logical Move You Find	Your Notation Beside Arrow	Skill Used
Deductive certainty (validity):		
—Deductively valid	OK—Ded. val.	3
—Modus ponens	OK—M.P.	4
—Modus tollens	OK—M.T.	4
—Disjunctive syllogism	OK—D.S.	3
—Hypothetical syllogism	OK—H.S.	3
—Universal syllogism	OK—U.S.	3
—Affirming the consequent	NO—A.C.	4
—Denying the antecedent	NO—D.A.	4
—Disproven by logical analogy	NO—L.A. disproves	5
Inductive strength:		
—Inductively strong	OK *or* Strong support	6
—Inductively moderate	Mod. support	6
—Inductively weak	NO—Ind. weak	6
—No support	No *or* No support	6
—Good analogy	OK?—Good anal.	9
—Weak analogy	NO—Weak anal.	9
Fallacies	NO—False Auth. (for example)	10

A SAMPLE MAP

Let's examine part of a speech on drug abuse* that U.S. Senator Hawkins from Florida delivered to the Senate on August 5, 1986:

> The university encourages physical fitness and good health; it discourages smoking and alcohol abuse. It follows then that institutions of higher learning have an obligation to wage war on drugs.

The senator has provided a clear conclusion indicator by using the phrase "It follows then that . . ." This portion of her speech can be mapped through steps 1 and 2 in the following way.

---

*The entire speech is recorded in the Congressional Record, *Volume 132, Number 105 (page S101307).*

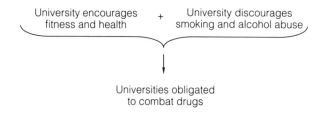

Unless you detect a clearly implied but unstated premise or conclusion, your map will look much like the preceding one. If you go on to step 3, your map may look like this.

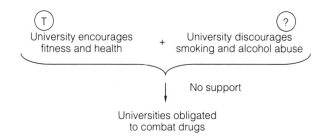

For this argument, the *T/F/?* premise signs may be assigned differently, depending on perspective. In the preceding map, a *T* has been assigned to the first premise because of the existence of interscholastic and intramural sports and various health programs; a *?* has been assigned to the second premise because discouragement of smoking and alcohol abuse is often token and unsystematic. Although these seem to be reasonable assignments, a focus on different aspects of the universities' approach to these problems might result in a different assessment. For this argument, however, that issue is not crucial because *even if both premises were true,* they would provide no real support for the conclusion.

Assume, for a moment, that both premises are true. Neither the universities' encouragement of fitness and health, nor their discouragement of smoking and alcohol abuse, nor these facts considered together, could possibly establish that universities have an obligation to combat drugs. Universities provide many services they are not obligated to provide, so the existence of the programs mentioned establishes no obligation of any sort. If it could be established that these fitness, health and smoking, and alcohol-abuse programs fulfilled actual university obligations, *then* an argument through analogy might be attempted. However, this has not been established. As the argument stands, the premises provide virtually no support for the conclusion.

Let's now return to Senator Hawkins' speech, adding the three sentences that she delivered immediately before the ones we have already considered.

Students are capable of individual and independent action. They are free to make decisions about their own lives. But they need guidance and leadership. The university encourages physical fitness and good health; it discourages smoking and alcohol abuse. It follows then that institutions of higher learning have an obligation to wage war on drugs.

Now steps 1, 2, and 3 might produce the following map.

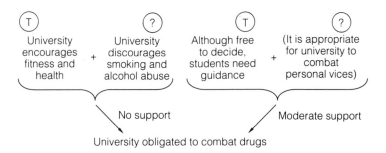

The three added sentences have been combined to read "Although free to decide, students need guidance." This is quite a compression of the three statements, but it seems to do no injustice to the intended meaning. Furthermore, to make mapping a useful and practical tool, we simply must combine and abbreviate. This three-in-one premise seems to function as a premise to support the conclusion we have already identified. Since the issue of the students' needing guidance is separate from the issue of which programs have actually been provided in the past, the additional premise is not linked to the two that we previously examined. A separate arrow joins this premise and the conclusion.

An unstated premise has been added to the map and joined with this new premise. The students' need for guidance would not lead us to believe that the *universities* are obligated to provide that guidance unless we accepted the unstated, but disputable, belief that it was appropriate for universities to provide such guidance. Actually, more than "guidance" must be allowed. We must accept that it is appropriate for universities to *combat* (whatever that may imply) personal vices. These two new premises join to provide at least a moderate degree of support for the claim that the universities are obligated to wage war on drugs. The premise that students need guidance has been assigned a *T* (though some people will disagree), and the unstated premise has been assigned a *?*. If the two premises were true, the conclusion would demand consideration, but the truth of the unstated premise requires examination.

We can increase the degree of support that these recent premises provide for the conclusion if we interpret the argument differently. Let's try an unstated premise that is more strongly worded. Consider the following map.

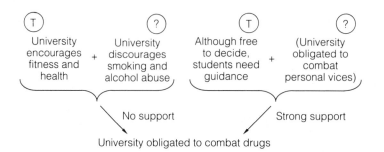

Here the unstated premise is considered to be "Universities are obligated to combat personal vices." While this premise definitely strengthens the degree of support provided for the conclusion, it is more contentious *and less clearly implied* by the senator's words than the other unstated premise we tried. This version of the argument is thus less accurate and less defensible than the last.

Despite the preference of the first interpretation of the senator's reasoning over the second, one more observation about the second map should be made. The two premises on the right side of the map might be said to produce more than an inductively strong argument. If, after all, every university is obligated to combat personal vices, then it is *deductively certain* that those universities are obligated to combat drug abuse. If we ignore distinctions between drug use and abuse, then, this part of the argument—this subargument—is deductively valid if we assume both that the drug activity to be combatted is a personal vice and that the claim "Universities are obligated to combat personal vice" implies that they are obligated to combat *all* personal vices.

REASSESSMENT
OF ARGUMENTS

When you have completed steps 1, 2, and 3, you have a map that displays (1) your understanding of the premise-to-conclusion structure of an argument, and (2) your evaluation of the argument's rational value. However, one great advantage of having your map laid out in front of you is that you can now go beyond your initial assessment of both the structure and adequacy of the argument. The map gives you a graphic basis for further consideration, and even discussion, of specific parts of the argument. Notice that, in the previous section, our original map served as a basis for an alternate map and for some subsequent thoughts on the correct interpretation of the argument.

After examining the map, you may find you had failed to see that a certain claim functioned not as a basic (unsupported) premise but as a transitional conclusion. You may recognize an important unstated premise or conclusion. You may change your mind about the appropriateness of the *T* you had assigned for one of the premises. You may conclude that the logical move you had labeled "NO—Ind. weak" is really a more legitimate move than you had previously thought. Record any reassessments. The change may require a new map if it is a major one or if you've simply run out of room to make legible alterations. If the change does not require a new map, just pencil in the change on the original map. Consider this a "working map" that is subject to reappraisal. This will allow it to be a means for opening rather than closing your mind to a proper analysis of the reasoning.

MODIFICATION OF MAPPING TECHNIQUES

You may want to personalize the mapping idea by changing some of the specific techniques that have been described here or by creating additional techniques of your own. Perhaps, for some reason, you can construct or read maps more easily by placing ultimate conclusions at the top rather than the bottom. Perhaps you want more, fewer, or different distinctions than the *T/T?/F/F?/?* signs that are assigned to premises; you may prefer phase-length premise assessments such as "possibly true, but not likely." Perhaps you will find that using different pencil or pen colors for various aspects of the map makes the map easier to scan.

Your changes might be more basic. Perhaps you will choose to draw a light *X* over minimally relevant or irrelevant (or even false) premises. To this you might add, above or beside the premise, a written phrase explaining the rejection. The premise may, for example, offer only fallacious support for its conclusion.

Ultimately, a system of mapping arguments must be workable *for you* if you are going to make good use of it in daily affairs. If you practice often, you will begin to construct mental maps—without paper—as a matter of habit. You will, in a significant sense, become more logical.

PARAPHRASING

Arguments often include parenthetical comments that are not very relevant to the line of reasoning (see the discussion of parenthetical statements in

Chapter 2), and they often include detail that is relevant but not essential to the gist or primary substance of the reasoning. A paraphrase of an argument is a shorter version of the argument that includes the essential evidence and conclusions. Effective mapping of arguments requires skill at paraphrasing because, very often, not all the statements in an argument should appear on the map; rewording, combination, and omission of statements are routinely required.

We can see some of this compacting in the mapping of Senator Hawkins' speech earlier in this chapter. For example, three sentences were reduced to one when our map showed the premise "Although free to decide, students need guidance," which served to represent this entire passage: "Students are capable of individual and independent action. They are free to make decisions about their own lives. But they need guidance and leadership." Notice that the entire map served as a paraphrase of both the content and the logical structure of the senator's argument. Once an argument is reduced to its "bare bones," it is typically easier to assess.

Some arguments, though lengthy as originally presented, permit consolidation into a rather small map through paraphrasing. Let's examine a few of these.

David P. Barash, in his recent book *The Arms Race and Nuclear War* (Wadsworth 1987), offers different perspectives on various policy issues. Here, he endeavors "to present each viewpoint as it is often expressed by devoted partisans." He intends each to be one-sided and recognizes that many are typically misleading. On the policy issue "Does nuclear deterrence work?" we can consider both the affirmative and negative answers. Following this, we will examine an article by newspaper columnist William A. Rusher. The first argument requires only a moderate amount of paraphrasing; the second argument requires more; the third requires most.

Does nuclear deterrence work? Yes. Despite varying levels of hostility since 1945, the U.S. and U.S.S.R. have not fought a war. Because of the nuclear weapons on both sides, the two nations have ample reason to back off from any serious confrontation. Although a world free of the threat of nuclear war would be highly desirable in itself, the elimination of nuclear weapons—even if it were possible—might not be desirable. Thus, conventional weaponry has become increasingly lethal, and without the inhibitions provided by the presence of nuclear weapons in an adversary's arsenal, international events could well be more tense and bloody than at present. Deterrence may not be lovable, but it is livable, and essential to keeping the peace. Our responsibility in the Nuclear Age is to maintain and strengthen deterrence, to see that it is not eroded.

The main thrust of the argument here might be mapped as compactly as this:

(T)

No U.S.-U.S.S.R. war since World War II

| Weak — Questionable cause
↓

Nuclear deterrence works

The conclusion "nuclear deterrence works" means that nuclear arsenals deter conflict and serve the national interest. The only evidence offered in support of this conclusion is in the first sentence: "since 1945, the U.S. and the U.S.S.R. have not fought a war." This premise is true. In the next sentence, we see that the arguer is connecting this with the notion of nuclear deterrence. Although the argument states only that "the two nations *have ample reason* to back off from any serious confrontation," it is intended to imply that they *actually have* backed off because of the nuclear potential. The person who is mapping might choose to translate that second sentence of the argument into a second premise: "the threat of nuclear conflict has halted confrontations in specific cases." In the preceding map, this was omitted because it was taken to be implied by the premise-conclusion pairing that was already on the map; if we think that the absence of wars establishes the effectiveness of nuclear deterrence, then this must be because conflict was avoided *due to* the nuclear threat. Still, it is not wrong to include the extra premise.

The remainder of the argument focuses on the issue of the importance of avoiding high-tech conventional war rather than directly on the issue of whether nuclear deterrence works. These four remaining sentences in the argument can be left unmapped because they do not directly support the central claim of the argument: nuclear deterrence works (or: nuclear arsenals deter conflict). If, however, we decide to fit this part of the argument into our map, we find ourselves with something like this:

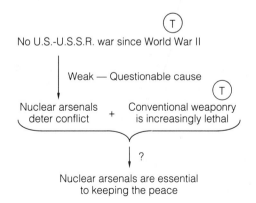

Notice first that the conclusion from our first mapping has been reworded. It now reads "Nuclear arsenals deter conflict" instead of "Nuclear deterrence works." Even with the rewording, however, the difference between this claim, which is now a transitional conclusion, and the new ultimate conclusion is not clear. In fact, the lack of precision in the ultimate conclusion has prompted simply a *?* for an evaluation of the logical move from its two premises. Does the phrase "essential to keeping the peace" mean that peace is impossible through other means? Should the conclusion merely indicate that "the nuclear deterrent is increasingly necessary"? We can't say how strong the logical move is unless the conclusion is free of this vagueness.

Finally, notice that the last sentence in the argument could be added to the chart. It would then become the ultimate conclusion.

Here is the opposing argument:

Does nuclear deterrence work? No. The assertion that deterrence works is counterfactual and cannot be checked, since we know only that something didn't happen—we don't know why it didn't happen. It may well be, for example, that the U.S.S.R. has not had any interest in attacking the U.S., nuclear deterrence aside. We cannot prove that the U.S.S.R. has been deterred by U.S. nuclear weapons, any more than the Soviets can prove that their nuclear weapons have deterred the U.S. The fact that something has not yet happened does not mean that it will not; indeed, you can just as well conclude that you will never die, because you haven't yet. Europe went through decades between World War I and World War II, longer yet between the Franco-Prussian War and World War I, and so on, but the next war always came. It is inconceivable that the world will go on indefinitely without nuclear deterrence failing somehow, somewhere. Moreover, deterrence has become an addiction, demanding ever more weapons. Our responsibility in the Nuclear Age is to get out from under deterrence as soon as we can.

A basic map for this argument can look like this:

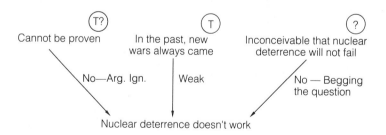

The first four premises of this argument provide the right sort of response to a questionable-cause claim such as the one we saw in the argument preceding this one, but as support for the conclusion that nuclear deterrence doesn't work, they do virtually nothing. In fact, if this kind of evidence *is* taken as support for that conclusion, the fallacy of argument from ignorance is committed.

The seventh sentence suggests, through the example of recent Europe, that new wars always come along. This observation carries very little weight because it does not counter the opponents' claim that nuclear deterrence—a brand new factor on the scene—is what makes the difference.

The eighth sentence simply begs the question, unless the word *indefinitely* misrepresents the opponents' position—in which case a straw man has been set up. The ninth sentence is parenthetical, having little bearing on whether deterrence works. Finally, the tenth sentence, as in the argument preceding this one, could be added to the map as an ultimate conclusion. In both arguments this addition would call for the inclusion of an unstated premise.

The final example of mapping demonstrates how very compact an adequate map can be in relation to the original material. William A. Rusher, a syndicated news columnist, wrote an article entitled "Church Isn't a Democracy" for publication on September 30, 1986. This is the article.

Commentary/William A. Rusher

Church isn't a democracy

As an Anglican, it behooves me not to go barging too breezily into the dispute now flaring between the Vatican and certain members of the American Roman Catholic hierarchy. On the other hand, the Roman Catholic Church is too important an institution in this world to be disregarded altogether by people who happen not to be members of it. Besides, the current controversy illuminates certain corners of political and religious philosophy not exclusively relevant to Roman Catholicism.

It seems quite clear that Pope John Paul II and his Vatican advisers have decided to rein in some of the American bishops and Catholic theologians who have been taking positions on moral questions at variance with the current teachings of the church. Since the proscribed positions are broadly of the "liberal" sort (tending to favor the ordination of women, contraception, a greater degree of sexual permissiveness, etc.), this has brought Rome into collision with major engines of liberal opinion in the United States, such as The New York Times.

Although the Vatican's notification to the Rev. Charles Curran in mid-August, that it considered him neither "suitable nor eligible" to continue teaching theology at Catholic University in Washington, D.C., has attracted perhaps the most attention, it is by no means Rome's only move in the direction of curbing dissent, nor even the most striking.

Early in September, the Roman Catholic archbishop of Seattle, Raymond Hunthausen—a flaming liberal on everything from personal moral issues to sanctuary for Central American refugees—was brusquely advised that his authority in five key areas over the 360,000 Roman Catholics in his archdiocese was being transferred to an auxiliary bishop who could be counted on to see things Rome's way. (The areas included such moral issues as birth control and homosexuality.)

(continued on next page)

(continued)

These moves have been countered, in the Times and other liberal watering holes, with the contention that polls of American Catholics indicate that a large majority of them are closer to the views of Archbishop Hunthausen and Rev. Curran than to those of John Paul and his Vatican advisers.

At first glance, it is a beguiling argument. Democracy is a highly popular concept in our society, and the news that a majority favors or opposes some particular policy carries considerable weight.

On the other hand, the Times would surely be among the first to agree that majorities ought not to prevail in all cases. What if (as is quite possible) a majority of Arkansas voters would like to see creationism taught in the state's public schools as an alternative to the theory of evolution? Would the Times tamely acquiesce? Or what if a majority of Japanese parents want their children to be taught a more "patriotic" version of the history of World War II than has hitherto been offered?

There are, in short, things that even the Times believes to be absolutely true, and as to which it would brook no disagreement. It merely happens to disagree with the pope about certain questions, and is therefore busily trying to undermine his authority to lay down answers to those questions on behalf of the Roman Catholic Church.

Rome is aware of the shortcomings of democracy, as well as its merits. Before there even was a church, Pilate asked the Passover crowd which prisoner he should free in accordance with the pleasant Passover custom—Jesus or Barabbas? The crowd roared "Barabbas"—and so it was Jesus who died.

As the late Bishop Fulton Sheen once put it, "right is right when nobody is right, and wrong is wrong when everybody is wrong." People who expect the Vatican to abandon that insight in pursuit of Dr. Gallup's evanescent majorities are advised not to hold their breath.

© 1986 Scripps Howard News Service. Reprinted with permission of United Media (NEA).

This is the map.

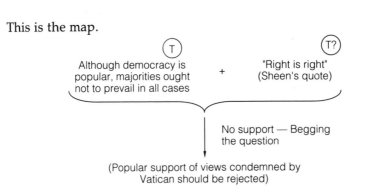

The primary reason the map can be so small is that two-thirds of the article (the first six paragraphs) is taken up with the presentation of background information. Up to the final paragraph of this introductory section, the only indicators of Mr. Rusher's stance are the title of the article (which he might not have written), the negative character of the phrase "flaming liberal" in reference to Archbishop Hunthausen, and the emotional charge tied to the phrase "liberal watering holes."

The conclusion is not stated as such but is clearly implied. Mr. Rusher's primary point is that the reader should not consider American Catholics' support of views condemned by the Vatican as relevant in determining the best moral and political opinions. The major support for this conclusion is the true claim that "majorities ought not to prevail in all cases." This, however, does not establish that majorities have no legitimacy in *this* matter. Thus, Mr. Rusher's premise offers virtually no support for his apparent conclusion. Following his presentation of this premise, he asks whether the *Times* would be willing to accept a majority rule on other specific matters. Although it is certainly important to think about which matters turn on public opinion and the extent to which they do, the determined focus on the *Times* appears to be no better than an attack on the person. Any bias or inconsistency on the part of the *Times* is still beside the point of whether public sentiment is relevant in *this* case.

The opening of the eighth paragraph ("There are, in short, things that even the *Times* believes to be absolutely true") joins with the first sentence of the tenth paragraph ("As the late Bishop Fulton Sheen once put it, 'right is right when nobody is right, and wrong is wrong when everybody is wrong'") to produce the second premise on the preceding map. While there may be truth in the general insight of this premise, if we offer the claim that "some things are simply right" as evidence for a specific conclusion, we just beg the question; the assumption must be that "some things" include "this thing." We assume the very point we intend to prove. The premise was mapped with a ⟨*T?*⟩ only because its clear-cut distinction is more or less appropriate, depending on the topic. Ignoring the last qualification, we can be reminded that true premises in an argument ensure neither deductive validity nor inductive strength. The content is fine, but the form—the relation between premises and conclusion—is not.

The ninth paragraph begins with the sentence "Rome is aware of the shortcomings of democracy, as well as its merits." Although this paragraph could be construed as a separate avenue of support for the conclusion, it's not clear that it adds something substantive and new to the argument.

Finally, we shouldn't fail to notice that at the very end of the article, after having dismissed the significance of majority opinion so heartily, Mr. Rusher even withholds his judgment that there is a majority in this case. This he does with a passing reference to "Dr. Gallup's evanescent majorities."

■

EXERCISES

6.1 Basic

Warm up to mapping by constructing a complete map for the arguments in exercise set 2.3 (pages 32–34). Then, doing only steps 1 and 2, construct a map for each of the following arguments. You may need to make major deletions and combinations.

1. From *Newsweek*, October 6, 1986:

The Case for Going to Mars

BY S. FRED SINGER

After placing men on the moon and instruments on Mars, America's space program has run into difficulties. The Challenger disaster has shaken our faith in NASA and dramatic action is required now to keep the promise of space exploration alive. We need to establish a specific goal that can fire our imagination with demonstrable scientific and economic results.

In its recent report to the White House, the national Commission on Space outlined a number of exciting projects, including a manned mission to Mars in 2010 and a permanent base by 2025. In my view, President Reagan should choose Mars as the focus for our future in space.

Many scientists agree that Mars is the right target—because of its similarity to Earth. Its mountains are higher and its canyons are deeper. Huge volcanoes have dominated its evolution and may still be active. It may have had oceans that disappeared as its climate changed from warm and wet to very cold and dry; water may now be locked up in deep permafrost. Life could have evolved before that. In specific locations, life may even exist today; after all, who would have guessed that primitive life forms would be found flourishing inside Antarctic rocks?

The scientific questions are truly important. How do planets evolve? Can life develop anywhere if conditions are right, and how would it differ from life on Earth? Why do planetary climates change? And can we use Mars to improve our models for weather prediction on Earth? Some of the answers would have immediate value: improved forecasting of weather and climate alone would save billions of dollars by reducing catastrophic losses to agriculture and industry.

Nonetheless, neither a manned mission to the surface of Mars nor the continuation of unmanned expeditions is the best way to explore it.

The easiest, quickest and cheapest way would be to send humans to Phobos and Deimos, the tiny Martian moons. From bases there, astronauts could carry out a program of research by remote control. Technically, such an operation means little more than transferring to Mars orbit a space station similar to the one presently planned for close Earth orbit. It would require less propulsion than a round trip to our moon and much less than a trip to the surface of Mars.

A journey from Earth to Phobos and Deimos and back would take 24 months, and a three-month stay would give us the time needed to explore the surface and subsurface of Mars with unmanned vehicles, remotely controlled and equipped to send back samples to a scientific laboratory on Deimos. Given its findings, another set of rovers would continue the exploration, but only at the most promising locations—a very effective scientific approach. And with some 20 to 30 unmanned rovers available, we could even afford to lose some as they traverse the difficult terrain and polar-ice fields of Mars.

As some astronauts control the rovers on Mars, others could sample its moons. Do they have the same composition, indicating a common origin and similar structure? Are they asteroids, captured by the gravity of Mars, or were they formed together with the planet? According to another theory, Mars's moons may well be original planetesimals—tiny bodies thought to be the building blocks of planets—which would then allow us to explore the origins of the solar system. Thus, by combining manned and unmanned techniques, we would be able to secure samples that are only a few hours old,

(continued on next page)

(*continued*)

an important time frame for the study of evanescent substances.

Radio signals: From the standpoint of science, the use of Phobos and Deimos as bases would be more rewarding than a manned landing on Mars. Because of the planet's terrain, humans wouldn't be able to venture far, nor could they operate a robot vehicle without the use of a satellite since Mars's mountains would block their view. They might as well be exploring Mars from Deimos. Using Mars's moons as a base would also be better than unmanned exploration directed from the Houston space center. Because of the distance, radio signals to and from Mars can take as long as an hour. And "driving" an unmanned rover from Earth, step by step, can become a time-consuming operation. Sample returns to Earth would take months instead of hours; follow-on missions would be years apart instead of days, further slowing the process of exploration.

The "Ph-D" mission, as I like to call it, is not only scientifically superior, it is also cheaper. A set of 10 unmanned sampling missions could cost $40 billion and extend over decades. By contrast, a Ph-D trip would cost less than $20 billion, just about half as much in today's dollars as Apollo cost us to put men on the moon. Most of the money would be spent on lofting into Earth orbit the components that make up the spacecraft plus the propellants for the

30 space-shuttle payloads.

Such a proposal represents a drastic change of attitude since I, like many other scientists who developed instruments for space observation, had always considered manned operations to be little more than an expensive stunt. Yet there are some projects—not too many, perhaps—where the addition of humans can make an operation better and even less costly.

It could also speed it up. For the race to Mars is now on and it won't be much of one unless we get into it quickly. Here the Russians are ahead of us. They have maintained cosmonauts in orbit for nearly eight months. And by the end of the decade they will have examined Phobos and Deimos, albeit with instruments. By announcing our intention to send Americans to Mars, we could transform a humiliating setback into a collaborative effort with parallel but independent programs.

Few remember that Phobos and Deimos were discovered in 1877 by an American astronomer, Asaph Hall. President Reagan now has the opportunity to make the moons of Mars the centerpiece of our future in space and to lay the foundation for manned exploration of the solar system.*

Singer, who pioneered the design of the earliest scientific satellites and directed the U.S. weather-satellite program, is currently eminent scholar at George Mason University.

2. From the *National Review,* November 7, 1986:

> Protectionism favors a cartel of producers at the expense of all consumers. We know that. We also know that these cartels will crumble if exposed to market forces. See the current headlines concerning OPEC. So how is it that President Reagan continues to give thumbs-up to a semiconductor pact, recently signed by the U.S. and Japan, that effectively creates a "high-tech OPEC"?

*S. Fred Singer, "The Case for Going to Mars," Newsweek, October 6, 1986. Copyright 1986 by Newsweek, Inc. All rights reserved. Reprinted with permission of Newsweek, Inc.

3. Letter to the editor (from R.S., London), *Time*, October 6, 1986:

   Drugs can satisfy a yearning that the various social systems, philosophies and religions are not able to fulfill. Attempts by the Government to educate people to the dangers of drug abuse while collecting sizable revenues from the sale of tobacco and alcohol look like self-defeating muddles. Perhaps those revenues should be used to perfect a chemical that would ease our craving for happiness without negative side effects. I exercise regularly, am a reformed smoker, don't drink and have no desire to inflict the zeal of the convert on the heathen. But life can get boring.

4. Stalin was a dictator and he was ruthless. Hitler was a dictator and he was ruthless. Castro is a dictator. So he must be a ruthless leader too.

5. From the State of the Union address by the President of the United States, Ronald Reagan, delivered on January 27, 1987:

   While the world is safer, it is not safe.

   Since 1970, the Soviets have invested $500 billion more on their military forces than we have. Even today, though nearly one in three Soviet families are without running hot water, and the average family spends 2 hours a day shopping for the basic necessities of life, their government still found the resources to transfer $75 billion in weapons to client states in the past 5 years—clients like Syria, Vietnam, Cuba, Libya, Angola, Ethiopia, Afghanistan, and Nicaragua.

   With 120,000 Soviet combat and military personnel and 15,000 military advisers in Asia, can anyone doubt their single-minded determination to expand their power?

6. Following is the introduction to "Filling the Leadership Vacuum: The Need for a National Education Plan" by Dennis M. Adams and Mary Hamm, *Educational Record*, Fall 1986:

   We've heard plenty of rhetoric recently urging the restoration of America's competitive position in the world economy by improving the knowledge, spirit, and overall educational quality of our youth. However, the whole debate is pointless if we have no national educational policy for pulling top talent into the teaching profession, training them, and providing ongoing professional development. Recognizing that American education is urgently in need of renewal is one thing, comprehensive strategic planning is quite another.

   It is time for the United States to formulate a deliberate national education policy.

We are the only technologically advanced country on the planet without effective educational leadership on a national level. A decentralized approach to the prime national educational objectives of training highly qualified teachers results in a dissolution of the issues. This does not mean that we can't extol the virtues of diversity and pluralism, yet we need a coordinated approach to defining our problems and resolving them.

7. The following letter on the AIDS threat, written by a physician in 1985, was read by William E. Dannemeyer to his colleagues in the United States House of Representatives on January 27, 1987:

> There is a sexually transmitted disease with a very long incubation period that is life threatening, and incurable. AIDS? No, syphilis prior to 1945. It was defeated by routine epidemiologic techniques. Everyone was tested when hospitalized, married, or inducted into the Armed Forces until the affected were identified, counselled, and all contacts followed.
>
> Prior to this public health effort, syphilis filled one-half of the hospital beds in the USA, just as AIDS will do in 5 years unless the federal government changes its lackadaisical attitude.
>
> Syphilis never had civil rights. Why is AIDS different? What about the rights of health care workers who frequently are not informed of those with ARC and AIDS, but are required to work with infected body fluids without giving informed consent? I feel the legal profession will have a field day when a health care worker and his family come down with AIDS and nobody warned them.
>
> Sincerely,
>
> Olva H. Alvig

8. From the Winter 1987 newsletter, "Senator Alan Cranston Reports to California":

'WOMEN'S WORK':
UNDERVALUED & UNDERPAID

FACT: In the 1950s women earned, on average, 64 cents for every dollar men earned.

FACT: Equal pay for equal work became the law in 1963 with the passage of the Equal Pay Act.

FACT: Today women earn, on average, 63 cents for every dollar men earn.

Why does that discrepancy still exist?

Sadly, equal pay for equal work still hasn't become a reality. But, today, the major part of the wage gap between women's and men's salaries results from the large concentration of women in certain jobs where the wages are unrealistically low.

Much of the problem stems from the fact that the work these women do is (*continued on next page*)

(continued)

undervalued and underpaid relative to jobs of comparable worth that are performed by men. Two different jobs involving similar levels of skill, responsibility, working conditions and training are considered to be of comparable worth.

The essence of comparable worth, or pay equity as it is often called, is that wages should reflect the value of the work performed and not the sex of the worker.

Pay equity is a matter of simple justice. For that reason, I have been a long-time supporter. In 1982, I was the first member of Congress to introduce legislation aimed at compelling those federal agencies responsible for enforcement of our federal equal employment laws to begin an aggressive campaign to enforce these laws, and to develop better tools for identifying sex-based wage discrimination. I introduced the same bill, S. 5, on the opening day of the new Congress.

While the Reagan Administration is strongly opposed to pay equity, polls show that men as well as women believe the value of "women's work" is underrated. In fact, a recent California Poll found that better than nine out of 10 women and men agree that predominantly female jobs should be paid at the same rate as predominantly male jobs if the jobs require similar levels of skill and responsibility.

It's long past time that women's contributions to the American economy were fully recognized and rewarded. Passage of S. 5 will be a giant step forward in making sure they are.

6.2 Difficult

For each of the arguments in the previous set of exercises, do step 3.

■

■

CHAPTER HIGHLIGHTS

- An argument should not be accepted or rejected until the line of reasoning can be followed, the premises are evaluated, and a serious assessment of the legitimacy of the logical moves is made.

- The *mapping of arguments* provides a deliberate and orderly way to do all of this. There are three steps to mapping:

    1. Using arrows to point from premises to their conclusions and placing the ultimate conclusion at the bottom of the page, draw the logical structure of the argument. Statements can be reworded and abbreviated on the map.

    2. Add unstated premises and conclusions, placing them in parentheses to distinguish them from the others.

3. Evaluate the argument by marking Ⓣ above true premises, an Ⓕ above false premises, a ⓀⒶ above questionable premises, and ⓉⓀ or ⒻⓀ above premises that are rather tentatively assessed as true or false. Then evaluate each premise-to-conclusion move by writing beside the downward arrow the strength of the logical move and, when possible, your identification of the kind of logical move that has been made.

The resulting map displays each significant element in the argument and your evaluation of these elements. This is not a process that leaves you with only a conclusion about the credibility of the argument; you have a diagram that invites discussion and reassessment of the argument. It is a "working" and revisable model of the argument. Modification of mapping techniques may be necessary to maximize their value for you.

■ A paraphrase of an argument is a shorter version of the argument that includes the essential evidence and conclusions. The paraphrasing skills of rewording and of combination and omission of statements are important in mapping arguments. In some cases, an adequate map of an argument will be surprisingly shorter than the original form of its presentation.

For Further Reading

Barry, Vincent E. *Invitation to Critical Thinking*. New York: Holt, Rinehart and Winston, 1984.

A textbook that offers, in chapters 5 and 6, a discussion of steps 1 and 2 of mapping.

Johnson, R.H. and J.A. Blair. *Logical Self-Defense*. New York: McGraw-Hill Ryerson Limited, 1983.

A textbook that offers "tree diagrams" for the reconstruction of arguments.

Thomas, Stephen Naylor. *Practical Reasoning in Natural Language*. Englewood Cliffs, NJ: Prentice-Hall, 1986.

A guide for mapping arguments.

Toulmin, Steven, Richard Rieke, and Allan Janik. *An Introduction to Reasoning.* New York: Macmillan, 1984.

A book with an alternate approach to mapping arguments.

C H A P T E R

SEVEN

Language

"I t's not just what you say, it's how you say it." This common expression reflects, among other things, the importance of carefully choosing your words when you are expressing a point.

As mentioned in Chapter 1, good reasoning and persuasion do not always coincide. While we know that persuasion often occurs without good reasoning (Who hasn't been talked into an injudicious act?), we should also remember that a good argument is occasionally less persuasive than it might have been if a premise or conclusion had been worded differently. We should strive to present our very best reasoning in the manner most suited to conveying our insights. Then, of course, we should listen openly to revise any faulty reasoning we may have used and to gain information we may not have had.

In Chapter 6 we found that the evaluative stage (step 3) in mapping arguments is sometimes difficult because both the truth of a premise and the strength of an argument could depend on wording that allowed more than one interpretation. With attention to clarity and precision, a fixed definition of terms, and emotional connotations in language, we can discern subtleties and vagaries in others' reasoning and avoid sloppiness in our own reasoning.

CLARITY

It is generally considered desirable to communicate clearly. The *correct use of grammar* is one tool for achieving clarity when you express yourself, whether you are informing, explaining, or presenting an argument. The structure of your sentences should enable the hearer or reader to grasp your point easily. (For example: Clauses must be placed so that their relation to the rest of the sentence is obvious. Run-on sentences must be avoided. The subject of your sentence and its associated verbs and pronouns must be consistently singular or plural.) Another tool for achieving clarity is *precision*. You should say—or write—exactly what you mean. Deficient vocabulary skills account for some imprecision, but much of it is a result of lazy thinking; at times we simply do not think about how a different choice of phrases would give the other person a more specific, more accurate, or more easily grasped notion of what we intend to communicate.

Vagueness and ambiguity can obstruct clarity through imprecision. Expressions that we hear, read, or originate on our own are occasionally vague or ambiguous. In either case, as well as when we simply use a similar but less accurate expression, the communication lacks precision. This may, depending on the situation, be undesirable for one or more of the people involved. Please see the skill box above.

Vagueness

An expression is **vague** when it is not specific enough to meet the needs or desires of the hearer or reader. In other words, when the speaker or writer is *too general* in presenting a point, we say that the point is vague. We also sometimes say that the person who originated the expression was "vague on that point."

When the teenager, on her way out the door, is asked by her parent, "Where are you going?" her answer may simply be, "Out." This is a vague answer, since the parent clearly knew that the teenager was going "out." The parent asked the question in order to get more specific—less general—information than that.

Here is another example of vagueness.

A student has asked his teacher to explain her reason for assigning an F to his report. The teacher answers: "I have assigned that particular grade because, on a careful examination of the report, no other grade is warranted. Applying the rule of determining the grade on the basis of the quality of the work, this is a justified grade." ∎

The professor's answer is vague. Notice that her explanation is so general that it could be offered to *any student* who was inquiring about an F that was given for *any assignment*. Clearly, the student in the preceding example wants the professor to discuss deficiencies that are specific to his report. The problem is not that the professor's response was false, but that it was not helpful because of its generality.

Is vagueness, then, always an error? Can we assume, for example, that any speaker or writer would avoid vagueness whenever he or she realized that the statement offered could be replaced by one that was more specific? For the answer to this question, think about the following exchange.

At a press conference, the president of the United States recognizes the news correspondent from a major television network and receives this question: "Mr. President, U.S. Marines who are armed for combat, although technically a foreign peace-keeping force, are presently in a tense situation as they hold their positions only two miles from a large contingent of hostile militia. I'm sure, Mr. President, that the American people would like to know what your response, as commander in chief of American armed forces, would be if these hostile troops advanced on the U.S. positions."

The president pauses, smiles, and responds. "I'm glad you asked that question, Mr. Bronno. I believe that the American people *are* concerned about this, and I believe that they deserve an answer. To every American who is concerned about how American strength will be wielded, I want to make it perfectly clear that if U.S. positions are advanced on, I will swiftly and without hesitation take every military or nonmilitary measure that is appropriate to the situation." ∎

Certainly the president's answer is vague. We know no more now concerning the U.S. response to the hypothetical militia advance than we did before his answer. The answer was simply too general to distinguish between alternate courses of action that are either under consideration or are being ruled out. Still, it is important to notice that the president undoubtedly *wanted* to be vague. Politically, a specific answer to such a question can be undesirable. Not wanting to call attention to the vagueness of his answer, however, the president speaks as if he were presenting a reasonably substantive reply.

Sometimes, indeed, we are vague on purpose. When asked about the host's strange-tasting wine or that atrocious dress someone has chosen, we may respond, "It sure is different." We are being vague to evade specifics. When someone asks our assessment of her unorthodox political or religious perspective, we may evasively respond, "It's a really interesting view." While it may be true that we've found the view "interesting," it would also have been possible, but perhaps not desirable, to say specifically how we felt. We employ vagueness in this case—again—to avoid a more specific answer.

We should recognize vagueness and, when appropriate, call for clarity. Some casual comments will be vague but will not warrant a follow-up demand for specifics. In other cases, the omitted specifics will be necessary for a fruitful interaction.

Precision in Thought and Words

Often, the reason for vague communication is that even the communicator has only a vague sense of the point being communicated. The problem here is not that the person is failing to say what he or she means; the problem is that the person simply isn't clear on the point in more specific terms. He or she must first think and observe more attentively, then choose the words that communicate the special character of the experience or concept under consideration.

Almost all of us are occasionally weighed down by a mental drowsiness that yields vague, minimally informative communications in place of precise and vivid ones. Consider our everyday conversations.

EXAMPLE

"How was the film?" you ask before Mom has even closed the front door behind her.

"It was great," Mom says. "It was just one of those very enjoyable shows. You know."

"What did you like about it?" you ask.

"Just everything," Mom responds with enthusiasm. "I don't know *when* I've ever seen such a good movie." ∎

With a bit of thought, Mom could probably enrich her own reflections on the experience as well as tell you what set it apart from others. Perhaps there were unique camera shots that constantly invited the viewer to change the perspective in which a person or object was viewed. Perhaps the plot involved an elusive puzzle that called for a certain sort of playful creativity. Perhaps the characters were portrayed with interesting contradictions in their personalities.

If Brent gave "the best" speech of any sophomore in the competition, it is probably worth considering the ways in which he excelled. Was the speech forceful, well-organized, humorous, emotionally moving, or insightful? Did Brent place his pauses so well that his main points were consistently underscored? Exactly what was so good about the speech?

If you're proud that your local high school is an "excellent" school, it is certainly worth considering the ways in which it may be distinguished from others. Is the faculty especially well informed or caring? Are effective teaching techniques used widely in the school? Do students learn research techniques especially well? Is there good school spirit? (How is this spirit displayed?) Exactly what is so good about the school?

If the book your friend had recommended so highly was "disappointing," it is probably worth considering the contrast between what you expected and what you feel the book offered. By taking the time to think, you can be specific in choosing your description. You can best communicate the greatness of your soccer coach or a certain disc jockey by reflecting, then being specific when choosing your description.

Efforts at precision in thought and self-expression yield a personal benefit: alertness to the rich variety of one's own experiences. In argumentation, the benefit is in the focus on premises (and conclusions!) that are specific, and thus more informative and less subject to misunderstanding and to the production of straw men.

Ambiguity

Ambiguity involves a lack of clarity, but it is not the same as vagueness. An expression is **ambiguous** when it can have two or more specific but different meanings.

According to this definition, some individual words, if considered apart from an actual effort at communication—that is, from a spoken or written statement, would be ambiguous. The word *bank* can refer to a financial institution or to the shoreline ridge of a river. The word *race* can refer to a contest of speed or to a classification of humans. However, this dual function of some words is seldom a serious problem for people who use the English language because the *context* (the sentence, the speaker's identity, the occasion) usually clarifies the intended meaning once the word is actually used in communication.

Statements can also be ambiguous, but here, too, the context usually clarifies the intended meaning. Examine one example.

EXAMPLE

Mrs. Rees, the high-school principal, leaned against the hallway wall of scarred lockers as she talked casually with Mr. O'Neil, the geography teacher, between classes. Students streamed by. Mrs. Rees was telling Mr. O'Neil about the hard work involved in planting a new lawn at her home. "Actually, it wasn't all just drudgery," she mused. "I became quite interested in grasses. There's a whole science of turf-building and turf management to learn about. Different types of grass have different qualities and require different growing conditions. Recently, I have devoted almost all of my free time to grass . . . ."

Just as Mrs. Rees was uttering that last sentence, a senior student was walking by on his way to class. The student heard only the last sentence. His steps slowed for a moment and his eyes widened at his newly acquired "knowledge" that Mrs. Rees *smoked marijuana!* Then he resumed his pace, smiling, anxious to tell his friends the scandalous news. ∎

The statement the student overheard was ambiguous because *grass* is a colloquial term for marijuana. Someone might, indeed, use the statement "Recently, I have devoted almost all of my free time to grass" to communicate an extensive use of marijuana. This would be an informal, but not grammatically incorrect, way of making the point. This is not, however, what Mrs. Rees meant. Her statement was ambiguous, but if it had not been separated from the context of the previous sentences, there would have been no misunderstanding.

Unfortunately, context does not always clarify ambiguity. In some cases, a statement is ambiguous even if it is not "taken out of context." Here is an example.

EXAMPLE

In a history of civilization textbook, the short section on the Romans and Carthaginians ends like this: "The Romans thoroughly defeated the Carthaginians, and, as a culture, they were never the same again." ∎

This closing sentence of the textbook section is ambiguous. On one way of reading it, *the Romans* were "never the same again" because of their victory; on another way of reading it, *the Carthaginians* were "never the same again" because of their defeat. It is unlikely that any preceding material in that section of the text would wholly clarify the writer's intention. The sentence is ambiguous even when delivered in context. This is the subtlest form of ambiguity. It is possible to follow the whole passage conscientiously and still misread it. The attentive hearer or reader is more likely, though not certain, to recognize such ambiguity.

∎

EXERCISES

7.1 Basic

For each of the following examples, decide whether the lack of clarity is due to vagueness or ambiguity. If vagueness is involved, describe how the communication could have been more specific. If ambiguity is involved, explain each of the possible meanings.

1. A classified ad:

   Wanted: Ranch hand for large cattle ranch—must be able to ride and brand cattle.

2. A news item from the Albuquerque *Journal*, December 26, 1984:

   Never withhold herpes infection from loved ones.

3. A news item from the *Adirondack Daily Enterprise*, January 17, 1985:

Potential witness to murder drunk.

4. *Question:* How did he react when you told him about the charges?

Answer: Appropriately.

5. From *Newsweek*, July 29, 1985:

About 24,600 Americans will develop leukemia this year and 17,200 will die . . .

6. From the bulletin of a church in Scottsdale, Arizona:

Today—Christian Youth Fellowship Human Sexuality Course, 1 P.M.–8 P.M. Please park in the rear parking lot for this activity.

7. An advertising claim for Popart's toy "Growbeasts":

Grows 200 times in water—shrinks back to original size when dry.

8. From a television commercial for *Finesse* shampoo:

. . . because no one wants to be dull.

9. A recent newspaper headline:

12th-graders score lower in all areas

10. Announced September 28, 1986, in the televised production of a professional football game between the San Diego Chargers and the Los Angeles Raiders:

The World Series was first televised by NBC in 1939.

11. From the *Los Angeles Times*, October 29, 1985:

Dizzy Dean, an 11–0 winner for St. Louis in the seventh game of the 1934 World Series against Detroit, made his mark on the bases in the fourth game when he was inserted as a pinch-runner.

Running to second on an apparent double-play ball, he was hit on the head by the throw of Detroit shortstop Billy Rogell and had to be carried off the field.

Said the headline the next day: "Dizzy Hit on Head; X-Rays Show Nothing."

12. After the November 1986 mid-term elections, the Democrats could claim control of both houses of Congress for the next legislative session. Senator Moynihan afterwards commented on the Republican President's veto of the Clean Water Act, unanimously passed by both House and Senate. The following statement was reported in *Newsweek*, November 17, 1986:

    The President could have avoided a confrontation with the new Congress. Now he has one.

13. A headline from the *San Diego Union*, February 10, 1986:

    Working Mothers Have Gotten Little Help with the Kids

7.2 Moderately Difficult

Rewrite these passages, making them more precise. Create the specifics from your own imagination.

1. It was such a nice wedding.

2. He's a good storyteller.

3. She's in poor health.

4. This newspaper is not worth the paper it's printed on.

5. I like the way the bartender handled himself when the customer threw her drink in his face.

6. A good time was had by all.

7. She has just the right qualities to be a good salesperson.

8. I'll tell you, as a realtor, that this is the best deal on a house purchase that you'll find.

9. Jimmy Carter was the best president we ever had.

10. Jimmy Carter was the worst president we ever had.

11. Clergymen just don't make good politicians.

12. We appreciate your applying for the job, but you're just not the right person for the job.

13. Money isn't everything.

14. That's not the way to talk to someone who is just trying to help you.

15. In some ways he's a good teacher and in some ways he's a poor teacher.

16. That was a boring baseball game.

17. That painting is beautiful.

18. I'm a reasonably good tennis player.

19. Professional sports in this country are a national embarrassment.

20. It's not possible to be honest and to be a successful politician.

21. From the Associated Press, in a report on the Mexican earthquake of 1985:

> Every increase of one number on the [Richter] scale means that ground motion is 10 times greater. A magnitude of 8 indicates a great earthquake. ∎

DEFINING TERMS

"Define your terms." This is the traditional wording of the demand that a person announce the way in which certain important words or phrases are being used. This demand, or a less abrupt and more specific version of it, is issued less frequently than it should be. People have argued for hours without realizing that each of them was using one or more key expressions differently. With attention to the need for definition, they might have saved both time and temper and made more progress in reasoning together. The task of formulating that definition is, of course, not always easy, but it will save you frustration in the long run. The box on page 168 focuses on the importance of defining your terms; take a moment to read it before you go on.

First, it is necessary to identify the vague or ambiguous expressions and to agree to one definition. Next, it is indispensable to be able to assess the adequacy of the definition.

Identifying Terms To Be Defined

In an exchange of reasoning, precision and effective communication may require more than careful word choice by each person. Even when a person has been reasonably attentive to the wording of his or her comments, misunderstanding can arise. Words or phrases that are central to the discussion

---

SKILL

Skill 13. Defining terms

Recognize (1) expressions that require definition and (2) definitions that are too broad or too narrow.

Why this skill is important

Lack of clarity concerning the definition of important words or phrases impedes progress in reasoning and can frustrate the thinkers so much that they simply give up on their task. ∎

---

may be used in different ways by different people. In such cases, those terms must be defined in order for everyone to be on "the same track."

In a discussion of communism, for example, one person may be arguing *against* a communism that would be defined as "any totalitarian political system in which Karl Marx is cited as a founder of the political philosophy." Another person may be arguing *for* a communism that would be defined as "any political system in which wealth and privilege are generally evenly distributed." Since these are different issues each of which is worthy of our attention, evidence to support one view may not be relevant to the issue that is on the other person's mind. If these people do not notice that the term is being used differently—and this happens often—they may spend unnecessary time and experience unnecessary frustration trying to make their points and come to an agreement. Straw men will hamper their communication until someone feels the need to ask, "What do *you* mean by 'communism'?"

Only in rare conversations does each person know the other's mind so well that there is no need to come to an explicit agreement on the meaning of a term like *communism*. Discussions of the existence of God also may suffer from a failure to recognize the need for definition. Topics like "just" wars, spying, and education may produce confused exchanges because of a failure to ask, "What do *you* mean by? . . ."

The need to agree on a definition is usually not limited to the term that identifies the central issue, however. A discussion of any of the topics mentioned in the last paragraph could easily involve the use of other expressions for which a person might not think to ask for clarification.

Central Issue	Related Terms That May Require Definition
Communism	Freedom Labor Workers
God	Faith Destiny Evil Love
"Just" wars	Aggression Self-defense Peace Security
Spying	National security The national interest Loyalty
Education	Good teacher The student's full potential Well-rounded person Basic skills

This is, of course, only a sampling of terms that might be used differently by different people. These terms are not usually multiple-meaning (ambiguous) expressions with specific but very different meanings. They are simply so general that the variation in their use may easily affect the strength of an argument.

When you are presenting your own reasoning, you should do your best to recognize terms that require definition and to specify your meaning before misunderstanding arises. When you are following someone else's reasoning, you should do your best to recognize such terms, and you should not hesitate to seek clarification when this is desirable.

Assessing the Definitions

The need for each person to use the same definition is clear. However, a "correct" definition is not always crucial to the argument. Consider, for example, the two conceptions of communism that were presented in the preceding section of the text. It is worth discussing the merits and shortcomings of "totalitarian political systems in which Karl Marx is cited as a founder of the political philosophy." It is also worth discussing the merits and shortcomings of "political systems in which wealth and privilege are generally evenly distributed." Here, it is more important that we carry on a clear and reasonable discussion than that we are "right."

In other cases, certainly, the accuracy of the definition we agree on is very important. If, for example, we are discussing "whether it is possible that the free press in the United States has, in any sense, undermined the democratic principles of the nation," we must be careful to define *free press* in a way that accurately describes the status of the press in this country.

An accurate definition is neither too broad nor too narrow. A definition is too broad when it includes items to which the term being defined does not apply—it includes too much. Consider an attempt to define the term *professor:* "A professor is a teacher." This definition is too broad. It includes kindergarten instructors and high-school teachers. Here is another definition: "A professor is a person who has acquired extensive knowledge in at least one area." This definition is too broad also. It includes physicians, architects, horse trainers, and watchmakers. Even if we combine those two definitions ("A professor is a teacher who has acquired extensive knowledge in at least one area"), the resulting definition remains too broad. Many precollege teachers have in fact acquired extensive knowledge in at least one area.

A definition is too narrow when it excludes items to which the term being defined does really apply—it includes too little. The following definition is too narrow: "A professor is a person who has an advanced degree and teaches at a college or university." It excludes those people who have been honored with professorships on the basis of nonacademic expertise; although most professors have advanced degrees, not all do. An accurate definition is neither too broad nor too narrow. It neither includes nor excludes too much.

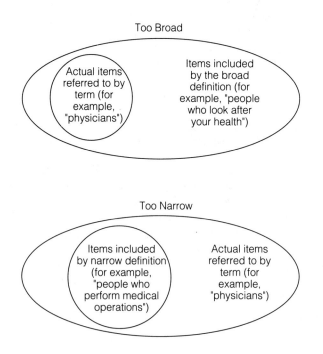

Too Broad

Actual items referred to by term (for example, "physicians")

Items included by the broad definition (for example, "people who look after your health")

Too Narrow

Items included by narrow definition (for example, "people who perform medical operations")

Actual items referred to by term (for example, "physicians")

Some definitions are *both* too broad and too narrow. These definitions include items that should not be included and exclude items that should not be excluded. If we were to hastily define *dictator* as "a cruel political

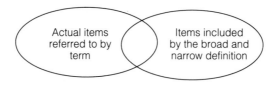

leader," our definition would be both too broad and too narrow. It would incorrectly exclude benevolent dictators who may not be cruel, and it would incorrectly include political leaders who are cruel but who are not dictators.

Accurate definitions are often difficult to produce. In some cases, they may be *impossible* to produce because of the variety of items to which the term may apply and because of irregularities in the common usage of the term.

■

EXERCISES

7.3 Basic

Is the proposed definition too broad or too narrow? Why?

1. Terrorist: A person who engages in acts of aggression.

2. Journalist: A person who writes articles for magazines.

3. Anger: A very strong emotion.

4. Government official: An advisor to the president of the United States.

5. U.S. senator: A member of Congress.

6. Science: The study of biology, chemistry, or physics.

7. Illegal aliens: Noncitizens who are living in the United States.

8. Drugs: Illegal substances that chemically affect the body.

9. Bribery: An attempt to obtain money or other gain illegally.

10. Blackmail: An attempt to obtain money from someone by threat.

11. Priest: A clergyman of the Roman Catholic church.

12. Saint: Someone who does good deeds.

13. Exports: Manufactured items that are sent out of the country for sale.

14. Civil war: An armed struggle between factions within one nation, with neither group having a legitimate claim to authority.

15. King: The supreme ruler of a nation.

16. Computer: An electronic device for manipulating information.

17. Mayor: An important person in a city.

18. Republican (politician): A conservative politician who favors increased defense budgets and decreased federal welfare budgets.

19. Famine: Food shortage.

20. Prison: A place to incarcerate those who are charged with or convicted of crimes.

7.4 Difficult

For each of the following expressions, construct the most accurate definition you can.

1. spy

2. traitor

3. terrorist

4. patriot

5. genius

6. war

7. saint

8. homosexual

9. family

10. democracy

11. immigration

12. executive

13. religion

14. citizen

15. private enterprise

16. remedial education

17. illiteracy

18. wisdom

19. progress

20. the military   ∎

EMOTIONALLY CHARGED LANGUAGE

The language we use to express ourselves varies not only from the general to the specific, but also from the neutral to the very emotionally charged. In each case, we often want to be somewhere between the extremes.

Humans are emotional beings. Emotions are a part of your life both when you are at your best and when you are at your worst. They constitute a grand and pervasive aspect of humanity, and life without them is close to inconceivable. Your emotions should often enter into your communications with other people, but not in a way that unfairly biases your reasoning or its presentation. The skill described in the box on page 174 can be invaluable to you in just about any communicative context.

Some expressions—words or phrases—generally have an emotional charge that is "positive." If we accept the statement that includes such an expression, we are more inclined to think well of whatever or whomever that expression characterizes. Some other expressions generally have a "negative" emotional charge. If we accept the statement that includes such an expression, we are more inclined to think poorly of whatever or whomever that expression characterizes. Certainly, if we use the terms *generous* or *thoughtful* to describe a person, we expect her to receive our comment as a compliment and not with indignation. Furthermore, we expect that people who hear our description will be at least somewhat well disposed toward her, unless they have a reason to reject that description. If, however, we use negatively charged terms like *selfish* or *rude,* we can expect that she and those who sympathize with her will be indignant or at least hurt because of the comment. We also expect that people who hear our description will think less of her unless they reject the description.

SKILL

Skill 14. Dealing with emotionally charged language

Recognize prejudice in wording. Identify positively and negatively charged expressions, fair and unfair language.

Why this skill is important

Good reasoning can be less compelling—and bad reasoning can be convincing—when we allow biases in language to lead to unsupported inferences. ∎

Adjectives are not the only words that can be emotionally charged. Nouns (*saint* and *sinner, gift* and *bribe*), verbs (*share* and *hoard*), and adverbs (*efficiently* and *wastefully*) can all be emotionally charged.

Two facts should be noted: (1) the emotional charge of an expression can vary, and (2) not every word has an emotional charge.

1. The emotional charge of an expression can vary with different contexts and with different hearers or readers. For an example of variation with context, consider the implications of "getting together with the old college *gang*" and "getting involved with a violent street *gang*." For an example of variation with different hearers or readers, consider the person for whom the normally positively charged word *immaculate* has a negative emotional charge because of his father's insistence, years ago, that his room be kept in "immaculate" condition. Other expressions, such as *conservative* or *work*, may as readily be positively *or* negatively charged; they may vary from person to person, with no exceptional circumstances necessary to account for the difference.

2. Not every word has an emotional charge. Normally, we do not anticipate that a person will react emotionally to words such as *plate, group, fabric, hear,* or *bring*; nor do we anticipate an emotional reaction to most pronouns or prepositions.

B.C. **BY JOHNNY HART**

Reprinted with permission of Johnny Hart and News America Syndicate.

People sometimes communicate impressions that they do not intend. The reason for this miscommunication can be a failure to distinguish between the emotional charge of two expressions that seem synonymous to the communicator. To one person, the difference between an "assertive" person or program and an "aggressive" one may be inconsequential. To another person, the difference may be great. If the first person is the communicator and the second is the intended recipient of the message, an unintended but strong impression may result.

Depending on the choice of words in the description, an incident or a person can actually appear to have either of opposite general characteristics. Examine Skill 14 once again and then consider the following sequence of occurrences.

EXAMPLE

Four of the five members of the city council were at their seats at the main table when the weekly council meeting began at the usual 7 P.M. time on Tuesday. The nameplate at the vacant seat had *SUE LASBURY* embossed on it. At 7:10, the door opened suddenly. Ms. Lasbury moved across the room with long strides and dropped quickly into her chair. She looked at the current speaker and nodded in silent agreement a few times. Soon the interruption was forgotten by almost everyone. ∎

Think of how this incident might be perceived or described by, first, someone who is sympathetic to the council member and, second, someone who is hostile to her.

If the late entrance were reported (in an article, to a friend, or however) from a sympathetic perspective, the description of the incident might run thus: "Several minutes into the meeting, missing only some preliminaries, Lasbury entered swiftly, strode confidently to her seat, and promptly sat down." From a hostile perspective, it might run like this: "A full ten minutes into this important meeting, Lasbury barged in, audaciously strode to her seat, and plopped herself down."

Which account is correct? To a significant extent, both accounts are correct. Each describes the same incident. Neither "makes up" occurrences that did not take place. If it is true that this was an important meeting and that only preliminaries were missed, the introductory phrase of each statement is correct. Choosing to stress the length of the tardiness and the importance of the meeting certainly leaves a different impression than choosing to stress the inconsequential nature of the meeting time missed, but each statement is nevertheless correct. Now, should we describe dropping "quickly into her chair" as "promptly sitting down" or as "plopping herself down"? Each way of putting it conveys a different impression about Ms. Lasbury's attitude, but neither is easily proven nor obviously false. Finally, was her stride "confident" or "audacious"? Again, neither is easily proven. Perhaps facial expression or body carriage would best reveal the truth of the matter, but the assessment may still remain very subjective.

To a significant extent, then, both accounts are correct and, beyond that, each is interpretive but not easily shown to be false. Furthermore, there might be *no intention to mislead* with either account! Because people can be naturally biased, or just lazy about observations and conclusions, either view might seem to its proponent to be "just the facts." To the hearer or reader, moreover, the account offered might seem to be "just the facts," true or easily shown to be false. ("Then she *didn't* really sit right down?") The problem is that some inferences (about character and attitude, in this case) that might be drawn from the particular account are not presented in a clear premise-and-conclusion form. Because of this, erroneous inferences may be harder to spot. *It probably won't occur to the hearer or reader that different word choice could, within the range of "the facts," present a different view.*

The vividness of emotionally charged language is usually unobjectionable and is an essential ingredient in pleasurable conversation or colorful description. When the choice of expressions blinds us to a clear analysis of evidence, however, our reasoning suffers.

Euphemisms

A euphemism is an expression that is used in order to avoid a common but negatively charged expression. The euphemism usually has no notable emotional charge.

In an effort to avoid the harsher expression, *lady of the evening* may be substituted for *prostitute, passed away* may be substituted for *died,* and *underprivileged* may be substituted for *poor.* Consider the shift from the term *pro-abortion,* which has taken on a negative emotional charge generally, to the term *pro-choice.* (In this case, the two components of the new expression—*pro* and *choice*—have a positive emotional charge rather than no emotional charge.) Consider the shift from the term *crippled* to the more general term *handicapped.* In education, the stigma of having "flunked" a grade in school led to the use of the now common expression *retained in the same grade.* (Of course, the result is the same: the student repeats the grade.)

Fair Language

You can learn by seeing the merit of other people's arguments—arguments that you would never have thought of on your own. You can learn by seeing how your own arguments fall short when measured against another person's insightful criticism. This is the profit in the exchange of ideas. At times, nevertheless, people make this kind of learning difficult for themselves. They think out their positions and word their arguments in ways that polarize, minimizing the chance that each person will learn from the other.

A confrontational "win-lose" attitude that precludes fairmindedness (see Chapter 1) is encouraged when you characterize the other's view with expressions that presume its inadequacy. By describing the other's view as "outdated" or "archaic," for example, you suggest that, however well the position may be presented and whatever its merits might be, you are not going to give it serious consideration. This invites an aggressive, confrontational response from the other person because people are often embarrassed or angered by the suggestion that their whole perspective is off-base.

The same effect is commonly produced by characterizing the person's entire view or approach with negatively charged expressions such as *foolish, extreme, outrageous, shallow, superficial, partisan,* and *irresponsible.* Although it is no shame to be a sophomore or an adolescent, the expressions *sophomoric* and *adolescent* also have strong negative charges in some contexts.

Rhetoric, in one sense, may be defined as "the use of language to persuade and/or to affect emotionally." At times you may choose to craft your language *only* rhetorically, in order to deliver your point as powerfully as possible. At other times (often, one would hope), when you want to be very fair and avoid prejudice and closed-mindedness, you will need to avoid language that is unfair because it biases the discussion of a specific issue. In a discussion of abortion, for example, if you refer to abortion as "murder," you discourage mutual learning for the reason expressed previously: the implication that you will not give serious consideration to a view easily gives rise to a combative frame of mind. Such language not only affects the other person but can psychologically commit you, in the continuing discussion, to the blind defense of such an impassioned stance. Similarly, referring to a social-welfare program as a "giveaway," a seriously religious person as a "Holy Roller," or the change of a hard-line position as "selling out" may contribute rhetorical punch to your argument, but it will probably do so at the price of an opportunity to expand the insights of each thinker who is participating in or observing the discussion.

"It's impossible for someone to defect from the United States. [Former CIA agent] Edward Lee Howard is not a defector. He's a traitor."— Michael Armacost, undersecretary of state for political affairs (reported in *Newsweek*, November 17, 1986).

EXERCISES

7.5 Basic

In each of the following examples, replace the positively or negatively charged expression with wording that is neutral or less charged, or that has an opposite emotional charge.

1. From *The Plain Truth*, May 1985:

   Earlier in this century both national laws and the medical Hippocratic oath protected the unborn. No one then questioned abortion being murder.

2. From the opening paragraph of an editorial entitled "Spy Panic," the *Los Angeles Times*, July 28, 1985:

   The news is full of spy cases, creating considerable worry about the nation's legitimate secrets and how to protect them. Unfortunately, Congress is reacting hysterically with quick-fix solutions that do not promise to stop the spying but do pose a serious threat to basic civil liberties.

3. From *Mother Jones,* August/September 1985:

> In recent months the Right has made great headway in its drive to devour Nicaragua.

4. From a law school professor's letter to the editor in the *Los Angeles Times,* August 13, 1985:

> To me, a graduate of the University of Southern California School of Law, Class of 1948, it is sad and sickening to read Moore's article (July 31).
>
> Moore says nothing about prosecutorial misconduct or lower court error resulting in the chief justice's decisions. The California Constitution provides for a given number of justices (7), with no allowance for "extra" law school professor "second guessers." The only "second guessers" allowed are members of the U.S. Supreme Court, who sit in Washington.

5. Written by a columnist for the *San Marcos Courier,* August 15, 1985:

> Let's deprive the pro-Soviet U.N. of our headquarters in New York and let them go to Russia or wherever they desire. One U.N. big-shot said if that happened they'd be glad to go to Geneva, Switzerland—I say, let 'em go.

6. From a column in the *San Marcos Courier,* August 8, 1985:

> Obviously, [Assemblyman] Bradley is quite willing and even anxious to spill blood for the political advantage of the coming Republican campaign. If he and his gang prevail in the next election, you can be sure that abortion, school prayers and the death sentence will be the main issues in the decade to come.

7. From a letter to the editor, *Rutgers University Alumni Magazine,* September 1985:

> Being a graduate of the University of California which comprises nine campuses, I cannot understand the stone-age mentality of the author who had trouble dealing with a system on only three campuses.

8. From *Newsweek,* November 24, 1986:

> The Iranian dealings once again showed the president carrying on his own seat-of-the-pants diplomacy, this time with most of his experienced advisers sidelined in dissent and only the gung-ho

staffers of the National Security Council on board to give dubious advice.

7.6 Difficult

1. Write two accounts of the same series of events. In one account, employ positively charged expressions to reflect favorably on a certain person, group, or process. In the other account, use negatively charged expressions to reflect unfavorably on that same person, group, or process. Do not change any factual claims in the second account. By changing the emotional charge, however, you will change the implied conclusions.

2. Write a pair of accounts as in the preceding assignment. This time, include within each account both a favorably described and an unfavorably described person, group, or process. The one receiving a favorable treatment in the first account should receive an unfavorable treatment in the second account, and the one receiving an unfavorable treatment in the first account should receive a favorable treatment in the second. ▪

▪

CHAPTER HIGHLIGHTS

- *Vague and ambiguous expressions* lack clarity. Vague expressions are not specific enough to meet the needs or desires of the hearer or reader. Thus, they are too general for the situation. Ambiguous expressions have more than one specific meaning. *Precision* in self-expression provides personal benefits and minimizes the chances that your reasoning will be misunderstood.

- *Defining terms* is sometimes necessary to avoid straw men. In some cases, it is simply sufficient to settle on *any* agreed-on definition. In other cases, when accuracy of the definition is important, the definition must be neither too broad nor too narrow. A definition is too broad when it includes items not referred to by the term being defined. It is too narrow when it excludes items that are referred to by the term being defined.

- *Emotionally charged expressions* can lead people to conclusions that are not well supported. An expression has a positive emotional charge if it typically inclines people who accept the description to think well of whomever or whatever is being described. An expression has a negative emotional charge if it typically inclines people who accept the description to think poorly of whomever or whatever is being described. Emotional charges sometimes vary with context and from person to person. Not all expressions have a discernible emotional charge. If we use *fair language,* we do not characterize another's view with expressions that presume its inadequacy.

For Further Reading

Fogelin, Robert J. *Understanding Arguments.* New York: Harcourt Brace Jovanovich, 1987.

A textbook that begins with a distinctive focus on rhetoric.

Moore, Brooke Noel, and Richard Parker. *Critical Thinking.* Palo Alto, CA: Mayfield, 1986.

A textbook with a good section (Chapter 2) on clarity.

C H A P T E R

EIGHT

Hypotheses and Statistics

S cience has come to be a part of our everyday lives. We
take for granted, with the push of a button or the turn
of a key, a dozen or more convenient mechanisms each day. We also read
and hear continually about technological innovation in genetic engineering,
health care, space travel, automotive production, disease treatment—the
list is long. While so many of the products of the scientific age are right in
our homes and offices, the principles of scientific reasoning that result in
the constant technological change may seem quite distant and alien.

Actually, some kinds of reasoning that are characteristic of the sciences
do become regularly involved in our everyday thinking. Two of these are
hypothesis formation and evaluation, and reasoning with statistics. The
formation and evaluation of hypotheses is quite a familiar process for us
all, but the scientist's attention to the systematic analysis of hypotheses
provides a skill—our Skill 15—that is worth learning. Reasoning with statistics, as physical and social scientists do through their own professional
investigations, has become important for all of us. News reports, magazines, and books present us with statistical claims and with conclusions
drawn from those claims. Recognizing good and bad patterns of statistical
reasoning—our Skill 16—is preferable to unreflective acceptance, skeptical
disbelief, or the shoulder shrug of those who always suspend their judgment.

HYPOTHESES

For the scientist, an **hypothesis** is an explanatory claim that is assumed to
be true for the purpose of testing it to determine if it is, in fact, correct. The
hypothesis is proposed as an explanation to account for an observed fact
or set of facts, or as a prediction based on inference from prior observation.
Observations and experiments are then arranged in an effort to confirm or
disprove the hypothesis. We also say informally, however, that any person

SKILL

Skill 15. Forming and evaluating hypotheses

Create plausible hypotheses and evaluate them critically, according to standards of consistency and verification.

Why this skill is important

We sometimes form our hypotheses hastily, then accept them without enough thought. Learning the skill of careful hypothesis analysis will minimize those occasions.   ■

who offers one of two or more possible explanations to account for an observed fact or set of facts is offering an hypothesis. Sometimes, little or no effort goes into the testing of that hypothesis. The general ways to choose and evaluate an everyday hypothesis are similar to the scientist's ways, though in everyday life we often pursue our actual investigations differently. Examine the skill box above.

Hypothesis guides inquiry in the sciences and in our own backyards and living rooms. We come up with explanations and expectations that can be evaluated by simply observing our world or by constructing experiments to test our hypotheses.

Alexander Graham Bell hypothesized in 1865 that speech could be transmitted by electric waves. He pursued the hypothesis through experimentation in 1875 and transmitted the first telephone message in 1876. (Usually, we need to determine the reliability of our hypotheses more quickly than that.) This is an example of scientific hypothesis that is predictive and is based on theory and on other knowledge. Sometimes we also encounter pseudoscientific claims. Pseudoscience, or "seeming-science," rests on theories, assumptions, and methods that are falsely considered to be rigorously scientific. Astrology is an example. A person who claims that the reason you were fired from your job today is that your horoscope read, "Beware of career obstacles" and that the stars were against you is offering an hypothesis. We encounter hypotheses not only in scientific and pseudoscientific contexts, but in the very ordinary speculations and discussions that we experience daily. Essentially, Dad's speculation that the recent poor health of the house plants is due to the dry heat of the furnace is an hypothesis.

None of these hypotheses—the scientific one, the pseudoscientific one, and the everyday one—is exempt from rigorous evaluation, though the testing process in each case is rather different. After some discussion about the formation of hypotheses, we will explore four considerations for hypothesis evaluation.

Forming Hypotheses

A scientist may spend much time and study formulating an hypothesis that will guide a string of investigations and experiments over a period of several years. On the other hand, an hypothesis may occur to the scientist almost instantaneously. Still, the investigation of the hypothesis is likely to take some time.

For the rest of us, also, one hypothesis may be pieced together over years and another may be chanced upon with sudden insight. For example, you might take years to come to a well-considered conclusion about why children learn some tasks so much more readily from other children than from adults, but you might see "in a flash," without a prior hint, a likely explanation for the poor air circulation in your house.

Of course, getting an insight "in a flash" is not an instance of magic or miracle. Intuition is based on an accumulation of information that is suddenly recognized as part of a pattern. Virtually all hypotheses are based on something; they are not absolutely blind guesses. Scientific hypotheses and most of the best general hypotheses are based on observation of the world, and they are confirmable or falsifiable through additional observations. Sometimes hypotheses are based on theory: a theory that is accepted implies or suggests the hypothesis. Of course, the theory is probably based on observations. Guglielmo Marconi, who shared the 1909 Nobel Prize in physics for his wireless telegraph, did not simply chance upon the telegraph or hypothesize on no foundation. Earlier work on electromagnetic waves had prompted his hypothesis that signals could be transmitted without wires. Sometimes hypotheses are created on the basis of authority alone. An orthodox religious belief, for example, can prompt an hypothesis that purports to show a relation between the data and the authority. Ultimately, then, hypotheses are not without basis, though they are sometimes without a *good* basis.

Reasonable hypotheses are, first of all, compatible with all of the known data; they "fit the facts" without ignoring some observable facts or overemphasizing others. The International Flat Earth Research Society publishes the *Flat Earth News* and insists that we live on a flat plane rather than a globe. This society maintains its hypothesis by downplaying innumerable scientific observations and contriving seemingly incredible arguments for its position.

The observations on which an hypothesis is built may be made incidentally in the course of daily events, or they may be gathered purposefully. The most rigorous observation-gathering in science takes place through controlled experimentation.

Reasonable hypotheses that are consistent with the data to be explained should be examined, but there is no need to consider only one hypothesis at a time. It is good to form several hypotheses, as long as they are all reasonable and not too unlikely. With those several hypotheses in mind, you can continue to observe, remain tentative in your judgment, and evaluate the hypotheses until it is time to act on the most promising one. The open mind is the one most likely to get at the truth.

Evaluating Hypotheses

It is easier to discredit an hypothesis than to confirm one. If enough counterevidence becomes available, the hypothesis must be rejected. However, many hypotheses are well established but still subject to being disproven through further evidence. They are at best the conclusions of inductively strong arguments that cite the supporting evidence as premises.

Good sense and honest reasoning require that we be especially wary of hypotheses we would want to be true and especially charitable toward hypotheses we are disposed against. Points of logical vulnerability take their toll, even from relatively levelheaded people. There are four considerations to keep in mind when evaluating an hypothesis, whether it concerns a technical scientific matter, a social issue, or a household topic.

Amount of Confirming Evidence Certainly an hypothesis becomes more reliable with additional evidence. The ancient Greek poet Homer told grand tales of Greece and Troy that historically have come down to us in the volumes *Odyssey* and *Iliad*. Some people have hypothesized that the cultural power of these epics stems from their being based on real events and places. At first, this was mere supposition, an hypothesis supported by some argumentation but no physical evidence. Then Heinrich Schliemann, who had been fascinated with Homer's tales as a boy, dedicated his life to proving that the stories were based on actual fact. In 1873 he unearthed walls, a city gate, and various artifacts that seemed to be from Troy itself. This evidence strengthened his hypothesis. After this success, he went to Greece in 1876 and discovered the Royal Grave Circle and other sites and objects from ancient times. His excavations were guided largely by his knowledge of Homer. Now his hypothesis was further strengthened. As the amount of confirming evidence increased, the credibility of his hypothesis increased. As the credibility of his hypothesis increased, the opposing hypothesis that the stories were wholly mythical was put into question. Notice that the burden of proof was on Schliemann: while the inductive strength of his conclusions increased with each discovery, the opposing hypothesis was supported primarily by a *lack* of physical evidence. Finally, it should be noted that some of Schliemann's finds were criticized as being inaccurately dated. Whether this lessens the strength of his hypothesis depends on an evaluation of those criticisms.

Consider a different kind of example. You planted a vegetable garden but harvested no vegetables. You cared for it well but nothing grew besides a few sickly sprouts that died quickly. You hypothesize that the soil in your yard is unsuitable for a vegetable garden and conclude that no garden will thrive here. Your hypothesis is weak, since not much evidence supports it. "You mean you just tried a garden once, and you're giving up?" someone challenges you. Certainly you would have a stronger hypothesis if you had planted and cared for a vegetable garden for the past several years and hadn't produced any eatable vegetables. Again, as the amount of confirming evidence increases, the credibility of the hypothesis increases. However, even with twenty years of crop failure as evidence (persistent, aren't you?), your hypothesis will gain no more than a moderate degree of strength. This leads to the next topic.

Variety of Confirming Evidence   Was the continually failing vegetable garden always planted in the same location? Might you have had better results at the other end of the yard? Are you a poor gardener, with even your best efforts seemingly doomed to failure in any garden? You failed for twenty years. The amount of evidence is relevant, but a variety of evidence would strengthen the hypothesis. If you had planted the garden in different locations in the yard, and other people—perhaps other family members or the previous owner—had also failed in their attempts to grow vegetables in your yard, then the hypothesis would be much stronger. A soil analysis would add yet better evidence for your conclusion. While you would have no practical need for all this evidence, you should maintain your hypothesis only rather tentatively without some variety of evidence. (Such variety is not possible for some hypotheses.) The desirability of having a variety of confirming evidence introduces the next topic.

Testability   "If this hypothesis is true, what else can I expect to find?" This question sets up valuable tests for an hypothesis. If a necessary consequence of the hypothesis turns out to be false, the hypothesis itself is false.*

The reasoning in this sentence reflects the form of a modus tollens argument: If the hypothesis is true, then the necessary consequence is true. The "necessary consequence" is false. Therefore, the hypothesis is false.

After the preceding question is considered and relevant kinds of evidence are acknowledged, the evidence must be found. This sometimes sparks the idea for an experiment. In the previous example about gardening, you might actually invite your neighbor to garden in your yard for a season, just to see how well he does. You hypothesized that no garden would thrive there because of the soil. What else, besides your own failures, would be true if the problem were the soil? A change in gardeners would not result in a decent garden. If the neighbor produces a good garden, your hypothesis about the soil is wrong.

A good hypothesis, then, has predictive strength. We should be able to deduce specific consequences to be expected under certain conditions. If these consequences are absent, three possibilities must be considered: these are not really necessary consequences, the experiment or observation was flawed, or the hypothesis should be rejected. In the quite simple gardening example, it's clear that the hypothesis should be rejected.

If your hypothesis were "schizophrenia is generated by genetic rather than environmental factors," the observation and experimentation would, of course, be much more complicated. (The false dilemma beckons here.) The social scientist's training would be invaluable in constructing appropriate investigations for this kind of topic.

Some hypotheses are not just more difficult to test; they are *impossible* to test. Among these, some are untestable because of practical limitations. Others, however, are untestable in principle. Such "irrefutable hypotheses" do not defy refutation because they are good hypotheses but because they are defended as if they were compatible with any possible state of affairs in the world. "All college professors who teach courses in Marxism are communist spies." Such a brash hypothesis invites challenge: Many of these professors behave very patriotically and defend the American way of life as well as the United States Constitution. "Yes," comes the response, "but this is just to make them appear to be loyal." It may be that nothing at all would count as evidence against this hypothesis for the biased witch-hunter. What could count against such an hypothesis?

Some of these irrefutable hypotheses are really "self-sealers" in the sense that their very wording rules out counterevidence. A person loses her job and is consoled with the remark, "That's just the way it was meant to be. There's nothing you can do about such things." More generally, the claim might be, "Whatever occurs happens that way because it was meant to be that way." What does this mean? It's certainly a vague claim, but it seems to mean that nothing could have happened differently and that there is some mystical intention, if not purpose, in every event. What can count as evidence against this hypothesis? *Nothing* can count as evidence against this hypothesis. If the woman lost her job, "that's the way it was meant to be." If she kept her job after almost losing it, then *that's* "the way it was meant to be." The hypothesis is compatible with any possible situation that could ever occur in the world. Then what does it tell us about the world?

It tells us nothing. It's true that no evidence can count against it, but it's also true that no evidence can count for it. The hypothesis is vacuous. The price for its being irrefutable is that it is also unsupportable.

Simplicity Rival hypotheses are incompatible explanations that are offered for the same data. PMS, premenstrual syndrome, was thought to be due to an imbalance between estrogen and progesterone in the body. More recently, two new hypotheses have been advanced. One suggests that opiates occurring naturally in the body diminish before menstruation and that PMS is a kind of narcotic withdrawal. Another hypothesis offers thyroid disorder as the crucial link to PMS. More research is required before the medical community accepts a single hypothesis.

Often, none of the rival hypotheses are obviously false. In fact, each of the rival hypotheses may be quite consistent with the data that are being explained. How, then, can a person decide between such rival hypotheses? Primarily, the way is to wait and watch for more evidence or to create experimental situations that will produce more evidence. If the conflict still cannot be decided, and there is a need to choose one hypothesis over the other, the principle of simplicity may come into play.

The principle of simplicity suggests that we endorse the simpler of any rival hypotheses. This principle was at work when Nicolaus Copernicus' hypothesis that the earth and planets revolve around the sun superseded the Ptolemaic hypothesis, according to which the moon, sun, and planets revolve around the earth. From the perspective of the sixteenth century, each hypothesis accounted for the data that described the observable movements of the heavenly bodies. The Ptolemaic hypothesis, however, had become complicated through modifications that were designed to preserve its predictive strength in the wake of more and more precise observations. The circular orbital paths this system described eventually failed to predict the correct location of a body, so epicycles—small circular detours—were added at a single point on those orbital paths. Then, when even with this modification the system was inaccurate, little epicycles were even added to those original epicycles. The hypothesis became unreasonably complicated. Copernicus' hypothesis was more efficient. It was simpler in its basic conception and displaced the other hypothesis.

Earlier, this "irrefutable hypothesis" was discussed: "All college professors who teach courses in Marxism are communist spies." Counterevidence would include the observations that many of these professors are not involved in anything worth spying for, that some offer harsh criticisms of present communist societies, that some have died for their country, and that some are fervent Christians or politically conservative. As qualifiers are added in defense of the original hypothesis, as farfetched explanations of each act are given, the hypothesis becomes more complicated *and less believable*. The principle of simplicity and common sense thrust us toward a simpler hypothesis: these professors teach these courses out of an interest or expertise in Marxism, without necessarily being Marxists or communists themselves.

EXERCISES

8.1 Basic

Create two or more hypotheses to explain each set of facts.

1. At the naval base at Jacksonville, Florida, the officers' restrooms are usually cleaner than the enlisted personnel's restrooms.

2. Males generally are better at math than females are.

3. If we compare people who have been child abusers with people who haven't, the former group has a larger proportion of people who were themselves abused as children.

4. Children with middle-class backgrounds get better grades in the public schools than do children with economically poorer backgrounds.

5. On November 17, 1986, the pilot and the two crew members on Japan Air Lines cargo flight 1628 spotted lights moving alongside them. As they descended from 35,000 feet to 31,000 feet, the lights moved with them. At one point, the pilot says, he viewed a huge flying craft unlike anything he had seen. When the plane landed, FAA officials found the men to be "professional, rational, well-trained people." Events of this sort have occurred before.

6. There are more psychology courses than philosophy courses in American universities.

7. Morning editions of newspapers are more successful than afternoon editions.

8. Success in school correlated more closely with the number of magazines the household subscribed to than with family income, the parents' education, or any other factor surveyed.

8.2 Moderately Difficult

1. Create an hypothesis. First, describe the facts to be explained. Then, state your hypothesis. Finally, evaluate the hypothesis according to

amount of confirming evidence, variety of confirming evidence, and testability. Is there any counterevidence against your hypothesis?

Do this as many times as are necessary to become familiar with these criteria.

2. Go back to the exercises in section 8.1. Evaluate your rival hypotheses according to the criteria mentioned in the preceding question. Also, evaluate the relative simplicity of each competing hypothesis if both hypotheses are so well supported that a choice is difficult. Otherwise, state which hypothesis is stronger and justify your selection. Remember that two hypotheses might complement rather than rival each other. Each might identify one contributing cause.   ■

STATISTICS

"Statistics don't lie." "Statistics speak for themselves." "The fellow had statistics to back up his point and I didn't have any. What could I say?" "You can't dispute statistics." "The numbers were right there in black and white."

Underlying these common expressions are the assumptions that all statistical claims are based on properly executed studies and that statistics cannot be misused and never mislead. Each of these assumptions is false.

Numbers present a mystifying world to many people. An engineer's complex formulas on paper are intimately and impressively related to the final product of a massive bridge that can bear hundreds of tons or to a successful space flight. Life in our modern scientific world easily generates awe and respect for the "power" of numbers.

Most of us do not deal with higher mathematics. We are not asked to work with them or to draw conclusions on the basis of some provided figures. However, we are invited to draw conclusions based on statistics, and sometimes the mystique of the numbers, their sources and implications, will overwhelm a person. Take a look at the skill box on page 191.

Here is an example of a statistical claim: "In 1978, 80 percent of Americans indicated that they would vote for a woman for president if she were qualified and nominated by the voter's preferred party." To assess this claim completely, we would want to know who did the research (it was the Gallup Poll in this case) and how it was done. We do not always have the leisure and resources or the interest to follow through with this line of investigation, but we should be aware of some relevant questions. Further, a complete assessment of the claim requires consideration of conclusions that such a claim would establish. The two general questions to ask, then, are "Is the claim justified?" and "What does it prove?"

SKILL

Skill 16. Assessing sources and implications of statistics

Identify basic questions to be asked about research that produces specific statistical information and recognize unjustified conclusions that are presented as following from statistical claims.

Why this skill is important

Since statistical information can be unduly impressive, people sometimes blindly accept questionable claims.　　　　　■

Although statistics can be applied to other areas, this book will focus on the social and behavioral sciences, which study human behaviors and beliefs. Much of the statistical information the average person receives through the media is of this sort.

This chapter offers suggestions about the kinds of questions a person should ask when evaluating statistical evidence and conclusions. It is meant to stimulate the creative process of evaluating such material so the reader will not only remember the questions considered here but also continually come up with pertinent questions of his or her own.

We will consider eight questions under three headings. This is the structure of the chapter:

Compiling Statistics

Is the researcher qualified?

Is the sample reliable?

Presenting Statistics

What if the data were organized differently?

Does the chart invite misunderstanding?

Drawing Conclusions from Statistics

Have other studies produced different results?

Is the fallacy of questionable cause committed?

Is the comparison reasonable?

Does correlation establish causation?

Compiling Statistics

Very often we don't know how statistical information was compiled. This warrants more concern in some cases than in others. At times, we do have some idea of how the information was compiled. In either circumstance, we should be aware of the kinds of questions that bear on the credibility of any study.

Is the Researcher Qualified?   To be qualified to direct a statistical study, the researcher must be competent with the method of research being used. This enables him or her to identify variables and to anticipate oversights. The person's "track record" of previous research can serve as a *general* guide to reliability. In other words, a researcher's previous work is a useful practical indicator of the quality of current work. Still, it is not a foolproof indicator, and information on the quality of previous work is not always easily obtained.

Even competent researchers can have a personal interest in producing one kind of result instead of another. They may resist, consciously or unconsciously, a result that would oppose findings already published under their name. This can affect the overall design of the study, the selection and presentation of data, and the drawing of conclusions. Political, moral, and religious commitments may also contribute to flawed investigation.

While assuring phrases such as "in research done by an independent research laboratory" or "in studies at a leading university" may be offered to imply objectivity, they provide no guarantee. In the first case, some "independent" laboratories are small and may not be professionally staffed to do the specific work for which they contract. Some labs must rely on the specific character of their results to ensure continued business. In the second case, although the reader may conclude from the phrase "at a leading university" that the studies were performed by university personnel or other qualified people, this is not literally claimed and is sometimes not true. Occasionally, with such a general reference ("a leading university"), no study at all has been conducted. One producer of a miracle weight-loss powder deleted such a phrase from newspaper advertisements when chal-

BLOOM COUNTY

© 1987 Washington Post Co. Reprinted with permission of the
Washington Post Writers Group.

lenged to name the medical school at which studies confirming the claims
had supposedly been done.

Is the Sample Reliable?   In a survey of people, those whom we actually
observe or question comprise the *sample*. In studies that are not surveys of
people, the sample may be comprised of objects, processes, or events. The
results are then generalized to make a prediction about a larger group, a
population. Generally speaking, very small samples produce less reliable
generalizations to the complete population than do larger samples. As information users who get most of our statistics from the mass media, we often
don't know the sample size for a particular study. The sample size can be
important because very small samples allow a greater margin for error. To
avoid a hasty charge that the sample is too small, however, we should know
that a sample of even a few thousand Americans can form a reliable basis
for the prediction of the outcome of a U.S. presidential election and can be
expected to be within two percentage points of the actual vote.*

*Ian Robertson, Sociology (New York: Worth, 1981), p. 37.

Since a minimally acceptable sample size is not easily determined by people who are not statisticians, let's watch for *obvious* deficiencies in sample size and become sensitive to the everyday form of the "small sample" error. People sometimes make broad generalizations on the basis of very limited observations. A parent may remark, for example, that he had never believed that infant boys and girls were very different, but that he now "knows better." In support of his conclusion, he may offer nothing but his own experience with his two children—a boy and a girl. Without the introduction of specific numbers, the parent's claim is only indirectly statistical. Still, he is projecting his observations to the population of all children. His sample is clearly too small. With only two observations—one of each sex—he should realize that he can justifiably project to neither a universal nor a general conclusion. Similarly, a sampling of fifteen New Yorkers, however carefully chosen, is not likely to provide a reliable basis for a statistical claim concerning New Yorkers generally.

The *composition* of the sample is important. If all, or an untypical proportion, of the people in the survey sample are from groups that are especially interested in the topic being investigated, or if they have personal characteristics that might affect their responses, then the sample is not representative. Suppose that, after conducting a survey at the front door of the local Baptist church, you were to conclude that most Americans believe in God. Your sample would be unrepresentative because we would, of course, expect that a higher percentage of those who attend church, in contrast to those who don't, are believers. Although 98 percent of the people who responded—the *respondents*—professed a belief in God, you would have no reliable basis for predicting that 98 percent of Americans would give similar reports.

Sampling through telephone inquiries—a frequently used method—can produce the same kind of problem because it excludes those who do not own a phone. Since we can expect that a significant proportion of those who do not own phones have severely limited incomes, the sample will be unrepresentative if the question calls for answers that may reflect financial status (for example, "Do you believe that welfare payments should be increased?"). If the sample is unrepresentative, then the results will be unreliable. Telephone sampling can also produce an unrepresentative sample by oversampling or undersampling people of certain occupations, and thus certain economic ranges or political perspectives. In the hours during which the sampling is conducted, some categories of people may be more or less likely than others to be at a home phone.

Small research firms often conduct marketing research for local clients. In an attempt to obtain a wide-ranging sample, the firm may ask questions of people who are entering or leaving a grocery market. When you are evaluating this sort of research, you should ask the following questions, among others. In what part of town is the market? Is the majority of shoppers female or male? Do many elderly people generally shop less frequently than younger people? As you can see, an unintentionally unrepresentative sample can be produced. On some topics, categories of people can be significant, distorting the results of the study.

Some academic psychologists have sought paid volunteers for studies by advertising on the college or university campus. Generally the respondents are students. This can easily introduce imbalance on the basis of age, and the monetary reward introduces another imbalance. Again, depending on the topic of research, the results may be distorted when generalized to the public. Masters and Johnson are famous for their research on the physiology of sexual response. Following initial study of female and male prostitutes, Masters recruited paid volunteers from a university and a medical school. This was certainly not a representative sample. The researchers' assumption, correct or not, was that the kind of sexual functioning they were studying—not merely through questions but through laboratory observation—did not vary significantly between individuals.

Certainly questionnaires that are printed in a magazine will, when returned, reflect an unrepresentative sampling if the results are generalized to the national population. A questionnaire printed in *Cosmopolitan* or *Playboy*, for example, would not reveal the sexual attitudes of the American woman or man unless it were by coincidence. Consider the omitted attitudes of people who would not be willing to buy or browse through such a magazine in the first place.

Presenting Statistics

The implications of statistical information can vary with the formulation or the format of its presentation. Here, an inquiring mind is essential if a person is to be aware of alternate manners of presentation that seem to change the significance of the data.

The first of the following questions is a general one concerning alternate presentations. The second question focuses specifically on graphic displays of statistical information.

What If the Data Were Organized Differently?   Kimble Auto Sales advertises its 100-percent increase in sales over last year, boasting the greatest increase of any dealership in Lancaster County. The consumer is invited to conclude that something phenomenal is occurring at Kimble: such an explosive burst of business must reflect both good management and exceptional deals on cars. Actually, Kimble Auto Sales has always been—and still is—a minor enterprise among dealerships in Lancaster County. While the major dealerships sell thousands of cars each year, Kimble is a vacant-lot operation that "moves" approximately one hundred cars per year. Last year was a particularly weak year in which only sixty-one cars were sold. This year, the sales are back up to, and slightly over, the average: 120 cars were sold.

If the increase had been expressed by stating the *number of cars* sold during the prior and present years, or if it were known that the previous year had been such a bad sales year, the advertisement would not have been impressive. Although the claim of a 100-percent increase in sales is not false, it will nevertheless be misleading to many people.

Data for statistics can usually be organized in different ways, with different apparent implications. In the preceding example, the data have presumably been intentionally manipulated to mislead. Sometimes, even with the intention to organize the information fairly, the problem is difficult to avoid.

The state-normed test scores for the third graders in the South Bay Unified School District have arrived at the district office and have been made available to the press. Should the local headline proclaim that the students have scored "8 percent higher than last year's South Bay third graders"? This is true and seems to be good news for the school district. In contrast, however, the headline might lament that the scores still fall below those of the neighboring districts. This is also true. In fact, the scores also fall below the statewide average. Perhaps this is what the newspaper's readers need to know. On the other hand, considering all the schools in the state that are of a comparable economic status, the district's third graders scored well. They were in the top 35 percent—almost the top third. Whatever headline is chosen for the news article, notice that all of this information except perhaps the "neighboring district" comparison should be presented to convey a full understanding and avoid false impressions. Perhaps additional perspectives should be included.

A similar array of claims may be revealed by applying such a variety of perspectives to business or government. In the case of business, the health of a company might be expressed in terms of total receipts, number of transactions or units processed, profit before or after taxes, or return on investment. For any of these contexts, a comparison might be made with previous years, other companies, or projections. Such a comparison might be in terms of raw numbers or percentages. Statistical claims that are considered in isolation from the body of data that generates them, or from other statistical perspectives, may mislead—not because they are false, but because they represent only part of the situation being described.

Finally, consider the ambiguous term *average*, which is used quite often in statistical claims. We are informed about the average annual income for a family in Boston, the average pay for a symphony musician, the average number of weeks a U.S. senator spends actively campaigning during a reelection year, the average age of an American astronaut, and the average number of marriages for a Hollywood star. The word *average* may convey any of three concepts:

1. *Median:* the item that is midway between the extremes, with an equal number of items occurring above and below.

2. *Mean:* the arithmetical midpoint, determined by computation.

3. *Mode:* the item that occurs most often.

Suppose that in our office the manager is paid $37,000 annually. His assistant is paid $35,000, and the bookkeeper makes $20,000. There are six others in the office. One is paid $14,000, another is paid $13,000, and four others are paid $11,000 each. The median is $13,000, since four people in the office make more money than this and four make less. The mean is determined by adding all the salaries (this comes to a $163,000 payroll), then dividing by the number of people in the office (nine). This yields a figure of $18,111. Notably, no one on the office staff makes this amount, and only one person—the bookkeeper—has a salary that is even near this figure. The mode is $11,000, since this is the salary amount that occurs most frequently on the payroll.

The "average" salary in the office, then, can be truthfully claimed to be $13,000, $18,111, or $11,000. This ambiguity allows misunderstanding and even intentional slanting of the data.

Does the Chart Invite Misunderstanding?   When statistical findings are compared in a graphic presentation, the format can affect the apparent significance of the information being presented. Examine these two graphs showing the size of the graduation class of Truman High School.

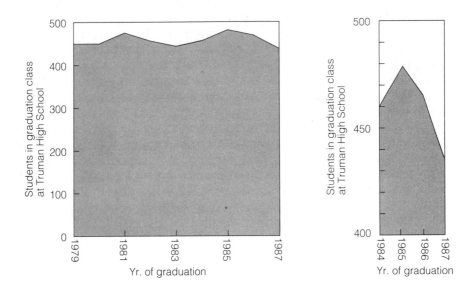

When we view the first graph, the size of the graduation class at Truman appears to be somewhat stable, despite fluctuations. The net loss of students from 1979 to 1987 has been only thirteen. When we view the second graph, however, we get the sense of a sharp and steady decrease. Parents in this school district, upon seeing the second graph, might wonder if a momentous shift has occurred. Actually, there is no contradiction between the graphs. Three related factors account for the difference in the apparent significance of the information on the graphs.

1. Line graphs have a horizontal axis and a vertical axis, each of which has scaled intervals indicating units of measure. The line that traces the data is altered when the size of the intervals on either side is changed. Although the data presented are the same in each of two graphs with different interval sizes, a person's impressions about the significance of this information might be different. Notice the greater distance between the markings for 400 and 500 students on the vertical axis.

2. The vertical axis on the second graph does not begin at zero. The descent of the data line is thus exaggerated.

3. The extent of data represented, meaning the years on the horizontal axis, is so much less on the second graph that no sense of the continuity of fluctuations is communicated. Even with the altered scale on the vertical axis that showed larger intervals and only a partial range, time's perspective would soften the sense that there is a disturbing drop in the number of graduates.

Although each of these three factors contributes to the second graph's capacity to mislead, not all of them are equally objectionable. A graph-wise person will not be bothered or misled by the "suppression of the zero," the elimination of the blank portion of the graph. This saves page space and allows an increased scale for the graph. The size of the intervals is not itself an issue, except that extreme changes in *both* axis intervals (one increasing while the other decreases) can radically alter the data-line pattern, inviting different interpretations of the significance of the data. In the preceding example, the factor that effects the contrast most is the range of years for which information is displayed. In the second graph, we simply get no sense of the regular ups and downs of the class size. This makes the already exaggerated descent seem noteworthy.

Bar graphs are generally simpler than line graphs in that there is usually only one scaled axis—either the vertical or the horizontal axis. Still, any of the three factors affecting the line-graph format can affect the bar-graph format as well.

This is a simple bar graph.

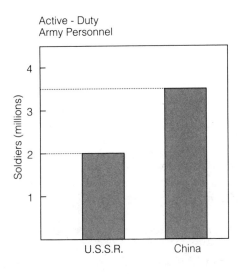

It clearly indicates that the U.S.S.R. has two million people on active duty in the army and that China has three and a half million. The bars give a visual impression of these proportions.

In an abuse of the bar graph, images are used instead of bars, with these images varying not only in length but in width as well. The preceding graph might have been designed like this.

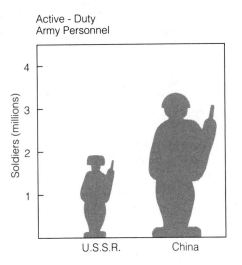

In the traditional bar graph, the two bars indicated the correct *proportion* to show the size relation between the two nations' armies. The image version of that graph displays an incorrect proportion. The total area representing the Chinese forces is now more than twice as large as the area representing the forces of the U.S.S.R. If you consider only the measurement from the bottom to the top of each image, the information is correct; if, however, the entire size of the images influences your assessment, the information is distorted.

Drawing Conclusions from Statistics

Even statistical claims that are well founded can provide a basis for faulty reasoning. When you draw conclusions on the basis of statistics, some of the following questions may be relevant.

Have Other Studies Produced Different Results? When the familiar phrase "in a recent study . . ." prefaces a confident statement of findings, one sometimes fruitful line of inquiry focuses on alternative studies. It would be worthwhile to know whether other investigation has either preceded or followed this particular study. If there have been no other reputable studies, then we should remember that the findings will be more credible when *replicated* (confirmed by others through similar studies). If, on the other hand, there have been other good studies, then it is important to know whether the results of those studies confirm or conflict with the results of the one currently being discussed. If there is a conflict, we should remain neutral on the issue or only tentatively accept the results of the study under current consideration. It is possible that "in a recent [perhaps poorly done] study," the findings run counter to much (or even all!) other research.

Is the Fallacy of Questionable Cause Committed? Statistics *do not* "speak for themselves." Failing to see different possible explanations for the available data will very frequently yield false conclusions.

"23 percent more women are seeking out-of-home employment now than in 1960. Women must be less content with the role of housewife than they used to be." The second sentence is offered as an explanation of the first. It is also a conclusion drawn from the statistical claim that is stated first. One might accept the pair of statements without question, but in so doing one would be committing a version of the fallacy known as questionable cause. If one assumes the accuracy of the first sentence by verifying or failing to question the source of the statistic, the second sentence reveals the apparently obvious *cause* of the increase in women who are seeking out-of-home employment.

Aren't there, however, other possible explanations for the increase? Keep in mind the possibility that there may be several contributing causes. Perhaps, with economic change, more two-parent families feel the need for both parents to work "just to make ends meet." Perhaps social disapproval of leaving young children in day-care situations has lessened. Certainly we have more single-parent families, most of which are headed by women. Furthermore, the population has grown; we have more men *and* women. (Notice that the reference was not to 23 percent of all women but to a 23-percent increase in the number of women.) This can be a contributing cause as well. Certainly there may be, as people say, "some truth," or even much truth, to the original claim that women are less content with the role of housewife than they used to be. Still, considering the other possibilities, this dissatisfaction may not be the sole cause for more women seeking out-of-home employment. For that matter, the preceding list of possibilities implies that *even if women were generally as discontent with that role in 1960,* the number of women who are seeking out-of-home employment could have increased.

The first explanation for why the data stand as they do is not always correct. The explanation that occurs to you may not reflect the only contributing cause. Furthermore, your points of logical vulnerability invite you to find an easy answer that confirms a prejudice. It is good to develop a habit of considering alternative explanations.

Is the Comparison Reasonable?   Perhaps you've heard the charge that someone is "comparing apples and oranges." The suggestion here is that a comparison is inappropriate because things of different—and, for the particular context, incomparable—kinds are being compared. This error can occur in the comparison of statistics as well as in other comparisons.

The means for computing our national unemployment figures are changed occasionally. Clearly, if we begin to include, or exclude, as "unemployed people" those students who are out of school for the summer, adults who are employed in household tasks and not seeking out-of-home employment, or marginally self-employed people, the national figures from before and after the change cannot be legitimately compared without prior adjustment or without reverting to the original definition. The same is true of changes in the computation of the Consumer Price Index (CPI) and other variable indexes.

When standardized test scores decrease in a school district, parents scowl and administrators squirm, but variables other than students' talent and education are occasionally involved. The recent version of the test may be more difficult than the last or have a different emphasis, making comparisons misleading. People have decried the decline in College Board (SAT) scores over recent decades, but attention should also be given to the fact that a larger proportion of high-school classes, which is to say not just the very best students, have been taking the test in many states.

As much as we would like to avail ourselves of quick comparisons, there's no use in comparing apples and oranges.

The statistical findings in studies on unemployment, inflation, psychological topics, opinion polls, or whatever are subject to some inaccuracy. The *margin for error* is the greatest plausible difference between the official figure and the actual rate. We should know the margin for error when we are comparing figures.

If a study of unemployment can be accurate to only two percentage points (2 percent), a published claim that unemployment is at 8 percent reflects the possibility that unemployment is actually as low as 6 percent or as high as 10 percent. Thus, if we observe that the rate was 8 percent last year and 9 percent this year, the margin for error (2 percent in this case) is greater than the difference between the compared figures, and unemployment *might* actually have decreased. In fact, it could have been as high as 10 percent for the first year and as low as 7 percent for the second.

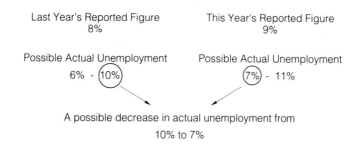

Last Year's Reported Figure
8%

This Year's Reported Figure
9%

Possible Actual Unemployment
6% - 10%

Possible Actual Unemployment
7% - 11%

A possible decrease in actual unemployment from
10% to 7%

Actually, the overall national unemployment figures are quite accurate. The margin for error is roughly two tenths of one percent (0.2 percent). For statistics that focus on a region (for example, Baltimore) or group (for example, blacks) or regional group (for example, blacks in Baltimore), the margin for error increases as the size of the sample and the estimate based on it decrease. In fact, for blacks in Baltimore, the margin for error is 16.3 to 23.4 percent.* For the relevant information for unemployment figures, contact your local Bureau of Labor Statistics office.

Clearly, we must be especially careful of our conclusions when the difference between compared figures is small and when the sampling and estimate sizes are small. In these cases, the diligent thinker will want to know the margin for error. This applies not only to unemployment figures, of course, but to statistical comparisons generally.

Does Correlation Establish Causation? Two things are correlated (co-related) when changes in one reflect changes in the other. Correlations are sometimes observed in statistical data collection and stated in statistical terms.

---

*Geographic Profile of Employment and Unemployment, 1984, *U.S. Department of Labor, Bureau of Labor Statistics, May 1985 (Bulletin 2234).*

A hypothetical example will illustrate how a correlation can be established. Suspecting a connection between cigarette smoking and stomach discomfort, the researcher sets up six groups of people. Group A includes people who do not smoke at all. Group B includes only people who smoke less than a pack of cigarettes each week. The other groups are as follows: Group C, one to two packs each week; Group D, up to a pack each day; Group E, one to two packs each day; Group F, more than two packs each day. The researcher finds that in Group A there is a very low *incidence* (number of occurrences) of stomach discomfort. She finds a higher incidence in Group B, and Groups C, D, E, and F display a continued pattern of increase. Should she conclude that there is a *causal connection* between smoking and stomach discomfort? Does one (smoking, in this case) cause the other (the stomach discomfort, in this case)? Perhaps she should be tentative about such a conclusion. While this may be the most obvious way to explain the correlation, another possibility (besides uncanny coincidence) does exist. Perhaps a *third* factor, yet unnoted, is the cause of both of these effects. If, for example, smoking was a common outlet for nervous tension and stomach discomfort was a symptom produced by the metabolism of a chronically nervous sort of person, then the smoking and the stomach discomfort might not be causally connected.

An inattentive researcher may too readily judge that a causal connection does in fact exist in such a case. While it is true that correlation does not prove causation, however, the failure to identify a "third factor" does not permit the discounting of intriguing correlations. The possibility or probability of a causal connection between the correlated items is compatible with continued vigilance for a third factor.

A Less-Than-Serious Example of Correlation Without Causation

Let's say that we are investigating the cause of Logician's Disease, which inclines its poor victims to mistake affirming the consequent for modus ponens and to mistake denying the antecedent for modus tollens. In other words, the victims see invalid conditional arguments as if they were valid. (There are stronger and milder cases of this disease, as you may know.) The frequency of occurrence and the severity of this disease are found to correlate inversely with years of schooling. (Additional years of schooling correlate with decreases in the frequency and severity of the disease.) We naturally conclude that Logician's Disease is caused by Education Deficiency. Later we discover that a third factor, "Apathetic Genes," is the direct cause of both Logician's Disease and Education Deficiency. The latter two were not causally related at all.

The expression *linked to* obscures the distinction between correlation and causation. We frequently read in the newspaper or hear on radio or television news programs that a certain food or other substance has been "linked to" a serious disease. Often, while the expression was justified by a discovered *correlation*, the person who is reading or hearing the report understands the expression to mean "caused by."

Many completely insignificant correlations can be constructed. Should you worry if you hear a report that "82 percent of all persons who committed violent crimes last year had eaten yogurt within a month prior to the crime"? You should *not*, of course, worry about such a report. Still, besides wondering about how the data had been collected, you should know how to demonstrate that this statistic is insignificant. The revealing question is this: "How often, on the average, do people eat yogurt?" If the frequency among violent criminals and the general public is the same, the statistic is insignificant. No significant statistical connection has been established between the consumption of yogurt and violent crimes.

By changing this silly example a bit, we can create a more credible argument. "Eighty-two percent of all preadolescent children who committed violent crimes last year had watched an average of six hours of television a day for the year preceding the crime." The inferred conclusion is, of course, that the television watching was the cause, or at least *a* cause, of the violence. What question now must be asked? "How much television, on the average, do preadolescent children watch?" If the percentage is similar, the implied argument has no strength at all. Here the general population of preadolescents functions as a *control group* to place into its proper perspective the specific claim about the children who had committed violent crimes. The control group in such a study is actually, to be precise, the sample of preadolescents that was used to generate the statistical claim about the larger population of *all* preadolescents.

■

EXERCISES

8.3 Basic

In each of the following examples of reasoning with statistics, an error is made or invited. Some types of errors have been covered in the preceding section. Others call for some reflective "common sense." Identify and explain the error.

1. A picture of Lee Iacocca of Chrysler Corporation is on the first page of a seven-page advertisement in the October 6, 1986, issue of *Time*. At the top of that first page, the following is printed:

    > Last year you made Chrysler the fastest-growing* car and truck company in America.
    >   The next seven pages are for anybody foolish enough to think we're resting on our laurels.

    In tiny print at the lower-left corner of the page, we find this:

    > *Based on market share increase, 1984 vs. 1985 model year.

2. From the Associated Press news service, reported locally:

    > The average price of gasoline, all grades and including taxes, was 84.63 cents per gallon Friday, compared to an average 84.73 cents Oct. 24, said Trilby Lundberg, publisher of the bimonthly [Lundberg Survey of 15,000 gas stations].
    >   "The drop was only a tiny portion of one cent per gallon, which was expected due to wholesale trends the past two weeks," Mrs. Lundberg said in a telephone interview from Houston, Texas.

3. Two excerpts from "Face-Lift for a Famous Test," *Time*, September 29, 1986:

    > As the [Minnesota Multiphasic Personality Inventory] has come to be seen as a beloved landmark of American psychology, it has also come under frequent attack as dated and culture bound. Since empirical work on the test was done among pre-war, white, rural Minnesotans in their mid-30s, it does not account for newer values and is often a particularly unreliable test for blacks, women and adolescents.

    > The revision committee is now testing two experimental booklets, one for adults, one for adolescents. Some 15,000 Americans and Canadians, randomly selected from phone books and replies to magazine ads in eight states and the City of Toronto, have taken the new forms of the test. Unlike the original sample—now regarded as "both small and parochial," according to Committee Member James Butcher of the University of Minnesota—the new group is carefully balanced by region, ethnic group, age, education, and gender.

4. From *Special Report on Tax Reform,* a letter Congressman Ron Packard sent to voters in his district:

   > This summer, I asked you and your neighbors . . . to evaluate [the President's] proposed tax reforms. The response to our survey was strong—10,000 families participated districtwide. The consensus was equally strong—overall, *76% supported the . . . tax reforms as our best course.*

5. Contrary to some claims, Americans are *not* losing their faith in God. In response to questionnaires sent to twenty thousand church members of different denominations, 70 percent reported that their religious beliefs—including faith in God—were as strong or stronger than ten years ago.

6. Despite all the women's-rights issues in the news, the American people are really quite content with the current role of women in our society. In response to a recent questionnaire printed in the magazine *Field and Stream,* 73 percent of the people indicated that they were content with the current role of women in society, seeing no need for major changes at this time.

7. People who are in good shape physically can bear 43 percent more mental stress than those who get no regular exercise.

8. Twenty-two percent of American families have incomes below the poverty level. That's because they're not interested in working as hard as the rest of us.

9. Two hundred complete skeletons of dinosaurs are yet to be discovered and unearthed on this continent.

10. Forty-two percent of the population has psychic powers of which they are unaware.

11. Less than 2 percent of all symphony orchestras are led by female conductors. Apparently music conducting is just something for which women don't have much talent.

12. Twenty percent more television sets were sold last year than in 1970. This is obviously a reflection of America's increasing taste for violence.

13. People in this nation are fed up with the welfare program. This was revealed in the results of a survey directed at readers of the *Wall Street Journal.* A majority of them—52 percent, to be exact—thought that all such programs should be scrapped completely.

14. It's definitely true. More people prefer our local Royal cola over Coke and Pepsi. In a recent test conducted at the county fair, more people chose Royal over either of the two big-name colas.

15. In "Reagan Aide: Pot Can Make You Gay," *Newsweek*, October 27, 1986, it is reported that White House drug adviser Carlton E. Turner

> says that when he visits drug-treatment centers for patients under 18, he finds that roughly 40 percent of them have also engaged in homosexual activity. "It seems to be something that follows along from their marijuana use," says Turner, who is convinced that the drugs come first, the homosexuality second.

■

EXERCISES

8.4 Difficult

A critique of each of the following examples of reasoning with statistics will yield a crucial question to be asked. For each of these examples, what is the question that provides insight into the implications of the statistics?

1. From "Are We Safe at Any Speed?" in *Newsweek On Health*, Winter 1986:

> The logic of the "double nickel" is as plain as can be: speed kills. The year the [55 mile-an-hour] limit was imposed, the highway death toll fell abruptly from 55,000 fatalities in 1973 to 46,000 in 1974. But what is mysterious is that since then, even though speeds actually driven have been rising, the national death rate has continued to fall. Last year there were only 2.48 deaths for every 100 million miles driven, down from 2.58 in 1984 and 4.24 in 1973. Especially on the interstates, which were engineered for speeds up to 75 mph, the death rate continued to fall as speeds rose.

2. From a letter to the editor of the *San Diego Union*, November 17, 1985:

> Your editorial (Nov. 21) asks the question, "Should minority students or any students receive preferential treatment in order to play football, or be in the marching band?" You then answer the question by stating, "Of course not."
>
> I can concur with the idea that the main purpose of school has been to encourage academic performance as a preparation for life,

but I believe that some exceptions need to be made for those students who cannot meet the scholastic requirements that are a prerequisite for extra-curricular activities.

Research shows that the young person engaged in extra-curricular activities remains in school. The model prisoners are those engaged in the athletic and artistic programs in our correctional institutions.

3. In September 1986 *Success!* magazine published "Marriage, Inc.," an article on spouses who have gone into business together as "mom and pop entrepreneurs—literally." Here is an excerpt from that article:

> The couple's rising fortunes are due, in large part, to women's increased training and expertise. Women today make up almost 40 percent of office workers and more than 50 percent of those in the professions. As a result of women's broadened business experience, husband and wife teams now represent one of the country's largest reserves of entrepreneurial energy. The Small Business Administration reports that the number of joint proprietorships—one of the legal forms that couples starting a business often use—has grown by 20 percent per year since 1980. That's almost four times as fast as other business proprietorships.

4. Again, from "Marriage, Inc.":

> Today mom has a C.P.A., pop has an M.B.A., and they're turning their store into a franchise. In 1974 only 1 percent of U.S. families, just 600,000, had an income above $50,000. Currently 16 percent, or almost 10 million families, earn that much. These new entrepreneurs—power partners, if you will—are finding that when it comes to doing business, two heads are often better than one.

5. From "Smoking: A Marital Minefield," *The San Diego Union*, February 1, 1987:

> A British study did not find passive smoking to be linked to lung cancer. The study, by a team led by P. N. Lee of the Institute for Cancer Research, said the risk of harm from smoke in the air is "at most quite small, if it exists at all." Valid statistical studies are difficult to make, the study found, because relatively few nonsmokers get lung cancer.

6. In January 1987 the Associated Press released the following story:

Nearly 40 percent of all violent crimes are done by friends

WASHINGTON—In nearly four out of 10 violent crimes, the attacker is a relative, friend or acquaintance of the victim, according to a federal study released Sunday.

The Bureau of Justice Statistics report says that less than half the 20 million violent crimes committed from 1982 through 1984 were perpetrated by people who were strangers to the victims.

The survey of 58,000 households conducted twice a year by the Census Bureau found that 46 percent of robberies, rapes and assaults were committed by strangers.

"It is often said that the fear of crime is largely a fear of strangers," bureau director Steven R. Schlesinger said in a statement.

But he said 10 percent of the offenders were known to the victims by sight and 39 percent of the violent crimes involved friends, relatives or acquaintances of the victim.

Friends accounted for 17 percent, or 3.3 million, of the violent crimes, while casual acquaintances accounted for 14 percent, and relatives accounted for 8 percent.

In the rest of the cases, the relationship of the attacker to the victim was not known.

From 1982 to 1984, friends, relatives or acquaintances were responsible for 40 percent of the rapes, more than 45 percent of the simple assaults, nearly 40 percent of the aggravated assaults and 20 percent of robberies.

The bureau, a Justice Department agency within the Office of Justice Programs, said it may be underestimating the number of crimes committed by people known to the victim.

"Individuals victimized by relatives may be reluctant to discuss the event . . . for fear of reprisal or out of shame or embarrassment," the report said. "Further, some victims of domestic violence may not perceive these acts as criminal."

In the 1.5 million violent crimes in which a relative was the offender, 77 percent of the victims were women.

Spouses or ex-spouses committed more than half of all crimes by relatives and about two-thirds of all crimes by relatives against women.

More than half of the crimes by relatives against women were reported by women who were divorced or separated.

The bureau cited FBI statistics for 1984 which found that 20 percent of the 19,000 homicides were committed by relatives and nearly 40 percent by acquaintances.

Reprinted with permission of the Associated Press.

7. From a letter to the editor of *The New York Times,* January 10, 1986:

Fred Hechinger (column, Science Times, Dec. 31) says that despite many calls for reform, "There has been no serious departure from the way the American school has been organized for more than 100 years." Why such resistance to change?

One answer may be that the testing system is the tail that wags the dog; we may need to trade in the old tests for new ones. Teachers are constantly training children to pass tests that certify them for passing into next higher levels. These tests require manipulating word and number symbols or regurgitating knowledge such as the difference between a paramecium and a euglena. The tests demand that the old system remain intact.

What old system? The system that classifies knowledge into such subjects as English, history, biology and math—the system that pins students to desks and forces them to swallow masses of material of little interest to them. Forty percent drop out of high school before graduating. Isn't there a strong message in that statistic? ∎

∎

CHAPTER HIGHLIGHTS

∎ Some kinds of reasoning characteristic of the sciences are regularly involved in our everyday thinking. Two of these are *hypothesis formation and evaluation* and *reasoning with statistics.*

∎ Whether in science, pseudoscience, or everyday matters, hypotheses are formed on some basis. This may be observation, theory, or authority. Reasonable hypotheses are compatible with the known data. They "fit the facts." The data may be observed incidentally or gathered purposefully. It is often helpful to form several reasonable hypotheses and to be open to evidence for or against any of them.

∎ Four considerations are central in the evaluation of the strength of an hypothesis. These are:

1. *Amount of confirming evidence.*
   Basically, more evidence strengthens an hypothesis.

2. *Variety of confirming evidence.*
   Different kinds of evidence generally confirm an hypothesis more decidedly.

3. *Testability.*
   "If this hypothesis is true, what else can I expect to find?" (Beware of the irrefutable but self-sealing hypothesis.)

4. *Simplicity.*
   A complicated hypothesis is generally less useful than a simpler one that explains the same set of facts.

∎ Statistical information is helpful, but one should not accept specific claims and conclusions uncritically. As a stimulus for the reader to identify additional questions he or she may need to ask, this chapter offered eight questions under three headings.

Compiling Statistics

Is the researcher qualified? A researcher's incompetence or bias can contribute to unreliable results.

Is the sample reliable? A sample can be too small to justify a generalization to the larger population for which conclusions are intended to apply. A sample can also be unrepresentative of the larger population. If the respect in which the sample is unrepresentative affects the result (that which is being measured), the generalization is unjustified.

Presenting Statistics

What if the data were organized differently? In choosing the way in which information is ordered for presentation, a person may invite false conclusions. Usually, it is useful to see the data in different formats.

Does the chart invite misunderstanding? People who are not graphwise may be misled by failing to consider the visual impact of a limited data range, interval size on an axis, bar-graph images, or deletion of the empty space on a graph (typically, from zero to a higher value).

Drawing Conclusions from Statistics

Have other studies produced different results? The study cited may show results that conflict with other research.

Is the fallacy of questionable cause committed? With a statistical claim as a premise, it is possible to draw an incorrect or partially correct conclusion about why that claim is true.

Is the comparison reasonable? Statistical comparisons should focus on measured items that are similar in kind. Also, awareness of a study's margin for error is especially important if the compared statistical claims are within a narrow range.

Does correlation establish causation? Although correlation is sometimes due to causation, in other cases a third factor is the cause and the correlated items are both effects.

For Further Reading

Huck, Schuyler W., and Howard M. Sandler. *Rival Hypotheses.* New York: Harper & Row, 1979.

A compilation of alternate interpretations of data-based conclusions.

Huff, Darrell. *How to Lie with Statistics.* New York: W. W. Norton, 1954.

A light-hearted introduction to the assessment of statistical claims.

Katzer, Jeffrey, Kenneth H. Cook, and Wayne W. Crouch. *Evaluating Information.* Reading, MA: Addison-Wesley, 1982.

A guide for users of social science research statistics.

McCain, Garvin, and Erwin M. Segal. *The Game of Science.* Monterey, CA: Brooks/ Cole, 1977.

An enjoyable discussion of scientific inquiry.

Moore, David S. *Statistics: Concepts and Controversies.* San Francisco: W. H. Freeman, 1985.

A well-written introduction to statistical analysis.

Quine, W. V., and J. S. Ullian. *The Web of Belief.* New York: Random House, 1978.

A philosophical discussion of rational belief and scientific thought.

Radner, Daisie, and Michael Radner. *Science and Unreason.* Belmont, CA: Wadsworth, 1982.

A readable, example-filled discussion of pseudoscience.

C H A P T E R

NINE

Research

The ability to determine whether, or to what extent, a conclusion follows from its premises is vitally important. Anyone will benefit from improved skills of this kind. However, this is not enough to ensure that a person will end up with the *right* conclusions!

In Chapters 3 and 4 we considered a distinction between an argument's form and its content. An argument has good form if its premises provide adequate support for its conclusion *apart from* the issue of whether the premises are true. An argument has good content if its premises are in fact true. Often, when you have no great difficulty in seeing the extent to which the premises support the conclusion, which means you can evaluate the argument's form, you still do not know whether to accept the conclusion: you don't know whether the premises that have been presented are true—whether the content is good. The questionable claim may concern the voting record of your state senator, the reversibility of damage to the earth's ozone layer, the ranking of your state or school district in terms of money spent per pupil in public education, the relative productivity of American and Japanese industries, or the frequency of teen pregnancies. The problem is that you simply don't know whether the premise is true. You may have your suspicions or you may clearly desire the premise to be true or false, but ultimately you just don't know.

In such arguments, you might accept your best guess, you might accept what you *want* to be true, you might suspend judgment and ignore the argument, or you could decide to find out if the premise is true. Where do you go to find out? Skill 17 enables you to find the information that is available in a library. Skill 18 focuses on assessing information from the news media.

LIBRARY RESEARCH

The most useful resource for evaluating the truth of factual claims is the library—public, private, or academic. Since everyone, at times, needs to verify a claim or to seek new information on a topic that is being evaluated,

---

SKILL

Skill 17. Doing library research

Locate desired information using a library catalog, periodical index, or special reference volumes and files.

Why this skill is important

Everyone encounters important reasoning that involves a factual premise requiring verification. ■

---

library research skills should be part of a person's general education. For our purposes, we are considering specifically the verification of premises for an argument. The box above will help you remember and use this essential research skill.

A library has a catalog, often called the card catalog, that is used to locate books. Periodicals—magazines and other literature that are issued periodically—are located by using an appropriate periodical index. A working knowledge of these information-locating tools is important. Familiarity with encyclopedias, almanacs, and other special reference sources is also desirable.

The Catalog

Every library has a catalog. Here, each book in the library's collection is recorded and its location on the library shelves is indicated. Periodicals are sometimes listed here as well. Many libraries have the traditional "card catalog," with three-by-five-inch cards filed in drawers of one or more filing cabinets. Although a major library may have a dozen or more large cabinets, locating a book is a relatively simple matter. The library's patrons—its customers—have direct access to the catalog, but the library staff should be quite willing to lend a hand if you need help. In some libraries, the catalog is recorded on microfiche (pronounced "microfeesh"), sheets of microfilm, instead of the traditional paper cards. In other libraries, access to catalog information is partially or wholly computerized.

Each book has at least three separate listings in the catalog. It is listed alphabetically by the author's name, by the book's title, and by the general subject of the book. Often, the author and title files are merged, and the subject file is separate. The organization of the catalog will, however, vary among libraries.

If you are looking for a specific book, you can use either the author's name or the book's title to discover whether the library has it in its collection and, if so, where it is located. If you want to find out the titles of all the books in the library that were written by a certain author, you can find them recorded alphabetically under the author's name in the catalog. If you have no specific book in mind, or if you have forgotten both the author's name and the book's title, you can use the subject listings to search the collection.

Searching by subject can be tricky. The subject category you have selected may list so many books that you must spend more time than you desire going through the list. Furthermore, you may be using the wrong subject category for your search. You may, for example, be looking within the category "Insanity," while the best book for your purposes is recorded under "Mentally Ill," a heading you haven't considered. To help with this problem you can consult *Library of Congress Subject Headings*, a two-volume work for standardization of subject categories and for cross-referencing categories, or *Sears List of Subject Headings*, depending on which is used by that library.

Many libraries—public, private, and academic—are part of a library network. These networks enable member libraries to borrow books from the collections of other member libraries for use by their patrons. For practical purposes, this can significantly extend the holdings of a library. Many of these networks maintain a catalog of books that is available on microfiche or by computer at each member library and branch.

In cataloging books, libraries use either the Dewey decimal system or the Library of Congress system, both of which classify books by subject. Each book in the collection has a different *call number*. This code, recorded with each catalog entry, is printed on the spine of the book and dictates the book's location on the shelves.

These are the major categories of the Dewey decimal classification:

000   GENERALITIES

100   PHILOSOPHY

200   RELIGION

300   SOCIAL SCIENCES

400   LANGUAGE

500   PURE SCIENCES

600   TECHNOLOGY (APPLIED SCIENCES)

700   FINE ARTS

800   LITERATURE

900   GEOGRAPHY AND HISTORY

Each hundred-level category is further divided according to distinctions within that area. For example, the 500 category contains the following classifications:

510   Mathematics

520   Astronomy & allied sciences

530   Physics

540   Chemistry & allied sciences

550   Sciences of earth & other worlds

560   Paleontology

570   Life sciences

580   Botanical sciences

590   Zoological sciences

For the Library of Congress classification, these are the major categories:

A   GENERAL WORKS

B   PHILOSOPHY, PSYCHOLOGY, RELIGION

C   AUXILIARY SCIENCES OF HISTORY

D   HISTORY: GENERAL AND OLD WORLD

E-F   HISTORY: AMERICA

G   GEOGRAPHY

H   SOCIAL SCIENCES

J   POLITICAL SCIENCE

K   LAW

L   EDUCATION

M   MUSIC AND BOOKS ON MUSIC

N   FINE ARTS

P   LANGUAGE AND LITERATURE

Q   SCIENCE

R   MEDICINE

S   AGRICULTURE

T   TECHNOLOGY

U   MILITARY SCIENCE

V   NAVAL SCIENCE

Z   BIBLIOGRAPHY, LIBRARY SCIENCE

Each single-letter category is further divided, as with the Dewey decimal system, according to distinctions within that area. For example, the Q category contains the following classifications:

Q   Science (general)

QA   Mathematics

QB   Astronomy

QC   Physics

QD   Chemistry

QE   Geology

QH   Natural history (general)

QK   Botany

QL   Zoology

QM   Human anatomy

QP   Physiology

QR   Microbiology

Let's now examine a card catalog's author card, title card, and subject-heading card for one book: *Juvenile Offenders and the Juvenile Justice System*, by Sol Rubin, published in 1986. These cards are typical of card-catalog entries, but the microfiche and computer formats may offer less information per entry.

Here is the author card for Mr. Rubin's book. It is located by finding the correct drawer in the card catalog and searching alphabetically. You might find this card in a drawer labelled ROY–RUD.

```
KF
9795       Rubin, Sol.
.R83          Juvenile offenders and the juvenile
1986       justice system / by Sol Rubin ; Irving
           J. Sloan, general editor. -- Dobbs
           Ferry, N.Y. : Oceana, 1986.
              131 p. 20 cm. -- (Legal almanac
           series ; no. 22)
              Includes index.
              ISBN 0-379-11150-0


              1. Juvenile courts--United States--
           Popular works.  I. Sloan, Irving J.
           II. Title  III. Series

           30 APR 86   12944879  CPDAnt     85-28481
```

The call number, KF/9795/.R83/1986, is at the upper left of the card. The first line of print shows the author's name. The last name is printed first, since it determines the card's placement in the catalog. Below the author's name is the book's title. On this specific card, the remaining information in that paragraph is a restatement of the author's name, the name of the editor of a series to which this book belongs, the place of publication, the publishing company, and the date of publication. Below this are listed the number of pages in the book and the book size. In parentheses are the name of the book series and the number of this book within that series. After the phrase "Includes index" is the ISBN, the book's international identification number. Near the bottom of the card is the subject heading under which this book is listed and its listings (besides author) in the author/title catalog. The codes along the very bottom of the card are for use by the library's cataloging staff.

Here is the title card for Mr. Rubin's book. It is located in the same catalog as the author's card.

```
           Juvenile offenders and the juvenile
              justice system
KF
9795       Rubin, Sol.
.R83          Juvenile offenders and the juvenile
1986       justice system / by Sol Rubin ; Irving
           J. Sloan, general editor. -- Dobbs
           Ferry, N.Y. : Oceana, 1986.
              131 p. 20 cm. -- (Legal almanac
           series ; no. 22)
              Includes index.
              ISBN 0-379-11150-0


              1. Juvenile courts--United States--
           Popular works.  I. Sloan, Irving J.
           II. Title  III. Series

           30 APR 86   12944879  CPDAnt     85-28481
```

Again, the call number is at the upper left of the card. The information on this card is the same as on the author's card. The only difference here is that the title of the book is printed at the top of the card, since this is what determines the placement of this card in the catalog.

Here is the subject-heading card for Mr. Rubin's book. In many libraries, remember, the subject-heading cards will be in a separate catalog from the author and title cards.

```
               JUVENILE COURTS--UNITED STATES--
                    POPULAR WORKS.
     KF
     9795      Rubin, Sol.
     .R83         Juvenile offenders and the juvenile
     1986       justice system / by Sol Rubin ; Irving
               J. Sloan, general editor. -- Dobbs
               Ferry, N.Y. : Oceana, 1986.
                    131 p. 20 cm. -- (Legal almanac
               series ; no. 22)
                    Includes index.
                    ISBN 0-379-11150-0


                    1. Juvenile courts--United States--
               Popular works.  I. Sloan, Irving J.
               II. Title   III. Series

               30 APR 86   12944879  CPDAsc      85-28481
```

This book was entered under the subject heading "Juvenile Courts—United States—Popular Works." The major subject heading is the first phase, "Juvenile Courts." After all the cards that are entered simply under "Juvenile Courts," the cards with subheadings are entered alphabetically by subheading. The subheading here is "United States." A further subheading under "Juvenile Courts—United States" is "Popular Works." Remember to check *Library of Congress Subject Headings* or *Sears List of Subject Headings* for direction in selecting a subject heading.

Periodical Indexes

Periodicals are sometimes included in a library's main catalog. If not, you can discover which periodicals the library subscribes to by consulting its serials list, an alphabetical compilation of the names of all of the library's periodicals. The way in which periodicals are filed varies among libraries. The current issue is usually available for patrons to read while they are in the library building. Previous issues ("back issues") may be in "closed stacks." This means that the shelves are not open to the patrons. If this is the case, the library staff retrieves the desired issue. If the library has "open stacks" for periodicals, the patron may go directly to the shelves that hold the previous issues. Periodicals may be ordered alphabetically or by call number on these shelves. Some libraries allow patrons to sign periodicals out of the library, but many do not.

Imagine that you have been presented with an argument that is inductively strong but has a factual premise that you simply don't know whether to accept or reject. If it is reasonably possible that the information you lack is available in articles from periodicals, you can quickly and easily search through years of issues for dozens, or even hundreds, of periodicals by using a periodical index.

You should know of the major periodical indexes and be able to use them. In the following paragraphs, the basics of the *Readers' Guide*, the *Magazine Index*, and the *National Newspaper Index* are discussed.

The *Readers' Guide to Periodical Literature*, better known simply as the *Readers' Guide*, indexes articles from over 160 periodicals. These periodicals are identified at the beginning of any of the volumes in the set. Published by the H. W. Wilson Company and with indexing back to 1890, these volumes list articles that you might use in constructing or evaluating argumentation. Fiction, reviews, and poetry are also indexed. You must exercise good judgment in using these sources, because the *Readers' Guide* does not screen articles for quality. In assessing the reliability of the material, you will have to consider the character and readership of the publication and available information about the author.

New articles are indexed and the index is published monthly for six months of the year and twice a month for six months. Each year, the material from the previous calendar year's monthly and semimonthly paperback issues is published in a single hardcover "cumulative" volume. The new volume then becomes a part of the permanent set of *Readers' Guide* volumes. (Before 1985, volumes were not based on the calendar year.)

Under subject and author categories, articles are listed alphabetically by title. Cross-referencing to related categories is provided where appropriate, so you won't have to guess about subject categories. Here is a sample entry.

Cancer research
    See also
  National Cancer Institute (U.S.)
The baffling standoff in cancer research. R. Teitelman.
  il *Forbes* 136:110-12+ Jl 15 '85
Can we conquer cancer? E. Horton. il *Sci Dig* 93:47
  O '85
Cancer: today's research tomorrow's hope. il *Curr Health
  2* 11:3-9 Ap '85
The search for a cure. J. Rogers. il *Macleans* 98:46
  Ap 8 '85
To conquer cancer [special section; with editorial comment
  by Oliver S. Moore] S. Hammer and others. il *Sci
  Dig* 93:4, 31-40+ Ag '85
                    Ethical aspects
Cancer researcher falsified records [case of W. T. Wallens]
  C. Ballentine. il *FDA Consum* 19:41-2 F '85
                       Canada
    See also
  National Cancer Institute of Canada
                     Egypt
    See also
  National Cancer Institute (Egypt)

This entry on cancer research can be found on page 358 of the 1985 volume of the *Readers' Guide*. The *see* or *see also* cross-referencing cue indicates that related articles are listed under "National Cancer Institute (U.S.)." Articles from *Forbes*, *Science Digest* (two), *Current Health*, *Macleans*, and *FDA Consumer* are listed next. "Ethical aspects," "Canada," and "Egypt" are offered as subheadings.

In alphabetizing the articles, an initial *a, an,* or *the* is disregarded. In the sample entry, then, the first article listed is "The baffling standoff in cancer research." The title is followed by the author's name: in this case, it is R. Teitelman. The *il* indicates that the article is illustrated. It is to be found in *Forbes*, volume 136, pages 110 through 112 and (*+*) is continued later in the magazine. The issue date is July 15, 1985. All of the entries can be read in this way. In some cases (two, in this cancer research entry), square brackets, which the publisher calls "title enhancement," are added to clarify the topic of the article. General instructions for using the *Readers' Guide* and a key to abbreviations are printed in the first few pages of each volume.

Here is a sample entry for which the category is a person's name.

> **Kennedy, Edward Moore, 1932-**
> The case against South Africa. il map *Ebony* 40:132+
> My '85
> Land of death and desolation. il pors *People Wkly*
> 23:26-36+ Ja 28 '85
> Should Congress act to convey line-item veto authority
> to the president [excerpts from debate, July 23, 1985]
> *Congr Dig* 64:266+ N '85
> South Africa: III. *America* 153:51-3 Ag 3-10 '85
> *about*
> Camelot (continued). C. O'Connor. il pors *Newsweek*
> 106:29-30 D 16 '85
> A dream deferred. C. O'Connor. il por *Newsweek* 106:19-20
> D 30 '85
> "I know I may never be president". E. Magnuson. il
> por *Time* 126:16 D 30 '85
> Kennedy exits, scrambles 1988 race. por *U S News World*
> *Rep* 99:14 D 30 '85-Ja 6 '86
> Kennedy the front-runner. F. Barnes. il *New Repub*
> 193:15-16+ N 25 '85
> Kennedy's '88 gamble: Senate or White House. J. W.
> Mashek. il por *U S News World Rep* 99:68 N 4 '85
> Kennedy's tilt at apartheid. N. Cooper. il por *Newsweek*
> 105:46 Ja 21 '85
> Ted Kennedy: the private side of a public man. G.
> Plaskin. il pors *Ladies Home J* 102:58+ Jl '85
> Teddy on safari. *Natl Rev* 37:19 F 8 '85
> Teddy's back. J. McLaughlin. *Natl Rev* 37:20 My 17
> '85
> An unlikely affinity. H. Sidey. il por *Time* 126:16 Ag
> 12 '85

This is the entry for Senator Ted Kennedy in the 1985 cumulative index. Articles Mr. Kennedy wrote are listed before articles about him. This is the standard procedure in the *Readers' Guide*. A portrait is included where *por* is indicated.

Besides the general *Readers' Guide*, H. W. Wilson Company publishes many specialized indexes: *Applied Science and Technology Index, Art Index, Biography Index, Biological and Agricultural Index, Business Periodicals Index,*

Education Index, General Science Index, Humanities Index, Index to Legal Period-icals, Social Science Index, and others. For these publications, indexing is the same as in the *Readers' Guide.* Other publishers produce useful periodical indexes too. One puts out an annual *Consumers Index to Product Evaluations and Information Sources.* Another produces *Access,* a recent index to supple-ment other general indexes. Many magazines publish indexes to their own back issues. *National Geographic, Scientific American,* and *The Saturday Review* are among these.

The *Magazine Index,* available at an increasing number of libraries, has an advantage over the *Readers' Guide:* It indexes over four hundred peri-odicals, more than doubling the sources of *Readers' Guide.* A disadvantage, however, is that it indexes articles in those periodicals for only the previous four years. (Microfiche records of the *Magazine Index* entries dating back to 1977 are available.) Each index, then, provides something the other doesn't. When you want a wide range of sources and you are interested in recent articles, you should choose the *Magazine Index.* On the other hand, when you need to research articles that are not recent, the *Readers' Guide* is the reference tool to use.

The *Magazine Index* is not bound in volumes that await you on a shelf. Instead, the information is displayed on the screen of an $18 \times 18 \times 15$-inch desktop machine. When you switch the machine on, you view an illumi-nated microfilm. You can locate the desired section of film by using the simple controls on the right side of the machine.

In the single index, you can find subject categories, author categories, product (brand name) categories, and entries for reviews of movies, restau-rants, books, and plays. The reviews are graded (A, B, C, D, F) to indicate the reviewer's general evaluation. A version of the *Magazine Index's* listings is now available on InfoTrac computer terminals.

Unlike the *Readers' Guide,* the listings within a category are not alpha-betical but are according to date, with the most recent articles listed first. If the same word refers to a subject or title and to persons (for example, "Carpenter"), persons are entered last. Finally, not all authors are listed. A person is listed as author only if that person is also the subject of an article that is listed in the *Magazine Index* or if a review of that person's work is listed in the index.

The *National Newspaper Index* is similar in format to the *Magazine Index;* both are products of Information Access Company, a division of Ziff-Davis Publishing Company. This index lists articles from *The Wall Street Journal, The New York Times,* the *Christian Science Monitor,* the *Los Angeles Times,* and *The Washington Post.* Again, recent articles are listed first. Many libraries also have back issues of certain newspapers and periodicals available on rolls of microfilm, which can be read on a microfilm-reader machine. There is a microfilm version of *The New York Times* for issues as early as 1851 and of the London *Times* for issues as early as 1785.

Special Reference Volumes

Sometimes the best source of information for your needs will be one of those volumes or sets of volumes that have been designed specifically for reference use. Hundreds, or even thousands, of useful publications of this kind await discovery in a full-service library. Several prominent ones will be mentioned under each of the following categories: encyclopedias, almanacs, atlases and gazetteers, and other reference sources.

Encyclopedias Although some single-volume or two-volume works are also termed "encyclopedias," the word typically refers to a set of twenty to thirty volumes. Informational topics are presented in alphabetical order, and the discussion of a topic may be as short as one paragraph or as long as ten pages or more. The presentation in a general encyclopedia is intended as introductory; specialized encyclopedias such as *The Encyclopedia of Philosophy* are exceptions. Topics included range from geographic locations ("Africa," "Alps," "Pittsburgh") to persons ("St. Francis of Assisi," "Theodore Roosevelt," "Mark Twain") to general topics ("livestock," "post office," "tariff," "chemistry").

The New Encyclopaedia Britannica is the most scholarly and generally the most detailed encyclopedia. The new format of the *Britannica* is designed to offer in-depth coverage without being cumbersome for the person who wants a quick and less-detailed presentation. Essentially, it is two complete encyclopedia sets: the *Micropaedia* for "Ready Reference" and the *Macropaedia* for "Knowledge in Depth." A companion volume, the *Propaedia*, offered as an "Outline of Knowledge," presents an extensive overview of the branches of human inquiry. Since 1986, there has also been a two-volume index. The *Britannica* has especiallly thorough presentations of scientific topics.

The other major adult encyclopedias are *Academic American* (the first encyclopedia available on-line), *Collier's*, *Encyclopedia Americana*, and *World Book*. These and the *Britannica* are surveyed in the accompanying chart.

Almanacs An almanac is an annual book of detailed statistical, historical, geographic, and miscellaneous information. In an almanac, you can obtain information about the following and more:

Nobel Prize and Pulitzer Prize recipients

The public debt, year by year

National capitals, populations, literacy rates, forms of government, languages

College faculty sizes and student enrollments

Title	Reading Level	Organization
Academic American Encyclopedia	High school/ college	21 Vols. Index—Vol. #21
Collier's Encyclopedia	High school/ college	24 Vols. Index ⎱ Vol. Bibliography ⎰ #24
Encyclopedia Americana	High school/ college	30 Vols. Index—Vol. #30
Encyclopaedia Britannica	College	30 Vols. 1-Vol. *Propaedia*: guide, outline, and table of contents for *Micropaedia* 10-Vol. *Micropaedia*: indexing and cross-referencing to *Macropaedia* with microview of subject matter 19-Vol. *Macropaedia*: In-depth coverage of material
World Book Encyclopedia	Junior high school/ high school	22 Vols. Index ⎱ Vol. Research guide ⎰ #22

Indexing	Updating	Special Features
Word-by-word by subject heading with subheadings and notations for: *Cross-referencing *Bibliographies *Map locations *Illustrations *Tables	Entire set—yearly Annual yearbook issued	Usage Guide in Vol. #1 *** Available in three electronic versions: *On-line *Laser video disc *CD/ROM
Letter-by-letter by subject heading with subheadings with comprehensive bibliography for entire set	Entire set—yearly Annual yearbook issued	An abbreviated guide to reference books located in index *** U.S. Census data published in a separate supplement
Word-by-word by subject headings with subheadings and notations for: *Cross-referencing *Maps *Illustrations *Book entries Selected subjects in index in the form of study outlines	Entire set—yearly Annual yearbook issued	Individual table of contents found at the beginning of lengthy articles *** Glossary of difficult/ technical terms *** Summary articles for each century A.D.
Word-by-word by subject headings Located in 10-Vol. *Micropaedia* (see organization column)	Entire set—periodically Currently in 15th edition plus annual yearbook issued	*Propaedia* provides an extensive outline of knowledge for research within the *Macropaedia*
Word-by-word by subject heading with subheadings and notations for: *Cross-referencing *Illustrations *Reading and study guides for selected topics	Entire set—yearly plus annual yearbook issued	User's Guide in Vol. #1 *** Instructional section, located in Index vol., titled "A Student Guide to Better Writing and Research Skills"

Locations and sizes of nuclear power plants

Television statistics

Employment data

U.S. defense budget

Volcano eruptions

History and membership of world religions

Geologic periods

Caloric content of foods

Spaceflight projects

United Nations charter, membership, and agencies

Declaration of Independence (text)

U.S. Constitution (text)

Qualifications for voting

Marriage and divorce statistics

Weights and measures

Imports and exports

Astronomical data and observations about weather patterns formed the heart of the earliest almanacs and are also normally included in modern almanacs. The favorite almanacs today are *Information Please Almanac, World Almanac,* and *Reader's Digest Almanac and Yearbook.*

Thematic almanacs focus on specific areas of interest. Examples of thematic almanacs are *Catholic Almanac, Women's Rights Almanac, The Statesman's Year-Book* (from Great Britain), and the two-volume *Europa Yearbook,* which contains details on all the nations of the world.

Atlases and Gazetteers   An atlas is a book of maps. The London *Times* sponsors the preparation of an excellent international atlas, *The Times Atlas of the World.* In the United States, major atlases are published by Rand McNally, Hammond, and *Reader's Digest.* Hammond's *Medallion World Atlas* includes an historical atlas section and maps of the Bible lands. The National Geographic Society and *Goode's* also publish good atlases. Thematic atlases are available as well.

A gazetteer is a dictionary of geographical information, defining names like Bavaria, Troy, Mount Whitney, Suez Canal, and Bay of Biscay. Correct pronunciation is also indicated. *Webster's New Geographical Dictionary* and the *International Geographical Encyclopedia and Atlas* are among the up-to-date gazetteers.

Other Special Reference Sources Even a general survey of additional reference sources would be extensive. Instead, a few specific sources will be mentioned. For a better sense of the range of special reference volumes, a visit to a good library is best.

Books in Print lists the title, author or editor, publisher, and price of almost every book that is published or exclusively distributed in the United States and is currently in print. Three volumes are indexed by author, three by title, and four by subject. In addition, there is a two-volume midyear updating—the supplement—and there are three volumes on paperbound books in print. A new fifteen-volume set is published each year. There is even a set called *Forthcoming Books.* The *Cumulative Book Index,* another publication, is the massive result of an attempt to list all books that have been printed in English, whether they are in or out of print. Each year, a volume listing new books is added to the set.

Facts on File is "a weekly news digest of world events with a thorough, cumulative index." Its issues are filed in large ring binders and they date back to 1940.

Many useful directories can be found in a library. *The College Blue Book* has five volumes of information on colleges and universities. Here you can determine which institutions offer programs in your area of interest. Also useful are *Lovejoy's College Guide* and *The Gourman Report: A Rating of Undergraduate Programs in American and International Universities.* Other examples of directories are *The Official Museum Directory* and the three-volume *Encyclopedia of Associations.* There is even a *Directory of Directories!*

The United States Government publishes many informative booklets and handbooks. For example, the Bureau of the Census produces the *Statistical Abstract of the United States,* an impressive collection of statistical data from private and public sources, focusing on the social, political, and economic structure of the nation. Another example is the *Occupational Outlook Handbook,* published annually by the Bureau of Labor Statistics. It assesses the prospects for employment in various occupations. *The U.S. Government Manual* lists government agencies and addresses. For an extensive list of government publications, many of which are free, you can write to the U.S. Government Printing Office, Washington, D.C. 20402.

■

EXERCISES

9.1 Basic

At the largest nearby library, exercise your research skills.

1. Locate on the shelves any book about a political party to which you do not belong.

2. Locate on the shelves any book about your own religion. If you do not have a formal religion, locate a book on humanism, atheism, or pantheism.

3. Determine the number of books available in this library on the topic of poverty.

4. Locate on the shelves any book on French politics.

5. Locate on the shelves any book on the nuclear arms race.

6. What is the call number of Plato's *Republic?*

7. What is the call number of *Autobiograpy of Andrew Carnegie?*

8. What is the call number of *The Golden Bough?*

9. Who is the author of *The Golden Bough?*

10. Locate, in the catalog, an entry (a card, if it is a card catalog) for a book authored by Henry Steele Commager or John Updike.

11. Locate a magazine article on drug abuse among athletes.

12. Locate a magazine article on farm income.

13. Locate the current issue of *Newsweek.*

14. Locate a past issue of *Time.*

15. List three articles authored by Martin Luther King, Jr., that were published during 1966.

16. In what magazine can a person find the following 1966 article on Martin Luther King, Jr.: "Doctor King's Case for Nonviolence?"

17. What is the capital of New Zealand?

18. Which country has the most Hindus?

19. What is the Magna Carta? What is the date of this agreement?

20. What happened at the Congress of Berlin?

9.2 Moderately Difficult

At the largest nearby library, exercise your research skills.

1. Determine the front-page headlines of the *Los Angeles Times* on September 2, 1987.

2. Locate a copy or microfilm of any newspaper dated November 14, 1986. What is the headline?

3. According to the most recent data you can locate, how many under-graduate students are enrolled at Princeton University?

4. Who won the Nobel Peace Prize in 1958?

5. What is the governor's term in office (in years) in Rhode Island?

6. What is the annual salary of the governor of Arkansas?

7. The purpose of the Emancipation Proclamation of January 1, 1863, issued by President Abraham Lincoln, was the liberation of slaves. Find the entire text of this proclamation.

8. Choose a book and locate every catalog entry for it.

9. How many magazines on health does this library subscribe to?

10. Which thematic almanacs are in the collection of this library?

11. Where is the village of Kodarma?

12. Locate two reviews of a film you have recently seen.

13. Find the title of a book written by William J. Steenrod, Jr. (For this task and the next, don't limit yourself to the library catalog.)

14. Find the title and author of any book on the Falkland Islands War.

15. Compare the *Readers' Guide* and *Magazine Index* listings under one subject. Which would you expect to have a more extensive listing? Which did?

16. Among the library's books on Albert Einstein's ideas, identify the one that is easiest to understand.

17. When and where did the Great Peace March across the United States end?

9.3 Difficult

At the largest nearby library, exercise your research skills.

1. Identify the source, date, and author of a magazine article about American soldiers in World War I.

2. Identify the source and date of a newspaper article describing the explosion aboard the U.S. battleship *Maine* immediately preceding the Spanish-American War.

3. Where in the U.S. Constitution is trial by jury in civil cases guaranteed?

4. Sometimes one copy of a book is in a library's reference collection, unavailable for circulation, while another copy of that book is else-

where on the shelves and available for circulation. Both will have the same call number except that the copy in the reference collection will have the designation *REF* at the beginning of the call number. Identify one such book in this library.

5. Give the title and author of a book that is no longer in print.

6. How many books did Socrates author?   ∎

NEWS SOURCES

"The news" is a fact of modern life. For this valuable informational resource, we do not have to visit the library. It is delivered to our homes on pages of newsprint, on glossy newsmagazine pages in the Tuesday or Wednesday mail, and on the screens of our television sets.

Much of the information that is deemed newsworthy centers on topics that are also the focus of daily reasoning disputes between family members, acquaintances, and workmates. Thus, it is a ready source of premise material. Here we find out what's in that new congressional tax or education bill and why it's stalled in the Senate. Here we find out about the new U.S.-Soviet accord on scientific cooperation or on the control of nuclear arms. However, since emphasis and point of view—indeed, even implied or stated conclusions—may vary from *The New York Times* to *The San Francisco Chronicle* or from NBC to CBS, it is important that we be alert and discerning consumers. Please see Skill 18 below.

SKILL

Skill 18. Evaluating news sources

Determine the character and perspective of news sources that you use.

Why this skill is important

The objective tone of both print and broadcast news can mask a slanting of the news.   ∎

It is foolhardy not to *know* your regular news sources. As good as you may be at evaluating evidence, drawing conclusions, and spotting fallacies, you are thinking with a disadvantage if you aren't clear about both the format and the perspective of those sources. Sometimes you will use news sources with which you are not very familiar, but for any news source that you use frequently, you should pay attention to its perspective on major issues and general politics. This helps you to analyze clearly what you read or hear.

Newspapers

If you consider newspapers as a source of information on current social and political events that would be likely topics for arguments, the two most important parts are the editorial sections and the news sections.

The Editorial Section The editorial (or "opinions" or "views") section of a newspaper is normally located on one or two pages somewhere in the first half of the paper. Often, an index on the front page will direct you to the exact page or pages. This section of the newspaper is of special interest to people who are interested in reasoning skills because the most explicit, and sometimes outrageous, argumentation is found here.

An editorial column, written by an editor or by an editorial staff member, will be a primary element here. In some newspapers, two or more editorials appear each day. This is also the location for an editorial cartoon, letters to the editor, and any guest commentary that the paper may recognize. Other general-interest columns, syndicated or unsyndicated, may be placed here or on a following page.

Essentially, there are three kinds of editorials. The *informational* editorial informs the readers about something—a new law or tax, plans for a city park, a good deed—with no strong persuasive effort. In the *rhetorical* editorial, there is a strong persuasive effort but very little relevant evidence. Emotionally charged language—and often sweeping, unqualified, and/or unsupported claims—are common in this kind of editorial, which incites emotions but does not encourage rationality. The *rational* editorial makes a clear effort to persuade and to present reasons that are worthy of consideration. While the evidence does not always adequately justify the conclusion, the editorial is still "rational" in the sense that reasoning, rather than the emotional response, is the primary focus on the writer. Some of the best of these rational editorials consider evidence on more than one side of the issue. (The mapping techniques of Chapter 6 are helpful with the rational editorial.) Finally, remember that many editorials will cross over the lines of distinction drawn between kinds of editorials.

An editorial cartoon is a drawing, sometimes with a caption, that portrays a political issue through a visual analogy. Elements from the actual situation are often represented as if they were different sorts of things in a

'YOU WILL HAVE NO MEMORY OF HOW WE TOOK OUR PAY RAISE. YOU WILL FORGET YOU WERE MUGGED BY YOUR CONGRESSMEN. YOU WILL RECALL ONLY MAKING A CHARITABLE CONTRIBUTION...'

different sort of setting. Simple labeling usually serves to identify the elements. Caricatures of famous persons are also common in editorial cartoons.

The insidious power of these drawings lies in a curious combination. While the cartoon normally brings no evidence to bear on the implied conclusion, that conclusion nevertheless will seem to have merit simply because of the cartoon's visual impact. In the end, the reader becomes more certain that the conclusion is true, but not on any rational basis. These cartoons are most effective at reinforcing a conclusion the reader already believes, but they are also very effective on issues about which the reader has no strong opinion. Seldom are they effective with persons who strongly differ with the implied conclusion.

Since letters to the editor, guest commentaries, and regular columns often have persuasion as a purpose, they provide a good opportunity for sharpening reasoning skills. Just turn to the editorial page and *analyze*. Be fair minded; don't simply look for the errors in alien viewpoints.

News Sections   The first page of a newspaper is usually devoted to national and international news and to the most important local news. Sometimes most of the entire first section has this "big news" focus. Other sections may include routine community news and general-interest items.

The articles in the news sections are typically characterized by a neutral, evenhanded tone of presentation. Because of this, and because of a perception of the newsperson's job as "just reporting the facts," readers might not be attentive to interpretive slants in the news.

Publishers, editors, and reporters, as well as the rest of us, have specific social, religious, and political backgrounds that can serve to push some relevant data to the forefront while other relevant data are passed over. In addition, we must remember that everyone's information is often necessarily limited.

A person should be aware of any consistent slanting of the news in the newspapers he or she reads most frequently. To discover slanting in the news section, you should monitor several newspapers, including your own, in their coverage of several selected issues. By reading articles covering the same story, you can see how different perspectives of the same event can result from specific word choices (see Chapter 7) and data selection. For example, in an article on a developer-versus-environmentalist confrontation, is there a focus on one side's excesses but not the other's? Keeping track of articles on the same topic, you may find that your newspaper is presenting a person, a group, or an idea in a consistently favorable or unfavorable way. The topics you choose to follow (for a month or more) should be selected carefully. They should not be "news service" stories, syndicated from elsewhere in the nation. Then, when you read about a labor-management dispute at a local factory, you may be in a position to say to yourself, ". . . but then, the *Morning Bulletin* seldom *does* present organized labor in a positive light." You should not, of course, commit the fallacy of attacking the person (source) by rejecting the entire account. However, you will be in a better position to weigh and utilize the information, and you will know that you need further sources before you draw your conclusions.

Your analysis of the news articles should include assessments of the following:

Word choice: Is a person, group, or event described with emotionally charged language that is either consistently positive or negative?

Headline: Does the headline invite a one-sided view? Many people will read *only* the article's headline.

Emphasis: Is the article "played up" with extensive coverage and attention-getting placement in the newspaper, exceeding an appropriate treatment of the issue? Is the article "played down" with limited coverage and poor placement in the newspaper, falling short of an appropriate treatment of the issue?

Event selection: Does the choice of what news to cover or which items to report within the context of one news story contribute to a one-sided presentation?

Photo selection: Are photographs that support a single perspective on a controversial issue chosen to the exclusion of those that support a different perspective?

Because of the news staff's practical limitations, such as time to prepare an article and space to print the entirety of a conscientiously prepared article, you will often find that a news report is lacking in some respect. When one newspaper's coverage of an issue is consistently slanted toward the same perspective, however, you as a consumer of information must read and reflect with that in mind.

Which Newspaper Should I Read? People often choose to read a newspaper that reflects their own social and political perspectives. This is understandable. Confirmation of a favored perspective is more comforting than the challenge of reasoning and rhetoric that support a suspect or despised perspective. Nevertheless, despite our inclinations and time limitations, the person who wants to have an informed and intelligent framework for thought on important issues would do well to read newspapers from diverse perspectives. Even if you choose to stay with one paper, it's worth knowing whether, in the editorial or news sections, some perspectives are more common than others.

Newsmagazines

Time, Newsweek, and *U.S. News & World Report* are three well-known newsmagazines of recent decades. They are published weekly and dated by the day the issue is scheduled to be replaced on the stands by the subsequent issue. Virtually everyone has seen copies of these on magazine racks, at the checkout counters of convenience stores, in waiting rooms, or elsewhere. They are frequently referred to in other news reports and in casual conversation.

These glossy, multicolor magazines typically cover major national and international political, social, and economic topics, giving general background information. This kind of overview is especially helpful for people who do not keep up with the major news stories on a daily basis. There are also sections on business, religion, the arts, and other topics of general interest. Sometimes commentary is provided in periodic opinion columns. Home subscriptions are available at prices that are well below the newsstand price.

A personal survey of these magazines, similar to the kind that was recommended for newspaper comparison, will enable any reader to interpret the reporting more intelligently. Again, you should follow similar stories in the different magazines to see if there is a consistent slant to certain news topics. One magazine might, for example, very often present the president as weak and indecisive, while another might just as often select language, pictures, and events that portray the president as a strong and very capable leader. One might typically present the woes of the economically deprived, while another might focus frequently on welfare abuses and excessive government spending on social programs. Here, as well as with newspapers, it may be advisable to be a regular reader of more than one of the news sources.

Television News

More people than ever before are relying on television as their main source for daily news, and the credibility of television news now surpasses that of any other news source.* Television is an enticing medium. We can actually *see* the news, we are reminded, "as it happens." This immediacy has the advantage of cutting out some "intellectual distance" between the interested citizen and the people in the news. We can see the overwhelming devastation of a massive but unexpected flood and feel compassion for those who are thrust into momentous circumstances—people who are obviously like us in many ways. The recent focus on the misery of an improverished Ethiopia produced an impact on viewers that newspapers, newsmagazines, and radio could not. Because the power of visual images is so great, television news has an impressive potential to inform and educate its viewers.

Televised reporting, like reportage through the print media, will reflect to either a reasonable or unreasonable extent the religious, social, and political backgrounds of the people who produce it. The wise thinker always "considers the source." To consider the source intelligently, of course, we must *know* the source. The viewer can assess television news programs, both local and national, through attentive monitoring. There is no justification for setting aside our healthy critical abilities—our reasoning skills—when we turn on a television set.

The television format is obviously different from that of the print media. This can have important consequences. First, the viewer's attention must be maintained throughout the broadcast. The viewer who is not interested in the lead story or the second story might change channels and "take his or her business elsewhere." Ratings will suffer if this happens often enough. If ratings decline sufficiently, the program is not viable from a business perspective. The reader of a newspaper or magazine, however, can simply turn attention to another story. The result is that a noteworthy story that nonetheless claims a limited audience (for example, a story on Basque separatism in Spain or on Spanish politics in general) is more readily excluded from the television news presentation than from the print media. This need to keep the viewer's attention also invites sensationalism—a focus on attention-getting and perhaps gruesome or pathetic stories that have no further value to the viewer.

---

*Public Perceptions of Television and Other Mass Media: A Twenty Year Review, 1959–78 (New York: Television Information Office, 1979).

The other important consequence of the television format is the lack of in-depth, detailed reporting, partly because of limited time and partly because of the need to keep the audience's attention. Television executives' response to charges of superficiality has been the emergence of the hour-long, or longer, TV "newsmagazine." Programs like CBS's famous *Sixty Minutes* and ABC's *20/20* provide the detail and the coverage of special topics that the regular programming cannot. Still, the visual premises that lead to our conclusions are limited and selected by the producers of the program. Are we being informed so that we can make intelligent inquiries for ourselves, or are we being shown "one side of the picture" for its entertainment value? After one of the televised "articles," the viewer should generally find that, since more aspects of different sides of the issue have been made clear, a conclusion is both easier (there is more information) and more difficult (the viewer sees the merit of more than one position). If, on the other hand, the program favors one side of a controversial issue and presents only a token countercase, then the viewer should not view the program as "just news."

With any of the news media, a tone of presentation that suggests objectivity should not lull us into a passive absorption of all that is presented to us. The most conscientious attempt to convey information fairly is not enough. The well-reasoned critical judgment of the person receiving the information is a necessary ingredient in the fruitful communication of ideas.

■

EXERCISES

9.4 Basic

The following are exercises on perspective or point of view in news presentations.

1. Rewrite a news article that shows a consistently positive or negative slant in word choice (as discussed in Chapter 7). Exchange negative for positive, or positive for negative, expressions so that the person, group, or event under discussion is seen in a different evaluative light. You may delete some comments instead of rewording them, but you may add only incidental claims to the story.

2. Choose an editorial cartoon for which there is a directly opposing view. What sort of cartoon and labeling or caption might be used to present that opposing view powerfully?

3. Follow the coverage of several controversial topics in three or more newspapers. Do not use news-service or wire-service items. Compare the treatments of the topic to see how the topic could be covered in

different ways. Continuing to monitor these papers, watch for patterns of favor or disfavor. Clearly explain your observations and your conclusions.

4. Repeat exercise 3 for the following three newsmagazines: *Newsweek, Time,* and *U.S. News & World Report.*

5. Repeat exercise 3 for television news programs, network or local. ■

■

CHAPTER HIGHLIGHTS

■ Very often, the open issue in the evaluation of someone's reasoning is whether a certain premise is true rather than whether the conclusion follows from the premises. Factual claims that we aren't in a position to judge as true or false are offered as premises. In some cases, it is worth the trouble to research the premise.

■ Libraries are an excellent informational resource. Each library has a catalog, often a card catalog, to index its books. Books are listed by title, author or editor, and subject. Articles from periodicals may be located by using the *Readers' Guide,* which indexes articles back to 1890, or the *Magazine Index,* which surveys more than twice as many periodicals as the *Readers' Guide* but covers only recent issues. The *National Newspaper Index* lists newspaper articles from *The Wall Street Journal, The New York Times,* the *Christian Science Monitor,* the *Los Angeles Times,* and *The Washington Post.* Many special reference volumes such as encyclopedias and atlases are also extremely useful.

■ A constantly used informational resource is "the news" from newspapers, newsmagazines, or broadcasts. Given the neutral, objective tone of most news presentations, we may not immediately recognize slanted presentations. Careful monitoring of news sources can help us identify perspectives that color the news.

For Further Reading

Katz, William. *Your Library: A Reference Guide.* New York: Holt, Rinehart and Winston, 1984.
An excellent guide for library research.

Decision Making and Problem Solving

Every day we make decisions that affect our own lives and others' lives. Sometimes the decisions have a great impact on these lives and sometimes the impact is less dramatic. Sometimes the "small" decisions turn out to produce quite significant consequences. Following both our heads and our hearts, we often make excellent decisions. Still, there are times when the need to grapple with a difficult decision is more than we care to bear. There can be so many factors to consider and so little knowledge of how to weigh them that we shirk the task and make a decision without efficient reflection.

Decisions cannot really be avoided. When you fail to act, certain consequences follow in place of those that would have followed if you had acted. In a sense, then, you have *chosen* to allow events to occur without your intervention. A responsible person must accept reasonable risks and act to bring about the best results that the available alternatives offer.

A GUIDE FOR MAKING DECISIONS

Although even the least complicated decisions are sometimes difficult to make, complex decisions that involve many elements, all of which must be kept in mind, present a special challenge. It is difficult to keep track of all the relevant considerations, even after we have identified them.

After we have considered a decision from many angles and mulled over many pros and cons, we might not recall some of those thoughts at the moment of the final decision. Bad decisions have been made on the basis

---

SKILL

Skill 19. Making decisions systematically

Use the decision-making chart or a variation of it to evaluate the alternative courses of action when a decision is required.

Why this skill is important

Some decisions require the consideration of so many factors that hardly anyone can keep them all in mind without a systematic approach. ∎

---

of those particular considerations that happened to have been on the person's mind in the moments or hours immediately preceding the decision, while some strong reason for deciding differently has been lost in the shuffle of ideas. It's simply too taxing to keep track of all those ideas. It seems to be beyond the capacity of most of us. The solution to this problem is to *write down* these thoughts as they occur and to order them in some way. One method for doing this, highlighted in the skill box above, is presented on the following pages.

Identify the Alternatives

Beware of the false dilemma! We sometimes are cautioned to look at *both* sides of an issue. It's easy to overlook *third* and *fourth* sides. We encounter the same kind of problem in decision making. We can fail to identify some alternatives simply by presuming that no more than the two obvious alternatives exist. In short, we sometimes don't even consider the possibility of other answers. In asking, "Should I bring grandma home to live with me or should I have her moved into a nursing home?" a person might neglect other possibilities. (Perhaps another relative might be willing, or even glad, to have grandma as a long-term house guest. Perhaps some settings other than nursing homes would meet grandma's needs.) We should at least think through possible alternatives. If there are several, it is helpful to list them on paper.

Consider the Consequences

One common method that people use to enumerate the consequences of a decision calls for drawing a line down the middle of a sheet of paper, dividing the page into left and right columns. *PRO* is written at the top of one column; *CON* is written at the top of the other. (This method clearly invites the false dilemma.) Then the desirable and undesirable consequences for each column are listed.

Pro	Con

The main benefit of this method is that it enables the decider to keep many consequences in mind while making an assessment. The next chart presented here is a variation of that simple two-column listing of consequences. This chart invites the listing of multiple alternatives and their consequences. To use this chart, first list your alternatives—your possible courses of action. If you think that you might have overlooked any, describe your situation to another person and ask if there seem to be other possible ways to deal with the situation. Then list the significant consequences of each alternative, regardless of whether the consequence is desirable or undesirable and regardless of whether it is a certain or a possible consequence. Again, you may want to enlist another person to help you think this through.

Alternatives	Consequences	Probability	Desirability	Kind of Gain/Loss

Assess the Probability and Desirability

The probability of a consequence is certainly relevant to the consideration of a course of action. Probable results generally concern us more than unlikely results. Still, if an unlikely consequence is very desirable (or undesirable), it may justifiably sway the decision more than some probable or certain consequences. Clearly, *both* the probability and the desirability must be considered and each must be considered in light of the other.

Evaluate the probability of a consequence before concerning yourself greatly with its desirability. This helps to avoid an irrational concern with a very desirable or undesirable but farfetched consequence.

For the chart, use symbols to indicate the probability (as far as you can determine it) of each consequence. You should feel free to devise your own set of symbols, but here is a suggestion.

C	Certain
AC	Almost certain
PROB	Probable
POSS	Possible (a reasonable possibility, but less than probable)
NL	Not likely

If, after entering the symbols for a few consequences, you feel a need to distinguish between two that have been assigned the same symbol, you can use a plus or a minus. For example, PROB+ is considered more likely to result than PROB. Further variations might be necessary.

Assign a numerical value to indicate the desirability of each consequence. Plan to assign a maximum of 5 for the most desirable and −5 for the least desirable. Remain flexible, however, and extend or change the numerical scale if that will clarify the options. When a single consequence has both good and bad sides, use the line below to add the opposing value.

Determine the *Kind* of Gain or Loss

Think about the standpoint from which each desirable consequence is desirable. Is there a personal benefit for you? If so, is this a financial gain, an improvement of reputation or character, or an opportunity for new experience, skill, or knowledge? Does it fulfill an obligation? If so, is it a legal or a moral obligation? Does fairness or sympathy call for this result? After deciding on this, write a word or phrase that will remind you of this when you scan the chart. For example, write MONEY, or REPUTATION, or CAREER, or COMMON DECENCY on the chart to indicate the kind of benefit that is to be gained.

Similarly, think about the standpoint from which each undesirable consequence is undesirable. Is there a personal harm or inconvenience? If so, is this a financial loss, jeopardy of career, or loss of reputation? Does it involve breaking a promise, or another sort of moral wrong? As before, write a word or phrase on the chart to remind you of this when you scan the chart. For example, write PHYSICAL COMFORT, or EDUCATION, or OTHERS' FEELINGS.

Scan the Chart

In some decision-making systems, you are told to compute the right decision by using a formula, sometimes a numerical one. While such a system has the advantage of avoiding mental and moral strain and putting the decider's mind to rest, it does so precisely because of its artificiality. No system can consistently produce the best decisions. Common sense and moral sensitivity are excellent tools in human judgment. If these can be aided by a means of tracking and remembering the consequences of each available alternative, there is seldom reason to yield important decisions to a contrived decision-making plan.

Just examine the alternatives. Think about the probability and desirability of the consequences of each possible choice. Strict adding, subtracting, or multiplying will not weigh the consequences better than you can generally weigh them informally. Think about the kind of gain or loss. Moral rights and wrongs do not automatically outweigh safety considerations, personal hurt, or even all cases of private gain. There is no simple ordering of such things. The issue cannot be decided without the integrated consideration of each of the columns on your chart.

None of us is absolved from making personal decisions and bearing the responsibility for these decisions. The chart is merely a list of items to keep in mind when weighing the alternatives.

■

EXERCISES

10.1 Basic

Use the decision-making chart to consider a decision in the following cases.

1. Choose a situation in your life that calls for a decision. Fill in the blanks on the chart. Consider your alternatives and their consequences.

2. Ask a friend or relative to let you use the chart to help her or him think through a problem that requires a decision. With that person's help, fill in the blanks on the chart, and give that person the chart.

3. Revise the chart itself in light of difficulties you have had in using it. Make copies of your revised chart for personal use. Share the revision with others who are using this book.

10.2 Moderately Difficult

Use the decision-making chart to consider a decision in the following cases. Add details to the example to fill out the chart.

1. Maria takes a bus to school each day. The fare is fifty cents. She gets a ride home for free with her neighbor, who leaves for school too late for her in the morning, but waits an extra hour at school each day to drive her home. Lately, the neighbor has been making casual comments about the inconvenience of staying the extra hour. Maria can't easily afford the dollar it would cost for a round trip each day. Her brother has offered to give her his old car, but she hates to take it because she knows that he needs the money he would get if he sold it instead of giving it to her. She is also aware that, despite the good mechanical condition of the car, maintenance and repair costs, together with fuel costs, might exceed the bus fare. If she gets a job to make more money, her studies will suffer. She wants help in deciding what to do.

2. The beautiful twenty-acre site just north of the shopping mall had been identified as the location for a city park. The city has no parks in the area now, and children between ages five and seventeen play on the roads and sidewalks. The park development plans may be abandoned because of the cost of constructing and maintaining the park. If the city were to develop the park, its support of the library and the annual parade might be cut drastically. There's a fifty-fifty chance that insufficient funds would remain for building a new elementary school in another part of town where the current school is overcrowded. Now a housing developer has offered to buy the land from the city at a handsome price that would virtually ensure that the needed school would be built and that additional funds would be left over. You are on the city council. Your votes on the park proposal and the housing proposal are important.

3. Study the newspaper and newsmagazine coverage of a topic of national interest that calls for a legislative or executive decision. Follow the television newscasts and discuss the issue with acquaintances. Then make an expanded chart and plot out the consequences of the most promising alternatives. ∎

A GUIDE FOR SOLVING PROBLEMS

We typically make decisions in order to direct specific actions. We may decide whether to renew a magazine subscription, whether to join a certain political party, whether to accept that new job offer, or whether to report a crime. Larger, less well-defined circumstances call for the creative processes of problem solving. Here, rather than starting with a focus on specific alternatives, we begin by surveying a general situation that calls for a kind of remediation that the problem solver has not yet identified. In such cases, it is often difficult even to know where to begin.

The distinction between decision making and problem solving is not always clear. Still, we will consider problem solving to be a creative process, even in the organization of data (see the skill box below). This organization gives us a way of approaching the issue.

Sometimes we solve problems intuitively or by haphazard approaches. Sometimes, however, a systematic approach to the problem is invaluable, and it need not be less creative for being systematic. Six steps will be presented in this guide to problem solving:

1. Statement
2. Quick start
3. Analysis
4. Incubation
5. Dialectic
6. Implementation

SKILL

Skill 20. Solving problems systematically

Apply the six steps of problem solving to create a solution to a complex problem.

Why this skill is important

Complex problems can be bewildering, leaving a person without a sense of where to begin the search for a solution. ∎

Each step is important:
Step 1 calls for a clear formulation of the problem.
Steps 2 and 3 include direct problem-solving techniques.
Steps 4 and 5 allow for review of the process.
The final plan is carried out in step 6.

Statement

People sometimes try to solve a problem without ever clarifying the nature of the problem. This can result in a confused search for solutions because the problem solver may inefficiently shift attention from one version or aspect of the problem to another without realizing that there has been any failure to stay on track (Skill 1). If more than one person is involved in the problem solving, the possibility of conceiving the problem differently or shifting focus is increased. Essentially, the problem is being *defined* at this point. Precision is important. Time and care taken at this point can minimize tangents and straw men later.

When there is more than one problem solver, a restatement technique is useful for achieving precision. After one person states the problem, another restates it, simply trying to put the first person's point into different words. The first person corrects any misunderstanding. Then they discuss which of the two versions is most appropriate. It may be that the *misstated* version—the second person's misunderstanding of the first person—is the better definition of the problem. The problem solvers restate the problem as often as necessary. However, if this step becomes tedious, it is advisable to go on to the second step, quick start, and to return later. Note that the completion of step 1 can occur incidentally during step 2.

In order to get a clear statement of the problem, a distinction between *means* and *ends* should be kept in mind. An end is a purpose or a desirable end-result. A means is a way to achieve that purpose or end-result. As far as possible, the problem should be stated in terms of ends rather than means. Consider, for example, the predicament of the owner of a public parking lot in the business area of a city. Although his lot is generally full, he makes little profit. He decides that he needs to restripe his lot so that more cars can be parked in the same space. He sees his problem as a need to determine where to paint the stripes to create more spaces. Restriping the lot, however, is a means to his actual end. What he *really* needs is to make more money from his property. By focusing on a means rather than an end, he unnecessarily limits his perspective. Although he has probably already considered raising his rates, other income-increasing moves may elude him. By focusing on a restriping pattern, he will be less likely to consider (a) hiring parkers to park the cars for the customers (they can arrange the cars tightly on an unstriped lot), (b) putting up a several-story parking structure (financing this may require separate problem solving), (c) selling the property and investing the money differently, or (d) converting the property to a different use.

Quick Start

After the problem has been stated with precision, or when further effort at definition would be counterproductive, it is time to jump right into the assessment and solution of the problem. Step 3 will dictate a methodical approach to this, but often it's worth letting enthusiasm and intuition run free to discover shortcuts. For the quick start, either brainstorming or categorical analysis can be used as a means to set forth (a) aspects of the problem that must be considered, and (b) solutions to the problem.

Brainstorming is a process designed for multiple problem solvers who are cooperating on one task. A moderator writes down on a list, preferably where all can see, each suggestion that a member of the problem-solving group mentions. The problem solvers offer any suggestions that come to mind, even though they may be unusual or not well thought out. There is no limit to the number of suggestions that one person, or the whole group, may generate. *No discussion of, or comment on, any suggestion is permitted while the list is being compiled.* After compilation, the moderator may help the group consolidate or eliminate items on the list. Any such action comes only after discussion and only by unanimous vote. The problem-solving group must be small—ideally two to ten members—and the list should be reduced to as few items as possible.

The group must understand which kind of suggestion is being sought: problem aspects to be considered or solutions to the problem. Clarification on the statement of the problem can also be the focus of the search, but this often occurs as a by-product of the other two kinds of brainstorming sessions. If only one person is attacking the problem, the basic brainstorming approach may still be useful, though much of the power of the approach comes from the cooperative effort of minds with different knacks and insights.

Categorical analysis, which professional problem solvers call morphological analysis, is another approach that can be used either to identify the problem's various aspects (this is its main strength) or to investigate solutions. It is a suitable approach for problem solving by individuals or by groups.

If we want to identify the various aspects of a problem, we simply list the most general aspects. Under each aspect, we then list specific facets of that aspect. For example, a factory manager who is grappling with low morale might list working conditions, supervisory personnel, pay, and job security. Under working conditions, then, he might list cleanliness, temperature, schedule, noise, and crowding.

If we want to identify solutions, we list the various kinds of solutions or causes for the problem. We then list specific possibilities within each category. For example, a student who is surprised to be getting low grades in a course might list course content, instructor, class setting, and study habits. Under study habits, then, he might specifically list note taking, text reading, review, time spent, and distractions when studying.

Brainstorming and categorical analysis are quick starts in the sense that these "scouting" processes, while meant to prepare the problem solvers for step 3, sometimes actually accomplish much of the business of the analysis step by calling on intuitions and creating an overview of the entire problem situation.

Analysis

If the problem appears to have been solved during step 2, the problem solver can skip step 3 and go directly to 4. If not, it is time to consider the problem in the light of current and desired outcomes.

Compare Current and Desired Outcomes   Keeping in mind the distinction (from step 1) between means and ends, the problem solver restates the desired outcome(s). The question here is this: What is the *desired* end-result in this activity or process that is seen as problematic? Then the problem solver states the outcome that is currently being produced. If several desired outcomes are identified, they are classified in order of importance.

Determine the Means to Get from Current Outcome to Desired Outcome   Clear thinking and creativity are indispensable. It may help to break the problem down into parts. For example, if the needs of many people are involved, the needs of each can first be considered separately, then need-conflicts can be recognized and a solution worked around these. At this stage, assumptions must be examined and the solution of previous similar problems must be explored.

Assess Alternatives   If more than one plan for getting from current to desired outcomes has been devised, these are assessed and compared for overall desirability. At this point the decision-making chart from Skill 19 is useful, since some of the same factors are considered—at least consequences, probability, and desirability. Note that the far-right column on the chart can be used or ignored, depending on the problem. The preferred solution is then identified by considering both the achievement of desired outcomes (remember that they have been ranked) and unintended negative features such as difficulty or inconvenience.

Incubation

A period of incubation, in which the problem solver "sleeps on it," follows the hard work of analysis. During this period of rest, the problem solver sometimes reflects on the problem but does not work with great effort unless the urge is compelling. Incubation ends either when ideas begin to flow freely, unravelling parts of the problem, or when the problem solver's schedule has dictated that incubation should end. The period of incubation is normally kept to a week or less. Otherwise, points of the preceding analysis fade in memory. Unfortunately, the incubation step in problem solving is often left out because of the pressing requirements of time. Nevertheless, this is a valuable step that has often been a key to effective problem solving.

Dialectic

Presumably, a solution is at least tentatively decided on in step 3, analysis. If not, the incubation step should cycle back to analysis for another examination.

When a sense of the proper direction toward a solution has been determined, it's time to enter into dialectic with other people or to pass by this step and begin implementation. Dialectic is simply the process of reviewing a solution by exposing it to the informal analysis of people who have not taken part in its formulation. A brief account of the problem and the solution is presented to another person, who is then invited to anticipate flaws in the solution. Worthwhile suggestions are written down for further consideration. The problem solvers follow up any suggestions that undercut the entire selected solution by asking for the critic's own intuitions about the best course of action. Crucial to the success of the dialectic is the general character of the interaction: the atmosphere must be relaxed, with the critic feeling that any suggestion, however hard to accept, is welcome.

Taking time for dialectic can obviously be helpful for both individual problem solvers and groups. It is usually more important for the individual problem solver, however, because a person often needs someone else to identify those almost inevitable mental lapses or idiosyncratic perspectives. The problem-solving group has already had a form of dialectic in its earlier idea-sharing.

Implementation

The final plan is implemented, or carried out, only with the serious commitment of everyone involved in implementation. Like programs within larger social systems, problem-solving plans are "only as good as the people involved." A plan has its best chance of being effective when it is implemented with intelligence and sensitivity. While one person or group can mechanically "go through the motions" the plan prescribes and fail or succeed only marginally, another can make the same plan shine by retaining the determined spirit of a good problem solver. In the implementation of the plan, personal interactions are designed to maximize cooperation, and good timing is always observed. Finally, the person or persons who are implementing the plan keep an eye on changing circumstances and adjust the plan whenever a reassessment demands it.

When these six steps in problem solving are followed in actual application, points of logical vulnerability may become involved. Functional fixation, a resistance to conceiving something apart from its usual function, may impede the process as well. Both of these hazards are well worth anticipating.

■

EXERCISES

10.3 Basic

1. As a lone problem solver, consider a personal problem of your own through application of the six steps in problem solving: statement, quick start, analysis, incubation, dialectic, and, if appropriate, implementation.

2. As a lone problem solver, consider a personal problem of someone you know well, using the first four steps in problem solving: statement, quick start, analysis, and incubation. If you feel that it is appropriate, discuss your thoughts with that person.

3. If you know another person, or other persons, who know these six steps or who would be pleased to try them after reading this section of the book, choose a topic and solve a problem with that person. Problems of home, work, or school are possibilities for discussion.

10.4 Moderately Difficult

1. Study (alone or with others) the news coverage of a topic of social or political importance. Use library research skills to find additional information. Identify a problematic aspect of that topic and apply the first five steps in problem solving: statement, quick start, analysis, incubation, and dialectic. You may choose to contribute to the likelihood of implementation through a letter to a legislator or by another means, depending on the problem and the nature of your solution. ■

■

CHAPTER HIGHLIGHTS

■ We often make excellent decisions informally, following our heads and our hearts. Sometimes, however, there is so much to consider that a systematic approach to decision making is helpful. We can use a chart to map out the factors involved in a complex situation that calls for decision. First, *list the available alternatives* on the chart. Second, *list both the desirable and undesirable consequences* for each alternative. Finally, *gauge the probability and desirability* of each and *list the kind of gain or loss* involved (for example, money or reputation). While no objective weighting of factors can replace a person's own good sense, the chart enables the decision maker to keep all relevant factors in mind while settling on one course of action.

■ Larger, less well-defined circumstances call for a different process, that of general problem solving. In this chapter, the guide to problem solving presents six steps: statement, quick start, analysis, incubation, dialectic, and implementation. Step 1, *statement,* involves the precise definition of the problem. Step 2, *quick start,* utilizes a person's initial enthusiasm and intuition about a problem. It offers two approaches to identifying the problem's aspects or possible solutions: brainstorming and categorical analysis. Step 3, *analysis,* requires the comparison of current and desired outcomes and the proposal of ways to move toward the desired outcome. Step 4, *incubation,* calls for time for these thoughts to settle and for new connections to be made. Step 5, *dialectic,* is more important for the individual problem solver than for the problem-solving group. It involves discussion with others. Step 6, *implementation,* is the carrying out of the plan that embodies a solution.

For Further Reading

Rubinstein, Moshe F. *Concepts in Problem Solving.* Englewood Cliffs, NJ: Prentice-Hall, 1980.

An innovative approach to explaining problem solving and decision making. The context for each explanation is the book-long conversation between young Alex and his uncle, Professor Gordian.

Sanderson, Michael. *Successful Problem Management.* New York: John Wiley & Sons, 1979.

A good introduction to problem solving.

A P P E N D I X

A

Venn Diagrams

W hen you are assessing the deductive validity of an argument, the distinction between adequate and inadequate (valid and invalid) arguments is clear-cut. Either the evidence establishes the conclusion in form or it falls short. Such a crisp line of demarcation between good and bad form can be tested with some convenient methods that simply would not work for the assessment of inductive strength. Venn diagrams—the focus of the skill box below—provide one way to check for deductive validity in certain kinds of arguments. They may be used in step 3 of mapping arguments (Chapter 6). The logical move indicated by the mapping arrow may then be labeled accordingly. When mapping, remember that a deductively invalid argument might still be inductively strong. Other methods and sources for testing deductive validity will be mentioned at the end of this appendix.

SKILL

Skill 21. Using Venn diagrams

Construct and read a Venn diagram to determine when an argument is valid or invalid in any reasoning for which Venn diagrams are effective.

Why this skill is important

Valid arguments sometimes seem invalid and invalid arguments sometimes seem valid. Because of this, we can incorrectly accept or reject someone's reasoning. For certain arguments, the step-by-step Venn diagrams will provide a means for assessing that validity. ■

With a certain kind of argument, a Venn diagram—a drawing that you can construct—can be used to test for deductive validity. While many arguments are not of this kind, others are well suited to such analysis. For those arguments that *are* appropriate for Venn diagrams, the advantage is that the simple steps that must be followed to determine validity require virtually no attention to the logical relation between the premises and the conclusion. You don't need to *think about* whether the premises prove the conclusion; you merely follow the unchanging rules about how to diagram an argument.

USING VENN DIAGRAMS

You have encountered the following argument several times in this book. Each time you have been asked to consider a different aspect of it.

All Italians are Roman Catholics.

Some Roman Catholics are dishonest.

∴ Some Italians are dishonest.

Please remember whether this argument sounded at least possibly valid when you were first asked to assess its validity in the exercises to Chapter 3. The argument is invalid, but it *appears* to many people to be valid, or at least possibly valid. A Venn diagram will show that the argument is undoubtedly invalid. Let's construct the diagram.

First, we need to know how to diagram each premise. We will be using four basic statement forms.*

Form A: All _____ are _____.
   Example: *All Italians are Roman Catholics.*
Form B: No _____ are _____.
   Example: *No Italians are Roman Catholics.*
Form C: Some _____ are _____.
   Example: *Some Roman Catholics are dishonest.*
Form D: Some _____ are not _____.
   Example: *Some Roman Catholics are not Americans.*

Circles can be used to represent categories of things. The plural form of common nouns (such as *pilots, rocks, parties,* or *arguments*) and noun phrases

*The traditional labels for Forms A, B, C, and D are A, E, I, and O.

(such as *good pilots, rocks that are too heavy to lift, birthday parties,* or *valid arguments that seem invalid*) serve to name categories for us. Categories identify kinds of things. A circle with an *X* in it is used to represent a statement claiming that one or more items in the world belong in that category, as if it were "marking the spot" where something lies within the category. A circle that is completely shaded out, as if there were no room for anything to be in the category, is used to represent a statement claiming that no items in the world belong in that category. So the statements "There are dishonest people" (a true one) and "There are no bad arguments" (a false one) could be represented, respectively, in the following ways.

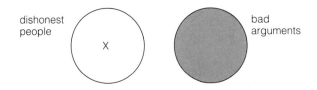

Now, the premises in the argument we are evaluating—and, in an obvious or subtle way, the premises and conclusion of any argument for which we will use Venn diagrams—include two categories, a "subject" and a "predicate" category. To diagram such claims, we need a circle to stand for each category, and these circles must overlap.

A new subcategory is now created visually. The football-shaped area, which is the intersection of the two categories, will be a *category* that includes everything falling in both, rather than just one, of the two main categories.

Any A-Form premise can now be diagrammed like this,

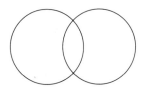

since if *all* items in the subject category are also in the predicate category, then *no* item that falls in the subject category (notice the "shading out") can fall outside the predicate circle.

Any B-Form premise can now be diagrammed like this,

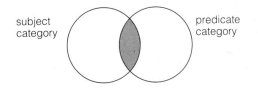

since if *nothing* in the subject category is also in the predicate category, the possibility of an X in the football-shaped section should be "shaded out."

Any C-Form premise can now be diagrammed like this,

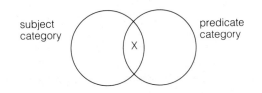

since if *something* (at least one item) in the subject category is also in the predicate category, then an X will mark that subcategory, which we know is not empty.

Any D-Form premise can now be diagrammed like this,

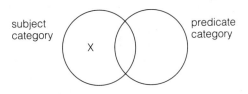

since if *something* (at least one item) in the subject category *does not* lie within the predicate category, then an X will mark this partial category that we know is not empty (that is, the category of items that are in the subject but not in the predicate category).

Therefore, a diagram of what is being claimed through the first premise of the "Italians" argument would look like this, reflecting the A Form.

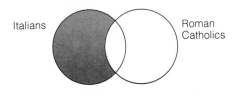

The claim is "All Italians are Roman Catholics." This means that nothing (no one) falling outside the category of Roman Catholics is an Italian. That is why the left crescent-shaped area is shaded: *nothing is there*. Note that since we are here concerned about validity but not soundness, the truth of the premise is irrelevant.

A diagram of what is being claimed through the second premise of the argument would look like this, reflecting the C Form.

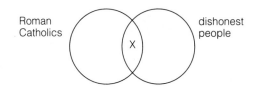

The claim is "Some Roman Catholics are dishonest." This means that there are people who fall into both categories, and thus into both circles: Roman Catholics and dishonest people. The adjective *dishonest* can be seen as labeling the group *dishonest people*. We have replaced the adjective with a noun phrase. You will never need to diagram a conclusion.

Now, to evaluate the complete argument for validity, we must consider the relations among three categories: Italians, Roman Catholics, and dishonest people. Three circles are required, one for each category. To allow for the possibility of affirming or denying an overlap of categories, each circle must overlap the other two circles. The traditional setup for the three circles is this.

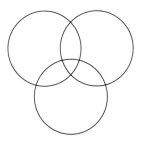

You are now ready to perform the four steps that lead to the answer to your question, "Is the argument valid?" The first step is to draw the three circles. Be sure that the "football" area of overlap for each pair of circles is not too narrow to draw an X within it. The second step is to label the circles. Write the name of the subject category outside the upper-left circle and the name of the predicate category outside the upper-right circle. One category named in each premise will not be named in the conclusion. This "mediating" category is represented by the lower circle, which you should label appropriately. For the "Italians" argument that we have been considering, the labeling should be done like this.

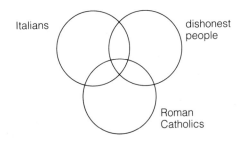

The third step is to draw each premise on the three-circle diagram pattern. For each premise, just think of how you would construct a regular two-circle diagram for that premise. Then, on the three-circle diagram pattern, find the circle that represents the subject category *for the premise you are now diagramming,* and find the circle that represents the predicate category. Turn your paper so that the subject circle is on your left and the predicate circle is on your right. Now, disregarding the extra lines, merely imitate the shading or X placement that you would use on the two-circle diagram. You must do this for both premises. A premise that calls for shading should be done before a premise that calls for an X. In our present example, this means that you would first do the A-Form premise, "All Italians are Roman Catholics." The result will look like this.

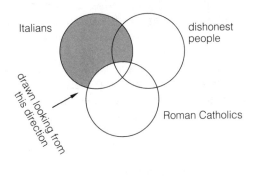

For the second premise, turn your paper again and notice that the football-shaped area (in which the X for the C-Form premise, "Some Roman Catholics are dishonest," belongs) is divided by a line from another circle. In this case, it is not possible to disregard the dividing line. Placing the X on one side of the dividing line indicates that the Roman Catholics who are dishonest are also in the category of Italians; placing the X on the other side indicates that they are not. The premise to be diagrammed, however, commits us to neither alternative. *So the X goes on the dividing line, indicating that, as far as we know from this premise, the X may fall on either side.*

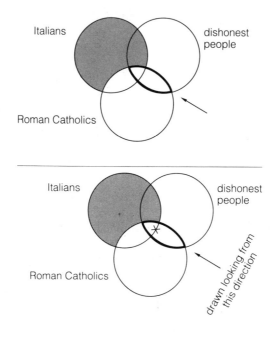

Now the diagram is completed. You should put your pen or pencil down and just *look* to see if the argument is valid. You must focus your attention only on the two top circles, disregarding the lines of the bottom circle altogether. An argument with an A- or B-Form conclusion is valid only if the entire area that should be shaded out for that form (A or B) is actually shaded out. If there is no shading or only partial shading in that area, then the argument is invalid. An argument with a C- or D-Form conclusion is valid only if an X is placed anywhere completely within the area that should have an X for that form (C or D). In our present example, the argument is invalid: the conclusion is a C-Form statement, but there is no X that is completely within the football-shaped overlap between the two top circles.

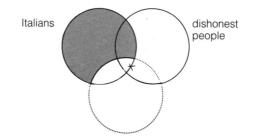

Our only *X* is on the "outside border" of that area. Remember that the *X* was placed on the line to indicate that the items might fall on either side of the line. Thus, our premises do not prove conclusively that there is anything in that subcategory of "Roman Catholics who are dishonest," despite our reasonable certainty that, in fact, there *are* such people.

The test for validity is now complete. We have constructed the three-circle diagram and we have "read" it to determine the validity of the argument. An additional comment is necessary. If the area in which an *X* is required is already shaded out by the previous premise up to the dividing line, then the *X* must be placed not on the line but in the remaining open space of that area.

This will be illustrated in a complete example shortly.

First, let's take the lessons learned from the "walk-through" of the "Italians" argument and state generally the steps that must be followed in using Venn diagrams.

The Four Steps for Checking Validity with Venn Diagrams

1. **Draw three circles.** Use the traditional pattern.

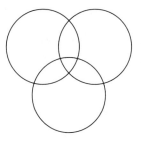

2. **Label each circle.** The subject category *of the conclusion* provides the label for the top-left circle. The predicate category *of the conclusion* provides the label for the top-right circle. A third category, appearing in both premises but not in the conclusion, provides the label for the lower circle.

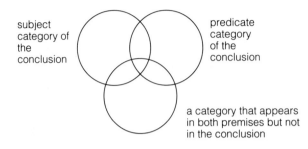

subject category of the conclusion

predicate category of the conclusion

a category that appears in both premises but not in the conclusion

3. **Shade or X for each premise.** Diagram one premise at a time. Placing on your left the circle that represents the subject category of the premise you are diagramming and on your right the circle that represents the predicate category of that premise, imitate the markings for an A-, B-, C-, or D-Form statement (whichever is appropriate to that premise).

Reminder:
If one premise requires shading and the other requires an X, diagram first the one that requires shading.

Reminder:
If a line from the disregarded circle cuts through the area in which you must place an X, place the X *on* that dividing line unless there is shading against one side of the line. In that case, place the X on the other side of the dividing line, but still within the appropriate area.

4. **Look to see if the top two circles show the form of the conclusion.** If the conclusion has an A or B Form, look for the appropriate shading in the top two circles. If the entire area that should be shaded for that form is actually shaded, then the argument is valid. Otherwise, the argument is invalid.

If the conclusion has a C or D Form, look for an X in the appropriate area of the top two circles. If an X appears anywhere completely within the area that should have an X for that form, then the argument is valid. Otherwise, the argument is invalid. Keep in mind that an X along the outside edge of that area does not count.

Let's now run through two examples for practice. First, let's examine this argument:

Some good thinkers are very emotional people

(but) no good thinkers are people who are consistently closed-minded.

(Therefore,) some very emotional people are not people who are consistently closed-minded.

Make your own assessment. Does this *appear* to be a valid or an invalid argument? After deciding on this, follow the four steps for checking validity with a Venn diagram.

1. **Draw three circles.**

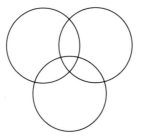

2. **Label each circle.** Be sure to assign each category label to the correct circle.

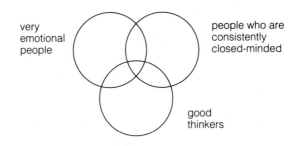

3. **Shade or X for each premise.** Since we have one premise that requires shading and one that requires an *X*, we will make a point of diagramming the B-Form premise before the C-Form premise.

   First, we diagram the B-Form premise.

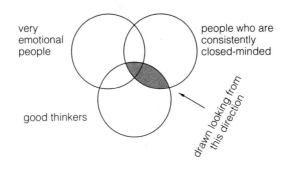

Then we diagram the C-Form premise.

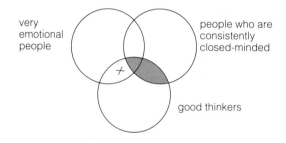

There was no choice in the placement of the *X*; part of the area of overlap between the "very emotional people" circle and the "good think-ers" circle is already shaded out, so the X is placed in the remaining open part of that area.

4. **Look to see if the top two circles show the form of the conclusion.** Focus your attention on the two top circles.

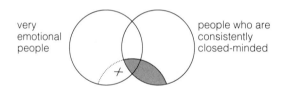

The conclusion of the argument is a D-Form statement. So, for the argu-ment to be valid, the left crescent-shaped area must show an X com-pletely within that area. This is what we would need:

We do have it! Although the *X* is not centered, it *is* completely within the appropriate area. If the premises were true, the conclusion would have to be true; there *are* very emotional people who are not in the category (circle) of "people who are consistently closed-minded." This is what the diagram shows. The argument is valid.

Here is another argument to examine:

Some psychologists are university professors,
(but since it's also true that)

some psychologists are not clinical researchers,

∴ (it follows that) some clinical researchers are not
university professors.

Again, make your own assessment. Does this *appear* to be a valid or an
invalid argument? After deciding, follow the four steps for checking validity
with a Venn diagram.

1. Draw three circles.

2. Label each circle.

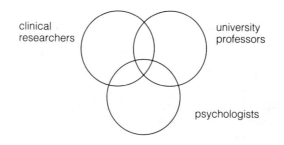

3. **Shade or X for each premise.** When both premises require an X, or when
   both premises require shading, either premise may be diagrammed first.
   Let's diagram them in the order in which they appear in the actual wording of the argument. The first premise has a C Form. The X is placed on
   the dividing line that falls within the overlap of the subject circle ("psychologists") and the predicate circle ("university professors").

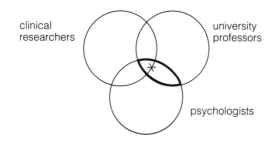

The second premise has a D Form. The *X* is placed on the dividing line that falls within the crescent-shaped part of the subject circle ("clinical researchers") that does not overlap the predicate circle ("psychologists").

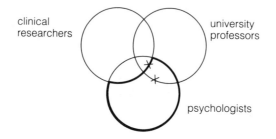

4. **Look to see if the top two circles show the form of the conclusion.** Focus your attention only on the two top circles.

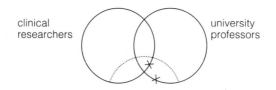

The conclusion of the argument is a D-Form statement. For the argument to be valid, we must find an *X* that is completely within the left crescent.

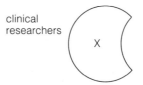

We don't find this on our diagram. The nearest *X* lies along the outer edge of that area. Therefore, the argument is invalid.

TRANSLATION

Two limitations of the Venn diagram method of evaluating validity restrict its usefulness. First, unless it is used by people who are very familiar with it, the method requires the evaluator to take the time to draw the diagram. While this is not a problem when reflecting privately on your own or someone else's reasoning, casual conversation does not usually allow for the required pause. Second, Venn diagrams do not work on all arguments.

This second limitation is unfortunate, but it is not as great as it would appear. Certainly, we don't often offer argumentation in which there are two premises and a conclusion that all begin with the word *all, no,* or *some.* However, many arguments that have premises and a conclusion can be worded differently so that, without a significant change in meaning, they conform to the now familiar A, B, C, or D Forms. Let's consider some examples of statements that are not in one of our four standard forms but could be "translated" into one of them.

Although the statement, "Every child has a right to the privacy of his or her own body" is not in a standard form, it does refer to an overlap of items in two categories, and it could be a premise or conclusion in an argument on which we use a Venn diagram. It can be translated into the following A-Form statement: "All children are people who have a right to the privacy of their own bodies." Here, we start with one of the standard introductory words, a subject category is named, the connecting *are* is used, and a noun phrase now serves as the name of the predicate category.

The statement "Any revolution could be averted with wise leadership" also translates into an A-Form statement: "All revolutions are events that could be averted with wise leadership." The statement "People like that are all out for a quick buck," despite the generality of the subject category, translates into yet another A-Form statement: "All people like that are people who are out for a quick buck." For a final example of translation into the A Form, consider the conditional statement "If you're a student at Stanford, then your family has money," which translates into "All Stanford students are people whose families have money." Note that *having money* is a casual phrase that means "being wealthy," or having *lots* of money.

The statement "There aren't any people who care about literacy any more" translates awkwardly but effectively into a B-Form statement: "No people are people who care about literacy." Here are three more examples of statements that translate into B-Form statements. "Not a single one of those concerned parents showed up for the meeting with the school board" translates into "No concerned parents are people who showed up for the meeting with the school board." The wording is stiff, but the premise (or conclusion) now fits into a Venn diagram. "A sane person cannot live in an insane world" translates into "No sane people are people who can live in an insane world." Finally, think about how you could translate the following conditional statement into a B-Form statement: "If a person voluntarily stays late at work without pay, then that person cannot be completely alienated from the workplace." The translation is "No people who voluntarily stay late at work without pay are people who are completely alienated from the workplace."

A standard C-Form statement can be produced from the statement "In some cases, the husband remains at home to do the household chores." The translation is "Some husbands are people who remain at home to do household chores." The statement "There are dissidents in the Soviet Union" also translates into a C Form. Either of the following translations will work: "Some dissidents are people in the Soviet Union," or "Some people in the Soviet Union are dissidents."

A Venn diagram works through the visual recording of two kinds of information about the subject and predicate categories. Inclusion or exclusion of the subject-category items within the predicate category is recorded. Also crucial is the recording of whether the *entire* subject category is being described or merely a *part* of it—only *some* of the items in the category. Since, on this last point, it is essential only that we know whether a complete or a partial subject category is being described, expressions like *many, few,* and *most* can be translated as *some.** Thus, the statement "A few angry senators managed to block the passage of the education bill" can be translated into a C-Form statement: "Some angry senators are ones who blocked the passage of the education bill." For another example, the statement "Many people who function well in society are, nevertheless, emotionally disturbed" translates into a C-Form statement: "Some people who function well in society are emotionally disturbed people." Note that, as in previous examples, the predicate category was created by producing a noun or noun phrase.

A standard D-Form statement can be produced from the statement "There are teachers who aren't happy in their work." The translation is "Some teachers are not people who are happy in their work." Here are three more examples of translation into the D Form. "Not all modern architecture is ugly" translates into "Some modern architectural structures are not ugly objects." The statement "In some instances, television programs are not a waste of the child's time" translates into "Some television programs are not programs that waste a child's time." Finally, consider the statement "There certainly *are* professional athletes who don't condone the use of recreational drugs." This can be translated into a D-Form statement: "Some professional athletes are not people who condone the use of recreational drugs." However, in this particular example, because the negation seems to fall *within* the predicate category, a justifiable translation could also produce a C-Form statement: "Some professional athletes *are* people who don't condone the use of recreational drugs."

In each translation, the standard-form statement, whether A, B, C, or D Form, consists of (1) the quantifying term *all, no,* or *some,* (2) a noun or noun phrase to identify a category, (3) a form of the verb *to be* (past tense may be used), and (4) a noun or noun phrase to identify another category. Every word in the translation must perform one of these functions. While the wording produced is sometimes awkward, there are no strict grammatical violations, and the fruit of the effort is the extension of the usefulness of Venn diagrams.

Such terms may be readily translated to "some" when they appear in premises, but not always when they appear in conclusions.

OTHER FORMAL METHODS FOR EVALUATING DEDUCTIVE VALIDITY

Truth tables can be used to assess the consistency and the validity of some kinds of arguments. *Truth trees* rely on a similar principle but are somewhat different in application and less cumbersome. *Natural deduction (derivation)* can be used to prove the validity of an argument but not to determine whether the argument is valid or invalid. All of these methods of evaluating reasoning with symbols are part of *sentential calculus,* which is useful for certain kinds of arguments for which Venn diagrams cannot be drawn. Sentential calculus is useful for arguments in which the truth of compound statements, which use connectives like *and, or, but, unless,* and *if . . . then. . . ,* depends on the truth of the shorter statements within them.

Dozens of books offer an introduction to sentential calculus. Use the catalog in your library (an academic library or a large municipal library would be best) to find these sources. Here are a few suggestions:

Introduction to Logic by Irving M. Copi, Macmillan Publishing Co.

A Concise Introduction to Logic by Patrick J. Hurley, Wadsworth Publishing Co.

Logic and Philosophy by Howard Kahane, Wadsworth Publishing Co.

These and other sources also provide an introduction to *predicate calculus,* which is quite flexible and can be used on many arguments for which neither Venn diagrams nor the methods of sentential calculus will work. In predicate calculus, the individual statements are symbolically broken into parts, while in sentential calculus only compound statements are.

■

EXERCISES

A.I Basic

Draw a Venn diagram for each of the following arguments and indicate the appropriate assessment: valid or invalid. Very little translation is required.

1. All students over the age of thirty-five are hardworking students, and all hardworking students get good grades. Therefore, all students over thirty-five get good grades.

2. Some jewelers are not interested in making a lot of money, but no bankers are jewelers. So at least some bankers *are* interested in making a lot of money.

3. Because some priests are intelligent and no priests are dishonest, there must be intelligent people who aren't dishonest.

4. No one who loves freedom is a communist, and no communists are American patriots. Consequently, no American patriots love freedom.

5. Since many existentialists are unhappy and some philosophers are existentialists, it must be true that some philosophers are unhappy.

6. There must be some archeologists who are teachers, because some anthropologists are teachers and many anthropologists are archeologists.

7. Many government agencies are very expensive to run, and some government agencies are not efficient. It follows that some of the very expensive programs are not efficient.

8.–17. Use Venn diagrams to demonstrate that the arguments offered in the exercise section for logical analogies (Chapter 3) are invalid.

A.2 Moderately Difficult

Translate each of the following statements into a standard Venn form so that if a Venn diagram were used, the statement could be diagrammed as a premise or "read" as a conclusion.

1. Not all logical people like to discuss controversial topics.

2. "Everyone has a price" (John DeLorean).

3. "No Greek god, not even Zeus, represents supreme good" (Lawrence Cunningham and John Reich, *Culture and Values*).

4. "Conditional arguments, by definition, involve conditional statements" (Z. Seech, *Logic in Everyday Life*).

5. "People under hypnosis have been able to recall . . . details of the babyhood experiences." (Patricia L. Garfield, *Creative Dreaming*).

6. "Communist societies are revolutionary societies" (Alfred G. Meyer, *Communism*).

7. Thousands of Americans gave to "Live Aid" to help the starving in Africa.

8. "Every evolutionary step is an addition of information to an already existing system" (Gregory Bateson, *Mind and Nature*).

9. "Almost every living thing is sensitive to light" (R. L. Gregory, *Eye and Brain*).

10. "There is indeed no culture of the past, and it seems there can be no culture in the future, which does not have religion in [the] broad sense . . ." (Erich Fromm, *Psychoanalysis and Religion*).

11. "The theory of science which permits and encourages the exclusion of so much that is true and real and existent cannot be considered a comprehensive science" (Abraham H. Maslow, *Religions, Values, and Peak-Experiences*).

12. "The essence of being a good reader is to be a demanding reader" (Mortimer J. Adler, *How to Speak, How to Listen*).

13. "We socialists agree that democracy is necessary and absolutely right" (Carl Cohen, *Four Systems*).

14. "Not everyone will agree with this view of religious ethics" (from *Fagothey's Right and Reason*, revised by Milton A. Gonsalves).

15. "All of us—writers and readers—want writing to be as specific as possible" (Alan Casty, *Improving Writing*).

16. "No evolutionist, since before Darwin, has wanted to claim that life is 'evolving' from nonlife" (Michael Ruse, *Darwinism Defended*).

17. "Each person, each day, moves in and out of the linear and nonlinear modes of experience" (Robert E. Ornstein, *The Psychology of Consciousness*).

18. "Many people used to believe that angels moved the stars" (R. D. Laing, *The Politics of Experience*).

19. "Most California birds are monogamous during the period of nesting and raising young" (Vinson Brown, Henry Weston, and Jerry Buzzell, *Handbook of California Birds*).

20. "Hens can be aggressive towards strange ducklings . . ." (Dave Holderread, *Raising the Home Duck Flock*).

A.3 Difficult

Draw a Venn diagram for each of the following arguments and indicate the appropriate assessment: valid or invalid. Translation is required in all examples. Provide unstated premises or conclusions that are necessary for the construction of the Venn diagram.

1. "The essence of a good reader is to be a demanding reader. A demanding reader is one who stays awake while reading, and does

so by asking questions as he reads" (Mortimer J. Adler, *How to Speak, How to Listen*).

2. All murderers are tax evaders, since all murderers are crooks and so are all tax evaders.

3. "All words are abstractions; that is, all words are mental tools. [Therefore,] They are not the real thing, the item in life itself" (Alan Casty, *Improving Writing*).

4. Since all stones are divine and everything divine is worthy of worship, any stone is worthy of worship (paraphrase from Hermann Hesse, *Siddhartha*).

5. Not all physicians are honest. Besides, some landlords aren't honest. It follows that at least some people are both physicians and landlords. ∎

A P P E N D I X

B

Longer Exercises Using Various Skills

1. The following newspaper article from the *Los Angeles Times*, Aug. 22, 1985, contains an example of Getting Personal and Setting Up A Straw Man (from Skill 1, Staying On Track). Both occur in the second half of the article. Find each and explain your choice.

Falwell, Jackson Trade Charges on South Africa

NEW YORK (AP)—The Rev. Jerry Falwell, leader of the Moral Majority, visited South Africa as an agent for the Reagan Administration, the Rev. Jesse Jackson charged Wednesday.

Falwell said he made the trip on his own and declared that blacks in South Africa do not support economic sanctions as a means of forcing South Africa's white-minority government to abandon apartheid.

During a five-minute debate on ABC-TV's "Good Morning America," Jackson reiterated his criticism of Falwell for calling the Nobel Peace Prize-winner, Bishop Desmond Tutu, a "phony."

The civil rights activist suggested that Falwell had a history of supporting apartheid, a system of racial segregation. "Falwell, you supported apartheid in southern America until it was over. Now you're supporting apart-

heid in southern Africa while it's still alive," he said.

Falwell denied the charge, saying, "I don't believe any Christian could support segregation, apartheid."

On disinvestment, Falwell said, "Most of the nonwhites in this country (South Africa) do not want sanctions. They're saying that to the American people (and) we're going to put it in prime time this week."

Falwell was referring to taped interviews with a group of black South African council members from Soweto. He said the interviews show blacks "who weep and say, 'Please, don't sanction. Don't cut (us) off; our children die.' "

Falwell, who supports reinvestment in South Africa and plans to kick off a $1-million campaign to persuade companies to invest more money there,

(continued on next page)

(continued)

said, "If we withdraw all sanctions, we lose all leverage."

On his return to the United States on Tuesday, Falwell called on Christian Americans to buy Krugerrands, the South African gold coins, and to invest in companies doing business in South Africa.

"We need to put more (money) there," Falwell said, "but with it more pressure on the South African government to move as rapidly as possible."

Jackson countered, repeating his statement from Tuesday that Falwell's identification with the Botha government was on a par with those who sided with Hitler over the Jews, Herod over Jesus and the Pharaoh over Moses.

"I heard that prose last night," Falwell said, laughing.

Jackson, who was an unsuccessful candidate last year for the Democratic presidential nomination, said, "And just as Reagan sent agents to represent his view on the *contras* to overthrow Nicaragua, I'm convinced you're operating, setting a climate for Reagan's policies in South Africa.

"It's an insult to those of us who are Christians and who care," Jackson continued. "You are not there on some mission to save black children, and if you are, start in Lynchburg where you live."

"As a born-again Christian for 30 years, God saved me from racism. I love everybody," Falwell responded, adding, "I'm sorry Rev. Jackson still thinks whites are bad people."

As "Good Morning America" host David Hartman informed the pair they were out of time, Falwell denied Jackson's charge he was sent to South Africa by President Reagan.

Jackson spoke from a Boston television station, while Falwell was interviewed from his Lynchburg, Va., home.*

*"*Falwell, Jackson Trade Charges on South Africa,*" Los Angeles Times, *August 22, 1985. Reprinted with permission of AP Newsfeatures.*

2. Read through this conversation between Judd and Marla. At the end, you will be asked questions about the reasoning both persons used.

Judd: If we ban all guns, then only the criminals will have guns. And if only the criminals have guns, then crime will be rampant in the streets.

Marla: You're wrong. It's easy to see that you're wrong. We only need to see what a radical you are on other issues to see that you're wrong here as well.

Judd: The good citizens of this country need to be able to protect themselves. We definitely should *not* ban guns.

Marla: But if there are no controls on guns, how do we keep track of them, trace them, or keep them out of the hands of criminals?

Judd: Look, I'm just saying that banning guns is a bad idea. First, it won't work. And second, it leaves us with no protection.

Marla: Wait a minute. What makes you think it won't work?

Judd: I'll tell you. It's just that if you put it into practice, it will be ineffective.

Marla: That's not so, because you can't prove it!

Judd: You're a fine one to argue against guns. Why should I listen to you? Don't your husband and your Dad both hunt? Isn't the pot calling the kettle black?

Marla: Now, just hold on one doggone minute. This conversation is worth pursuing if you want to talk about the issue. But it's clear that you want to talk about me, not the issue. So this particular conversation is just not worth pursuing. Let's drop the whole topic.

Judd: Good idea. Let's talk about something we agree on.

Questions about the Conversation

A. Find an example of setting up a straw man. Where does this occur?

B. Find four fallacies. Explain where and how they are committed in the preceding conversation. In each case, explain how the reasoning conforms to the definition of the fallacy you have named.

C. What is the unstated conclusion in Judd's opening comments? Is that argument valid? Is it sound?

D. Find a conditional argument. (No unstated conclusion or premises are needed to reconstruct this as a conditional argument.) Write out the two premises and the conclusion. Is the argument valid? If it is invalid, name the formal fallacy that is committed.

E. What is the unstated premise in Marla's opening argument?

3. Read through this conversation, looking for fallacies and problems in staying on track. At the end, you will be asked to name and justify your choices.

Kurt: There's a lot of immorality in politics.

Thane: Oh, nonsense. It's ridiculous to think, as you've just claimed, that everyone in political life is immoral.

Kurt: Let me explain my position and my reasons for believing it.

Thane: Anyone who has reasoned as you have in the past isn't going to make sense this time either. I can tell you right now that your reasoning and position are wrong. I don't need to hear them.

Kurt: Now, either you shut up and listen to me right now or you're just going to go on believing the same nonsense you always have until the day you die.

Thane: You always want to give reasons for your political beliefs. You want me to give reasons for mine, too. But I don't need to do that.

Professional politicians seldom give sensible defenses for *their* positions. They just hold whatever position is in their interest. If that's what they do, then it's certainly okay for me to do it too.

Kurt: You're an idiot. Do you know that?

Thane: You're just saying that because you know that you're wrong about this politics business.

Kurt: I'm not wrong. The problem is with your reasoning. The conclusion never follows.

Thane: And why is that so?

Kurt: Because the premises don't *support* the conclusion.

Thane: This conversation is getting nowhere.

Thane is right. This conversation is getting nowhere. Using Skill 1, find two "sidetracks" and, using Skill 10, five fallacies. Where does each occur? Explain how each fallacy fits the definition of the fallacy you have named.

4. Read through the following conversation. Myra and Thad are discussing the kind of topic that tends to bring out a stubborn side in folks on both sides of the issue. (Does *both* imply a false dilemma?) Questions will follow.

Myra: There is no God. There would be no evil in the world if God existed. Yet there certainly *is* evil in this world.

Thad: God certainly does exist. There is no doubt in my mind on the matter.

Myra: There should be, Thad.

Thad: Why? What makes you so sure that there isn't a God?

Myra: You do. Every time you try to explain your reasons for believing in God, you end up unable to produce even one decent argument. It becomes obvious that your belief is simply a false one.

Thad: Then give me one argument for *your* position.

Myra: No problem. There can be no God simply because a being of that type would be impossible.

Thad: You're wrong. You just disbelieve in God so you can justify some of your immoral habits.

Myra: I have no immoral habits.

Thad: Let's get back to the topic. God *does* exist. Hardly anyone doubts that, and anything that so many people believe must be true.

Myra: Nonsense. As a matter of fact, as evidence that there is no God, I would like to draw your attention to the fact that some very famous people acknowledged that humans made up the idea of God just for our emotional satisfaction.

Thad: Who do you have in mind?

Myra: Sigmund Freud.

Thad: Oh, his reasoning isn't worth considering. He was a real pervert, always thinking about sex.

Myra: Let's stop this arguing and go out for dinner.

Thad: Good idea. We can talk about it over dinner.

Questions

A. Myra opens this conversation with a conditional argument. Is it valid or invalid? If it is invalid, name the formal fallacy committed.

B. What is Myra's ultimate conclusion? What is Thad's ultimate conclusion? Does it contradict Myra's?

C. Find six fallacies. Where are they? In each case, explain how the reasoning fits the definition of the fallacy you have named.

5. Read the following letter from Andy to his friend Karen and list any bothersome reasoning that you encounter.

Dear Karen,

How are you? I haven't written to you for quite a while because I've been busy with my schoolwork.

I'm going to Trenton College now. I realized that I could either spend the rest of my life doing odd jobs or I could get an education and make something of myself.

If a person is really going to get ahead in life, then that person is someone with a college education. Since I'll have a college education in four years, that's when I'll start getting ahead in life.

Some of my courses are interesting. I want to get a good start in school, so I have avoided math courses. Any fool knows that those are the hardest courses in college. I have a course in geography. That one is harder than I thought it would be. I thought I would just have to memorize countries and their capitals and do that sort of thing generally. But there's really much more to it than that. (I won't go into all that right now.) My psych course is easy. I've managed to get the answers to each test ahead of time. My Mom would kill me if she ever found out how I'm passing that course. But it's really no big deal. A lot of other students are managing to do the same thing. My logic course is ridiculous. I sleep through class and still get A's. I just wish I didn't snore. Everyone is always staring at me when I wake up.

But enough about me. How are you? Is your job going any better now? You know, if you had gone into real estate, you would be rich by now. But that's all "water under the bridge." I hope your Mom is feeling better. She really should take better care of herself. I'm sure she has pneumonia, not just a cold. After all, none of those doctors has been able to show that that nagging cold of hers isn't really a mild case of pneumonia.

Oh, speaking about your mother . . . Don't listen to a thing George has to say about putting her in a nursing home. You and I both know that he has his own very personal reasons for wanting her there. I hope you can be strong on this. I would hate to see him win you over.

Well, I guess I'd better go for now. I need to get to my geography class. I can't afford to miss the lecture.

Say hello to Tommy and Mary for me. I'll write again soon.

Love,

Andy

6. In *USA Today,* on August 7, 1985, the editorial topic was the use of polygraphs, commonly known as lie detectors. A full page was devoted to columns presenting various views on the topic. One of these articles appears on page 277. Read through it. Then list any concerns you have about this author's presentation of his point of view.

7. R. Gregory Nokes, Associated Press diplomatic writer, quoted the president's press secretary, Larry Speakes, on the topic of bringing about a democracy in South Africa (July 1986):

Speakes said, "I don't think we've ever said one-man, one-vote, but we're certainly talking about a democratic system that would allow full participation by all elements of society.

"It would include a democratic system in which a majority would rule," Speakes said. However, he said that didn't necessarily mean black rule because blacks wouldn't necessarily vote as a block.

Analyze Speakes's comments, evaluating the clarity and consistency of the view he presents here.

Attention: The remaining exercises in this appendix call for the use of Venn diagrams, which were presented in Appendix A. If you have not learned this skill, you may still do these exercises, simply omitting the questions that refer to Venn diagrams.

8. Read this paragraph and answer the questions that follow.

Contrary to the claims of some, there are people who have both quantitative and artistic talents. Scientists, for example, are without exception competent at math, and thus have a quantitative talent. Furthermore, there are many scientists who love the arts and have artistic talent. Now, since some people have both kinds of talent,

FRANK HORVATH/An opposing view

Detectors accurate and are reliable tools

RENO, NEV.—Polygraph testing is widely used in the USA, Canada, Japan, Israel, and a number of other countries.

It plays a role in almost every major investigation, and, contrary to common belief, it is admissible in many courts.

It is now common to find polygraph tests used both to screen job applicants and to investigate losses in business and industry.

The accuracy of polygraph testing is about 90 percent; critics say it is 70 percent. These statistics miss the point. The only fair and realistic question is: "How accurate is polygraph testing compared with other things we rely on?"

Psychiatrists are commonly believed to be wrong 50 per cent of the time.

Eyewitness identification is similarly regarded.

Our court trials, the most elaborate and careful in the world, do not always produce accurate results.

In comparison with these and other alternatives, polygraph testing fares very well.

Because errors are sometimes made does not mean we should prohibit polygraph tests. It does mean we should use them with caution.

No one should be denied employment or convicted of a crime solely because a test shows he or she lied; no one should be given a job or acquitted solely because a test showed he or she told the truth. A polygraph test outcome should be considered along with other evidence to make decisions.

All of the scientific surveys of people who have actually taken polygraph tests show that the great majority do not find the test to be offensive, objectionable, or an invasion of privacy.

The reason for this, despite what the critics say, is that during a properly carried out polygraph test there are no surprise or unreviewed questions, and there are no questions about matters that are not related to the issue at hand.

There are abuses in the polygraph field, just as in other fields. The critics' answer to these is prohibition. That solution is simplistic and misinformed.

We ought to license and strictly regulate the polygraph industry as is now done in 30 states; standards of training and qualifications should be uniform.

More important, polygraph examiners and the users of their services ought to be held accountable for abuses.

Proper, rigorous regulation and control is the only rational way of balancing the competing interests in this area.*

Frank Horvath is a professor at the school of criminal justice, Michigan State University, and director of the American Polygraph Association Research Center there.

Frank Horvath, "Detectors Accurate and Are Reliable Tools," USA Today, August 7, 1985. Copyright 1985 USA Today. Reprinted with permission of USA Today.

we can see that neither of the two hemispheres of the brain *necessarily* predominates over the other.

Questions

A. What is the ultimate conclusion in the preceding passage?

B. Is there a transitional conclusion? If so, what is it?

C. Part of this reasoning can be analyzed by drawing a Venn diagram. Draw the diagram correctly and indicate whether that part of the reasoning has been shown to be valid or invalid.

9. Read this paragraph and answer the questions that follow.

Belmont High would certainly be a good school if all the instructors were good ones. And we do know that Belmont is a good school. Thus, all of the instructors there must be good ones. Any good instructor, I might add, is concerned about her or his students. Therefore, all Belmont High instructors are concerned about their students.

Questions

A. What is the ultimate conclusion in the preceding passage?

B. Is there a transitional conclusion? If so, what is it?

C. There is a conditional argument in this passage. Is it valid or invalid? If it is invalid, name the formal fallacy that is committed.

D. Part of this reasoning can be analyzed by drawing a Venn diagram. Draw the diagram correctly and indicate whether that part of the reasoning has been shown to be valid or invalid.

10. Read this letter to the editor and answer the questions that follow.

"THE U.S. AND THE NORTH ATLANTIC TREATY ORGANI-ZATION (NATO)"
In Europe, communists are everywhere. It's common knowledge that any European is at least reasonably sympathetic to a communist perspective. So, since the French are all (obviously) Europeans, we can see that any French person will be a communist sympathizer.

Now, if the French people are all sympathetic to communism, there is no hope for a meaningful NATO alliance with them. Clearly, then, there is no such hope. You must admit that my view is true, since there is no way to demonstrate that such a hope for a meaningful alliance really does exist.

We must extricate ourselves completely from NATO. If we don't, we'll find ourselves first mired in more foreign treaties that obligate but do not benefit us, then coming to the military aid of nations that are not essential to the strategic interests of the United States, and ultimately involved unwittingly and unnecessarily in World War III. After all, my grandmother predicted this course of events fifty years ago, and my grandmother was a very wise woman.

Actually, it's quite a shame. If we hadn't got involved in NATO in the first place, most of our international diplomatic problems never would have arisen.

Questions

   A. Find three informal fallacies in the preceding passage. Being precise, show where they are committed and explain how that reasoning fits the definition of the fallacy you have named.

   B. Find an argument within the passage that can be analyzed with a Venn diagram. Draw the diagram properly and indicate whether the argument is thus shown to be valid or invalid.

   C. Find a conditional argument in the passage. Is it valid or invalid? If it is invalid, name the formal fallacy committed.

11. Read this dialogue about movies and answer the questions that follow.

Lloyd: I heard that you saw the movie *Dune* twice.

Eric: Yes. I had already read the book. The movie really left out a lot.

Lloyd: Well, why did you see the movie *twice* if you didn't like it the first time you saw it?

Jamie: Did either of you see *Amadeus*? I haven't seen it, but I've heard that it's a classic!

Lloyd: Then I'm sure the movie was lousy. The last two movies you expected to be good were both a waste of money. If you had ever been right about which movies we should see, it would be worth listening to what you have to say. But you never *have been* right!

Jamie: Maybe so, but lots of other people said it was good. Didn't you say you liked it, Eric?

Eric: Yes, I saw it and it *was* excellent. I highly recommend it.

Lloyd: Is it playing anywhere in town now?

Eric: It's playing at the Welton Theater in the Broadway Mall.

Lloyd: Is it R-rated?

Eric: No, I don't think so.

Lloyd: Did it have any explicit sex scenes?

Eric: Not really. Why?

Lloyd: I don't like movies that have scenes like that. And I'm sure that some films at the Welton are like that because many films at the Welton are at least R-rated. And most films with that rating have explicit sex scenes. Movies like that have no productive social value.

Jamie: I don't agree with that last statement.

Lloyd: It's true! And the reason they don't is that they perform no significant function in society.

Jamie: Well, that's just the way movies for adults are made these days. You might as well get used to it. The alternative is watching the kiddie cartoon movies by Walt Disney.

Lloyd: Quit giving me a hard time. Let's go to a movie. Then we can go get a cup of coffee and argue about whether it was any good.

Questions

A. Using Skill 1, find a failure to "stay on track" that occurs early in this conversation. In which statement does this move occur? Which of the four kinds of shifts is it?

B. Find three places where a fallacy is committed in this conversation. Where is each committed? Which fallacies are they? Explain how each is an example of the fallacy you have named.

C. In one of his comments, Lloyd offers an invalid argument that a Venn diagram could show to be invalid. Draw the diagram.

D. Either Jamie or Eric could have shown the argument from question C to be invalid with a logical analogy. (This would be a more tactful way of making the point than drawing a Venn diagram for Lloyd!) Construct a logical analogy that should be effective.

E. Find a conditional argument that has an unstated but clearly implied conclusion. What is the conclusion?

F. Is that conditional argument from question E valid or invalid? If it is invalid, name the formal fallacy committed.

■
Answer Key
FOR INITIAL ITEMS
IN EXERCISE SETS

Skill I

Exercises 1.1

1. Setting up a straw man.

   Mr. Smith's argument against telepathy attacks a position that is a misrepresentation of the actual position held by advocates of telepathy. While it is true that normal social relations would be disrupted by constant and lucid mind-readings of every person by every person, this is not what those who believe in telepathy actually suggest. They hold that certain persons occasionally intuit vaguely (and sometimes more clearly) the feelings or thoughts of another.

2. Setting up a straw man.

   Mr. Helband responds by saying that "there isn't one document that is all-important." In other words, no single aspect of a college application is used as the sole determinant for admission. The *U.S. News & World Report* question, however, was whether the applicant's essay was more important than the other parts of the application. Certainly it might be more important than grades or reference letters, for example, without being all-important.

3. Pursuing a tangent.

   In this rambling discussion, the two announcers are diverted from their task of reporting the game. Since Claudell Washington had struck out three times and hit a home run, the announcers' discussion of the value of such performance on a daily basis is not irrelevant to their reporting of the game. As you see, however, the discussion goes far afield.

4. Getting personal.

   The author refers to Professor Buchanan's salary, noting that it is "higher than that of the members of Congress whose big-spending ways he deplores." Since Buchanan is not objecting to their salaries and personal expenditures but to their handling of government monies, the author's personal reference to Buchanan's salary is irrelevant and off-track.

5. Shifting ground.

   Rubens insists he claimed only that in "big-time national politics" corruption had touched every politician. Of course, this is not what he actually said. If this is what he originally meant, then he expressed his view incorrectly. If he is now changing his mind, he should acknowledge this.

Skill 2

Exercises 2.1

1. That house is too expensive for you.
2. Some Italians are dishonest.
3. The Astros are likely to win the division again.
4. There's no way I could pass that math course (even if I *did* register for it).
5. I will have to move out.

Exercises 2.2

1. You'll get the job.
2. This will be a good Christmas.
3. I need a computer.

Exercises 2.3

1. Ultimate conclusion: Our government's covert and overt support of the contras is an act of international terrorism.

   Unstated premise: Any action condemned by the court is, in fact, morally wrong. (The unstated premise may be stated differently, but it must link the court's judgment with U.S. guilt.)

2. Ultimate conclusion: No college student's schedule should omit foreign language (even if it is not required by the school).

   Transitional conclusion: Foreign language is an important subject of study for college students.

3. Ultimate conclusion: Steve ought to find a place for foreign language in his college career.

   Transitional conclusion: No college student's schedule should omit foreign language (even if it is not required by the school).

   Transitional conclusion: Foreign language is an important subject of study for college students.

   While a few unstated premises do function as part of the argument, they need not be called to our attention. One unstated premise would indicate that Steve is a college student. Two others would indicate that it is important for college students to learn about diverse cultures and that it is important for them to learn about conceptualization.

4. Ultimate conclusion: Ronald Reagan is a fine man.

   Transitional conclusion: Ronald Reagan has a gift for sentiment without sentimentality.

   Unstated premise: Ronald Reagan was not wholly motivated by political considerations in these cases.

5. Ultimate conclusion: We'll be out of the theater in time for dinner.

   Transitional conclusion: We can't go to the State Theater. ("The State isn't really a possibility.")

   Unstated transitional conclusion: We will go to the Diamond Theater.

The first sentence in this argument is neither premise nor conclusion. In this sense it is parenthetical, but it provides a context for the reasoning.

Skill 3

Exercises 3.1

1. Invalid. The evidence does not establish that *all* Italians are intelligent.
   Unsound. If it is invalid, it fails the first test for soundness.
2. Invalid. Unsound.
   Unsound. The first premise is false. The second premise is false, but less easily demonstrated to be false than the first.
3. Invalid. Although it is likely that Harcourt committed the murder, he might not have. In television dramas we are often shown that the strongest of circumstantial evidence might point in the wrong direction.
   Unsound. If it is invalid, it must be unsound.
4. Invalid. To establish the conclusion with certainty, the word *most* would have to be *all*.
   Unsound. Again, soundness presupposes validity.
5. Valid. If the premises were true, the conclusion would have to be true.
   Unsound. The first premise is false. The second is contentious on various grounds.

Exercises 3.2

1. Valid. If we disregard the truth of the premises, the evidence establishes the conclusion that California is a desert.
   Unsound. It does rain in California. Therefore, one premise is false.
2. Invalid. Even if all Coast Guard personnel are government employees, the government employees with top-secret clearances are not necessarily Coast Guard personnel. Do not allow your knowledge of the truth of the conclusion to mislead you. Although the conclusion is acceptable on other grounds, it is not established by these premises.
   Unsound. Although both premises are true, the evidence does not establish the conclusion. Since the form of the argument is invalid, the argument is also unsound.

Exercises 3.3

1. The reconstructed argument, which includes two subarguments, looks like this:
   All career military officers are neurotic.
   Some neurotics are dangerous to society.

   ∴ Some career military officers are dangerous to society.
   Many people who are dangerous to society have had sexual problems as adolescents.

   ∴ Some career military officers have had sexual problems as adolescents.
   Both subarguments are invalid and unsound. No assessment of the content—the truth of the premises—is required, since the form in each case reveals an

invalid argument. This is one of those discussions in which the arguer is more likely to accept criticism of form than criticism of content. Just imagine the disputes you could get into with these premises!

Skill 4

Exercises 3.4

1. Invalid. Affirming the consequent.
2. Valid. (Modus tollens because it denies the consequent.)

Exercises 3.5

1. Valid. (Modus tollens because it denies the consequent.)
2. Valid. (Modus ponens because it affirms the antecedent.)

Exercises 3.6

1. First conditional argument:

   Whenever (if) Dad takes the medicine, he will feel dizzy.

   Dad feels dizzy.

   ∴ He took the medicine.

   Invalid. Affirming the consequent.

   Second conditional argument:

   If he took the medicine this morning, then he won't be alert enough to go to the game.

   He took the medicine. (This is the conclusion from the previous argument.)

   ∴ He won't be alert enough to go to the game.

   Valid. (Modus ponens because it affirms the antecedent.)

   There is another modus ponens at the end of Chris's last comment. The conditional premise is unstated in this incidental argument.

Skill 5

Exercises 3.7

1. Some R are PC

   Some R are ALAP (advocates of liberal abortion policies)

   ∴ Some PC are ALAP

   Any argument with this form and with obviously true premises and an obviously false conclusion will serve as a logical analogy to this argument.

One possible logical analogy is this:

Some dogs are German shepherds

Some dogs are Chihuahuas
_____
∴ Some German shepherds are Chihuahuas

2. All S are CEP

Some CEP are PAT (people with artistic talents)
_____
∴ Some S are PAT

As always, there are many possible logical analogies for the invalid argument. Here is one:

All scientists are college-educated people

Some college-educated people are nonscientists
_____
∴ Some scientists are nonscientists

Exercises 3.8

1. The reconstructed argument looks like this:

All physicians are wealthy

Many wealthy people are not compassionate people
_____
∴ Some physicians are not compassionate people

The argument's form is:

All P are WP (wealthy people)

Many WP are not CP
_____
∴ Some P are not CP

Here is one of the many possible logical analogies:

All physicians are wealthy people

Some wealthy people are not members of a health profession
_____
∴ Some physicians are not members of a health profession

2. All I are BP (bilingual people)

Some BP are PGM (people with good memories)
_____
∴ Some PGM are I

Any argument with this form and with obviously true premises and an obviously false conclusion will serve as a logical analogy to this argument. One possible logical analogy is this:

All apples are fruits

Some fruits are oranges

∴ Some apples are oranges

Skill 6

Exercises 4.1

1. R: Yes. The reasons offered for believing that Arnie would be a great teacher are the right kind. Both of the mentioned characteristics are important ones in teaching. The reasons are relevant.

   E: No. Other characteristics like patience and good interpersonal skills are also relevant and, to some extent, necessary for a good teacher. So the reasoning Gail offers has only a moderate degree of inductive strength. This is the best assessment we could give the argument even if the conclusion were merely that Arnie would be a *good* teacher. The conclusion here is that he would be a great teacher. Perhaps Gail has some of Arnie's other characteristics in mind as well, but the reasons she has given us should not in themselves convince us.

2. R: No. The number and title of the professor's advanced degrees is virtually irrelevant as a guide to the difficulty of the course. Professors with impressive academic degrees might conduct relatively easy or difficult courses; professors with less impressive degrees might offer relatively easy or difficult courses. Even if the school granting the degree were known, this reasoning would fail the R test of the R-E-T method. (Moreover, a course that seems difficult to one student may not to another.)

Skill 7

Exercises 4.2

1. Relevant kinds of evidence:

   The career success of graduates of this and other schools that might deserve the distinction.

   The success at changing occupations for graduates of this and other schools.

   The breadth of course offerings for this and other schools.

   The kinds of assignments that are made in courses.

   The other teaching methods that are used regularly.

   The performance of graduates on appropriate standardized tests.

   The list could be extended. To determine what evidence is available within each of these categories, research is almost certainly required. You can thus use Skill 17, doing library research, to complement your own knowledge.

2. The modifying term *basically* requires definition. Skill 13 focuses on this skill. Still, we can name two relevant kinds of evidence:

   Whether it is always/usually possible to identify a self-serving motivation or result. (Again, we need to define. Are we assessing motivations or results?)

The actual motivation of acts that can be explained either as self-serving or otherwise.

How much of this information is available?

In the first category, we can observe results and see that people often act contrary to their desired and desirable ends. If we analyze motivations, however, we find that most or many acts can be accounted for by reference to self-serving purposes.

In the second category, we find that we sometimes cannot make final judgments concerning motivations because the information is not available. Actually, the issue rests largely on definition.

Exercises 4.3

Part A of the directions calls for the same analysis as the items in exercise set 4.2. Part B is subjective and will vary from person to person.

Skill 8

Exercises 4.4

1. Universal statement. The expressions *no* and *has ever been* indicate that Mr. Will would not believe that there have been exceptions.
2. Although the word *all* makes this appear to be a universal statement, that interpretation is open to question. A reader could imagine that all through history, class struggle has generally characterized social interactions but that not every incident should be understood in terms of class struggle. With this reading, the statement is a generalization. Marx and Engels's intention, nevertheless, seems to be to offer a universal statement.
3. Generalization. According to Mr. Kuhn, such suppression occurs not always but "often."

Skill 9

Exercises 4.5

1. Here we have a double analogy. The discharge of toxic waste into our natural environment is compared with two things: the discharge of different kinds of toxic waste in birds' nests and in humans' houses. In each case it is seen as a threat to healthy survival (and it is implied to be unwise). The analogy is simple and acceptable.
2. "We can't cut one suit and have it fit everybody." This old saying is literally true. The suit that is tailored to fit a six-foot-five, two-hundred-pound person will not fit a five-foot-six person who is forty pounds lighter. Mr. Robinson perceives a similarity between this and a matter of school curriculum. As one suit cannot serve the physical needs of all body sizes, he reasons, one curriculum cannot meet the academic needs of all mental sizes or all scholastic capabilities.

   There are two questionable points in the comparison. First, is it as certain that (1) one general curriculum cannot be flexible enough for varied student needs as that (2) one suit cannot stretch and shrink to all sizes? (The breadth of the term *curriculum* is at issue here.) Second, is it as certain that (1) not all students can meet rigorous standards as that (2) short adults cannot grow taller? (The answer to this would depend on the rigor of the standards.)

3. Visiting different churches and enjoying their services instead of giving your time and effort to the development of one church is objected to here. It is compared with eating out of other people's baskets whenever you are on a picnic. In each case, you are enjoying the benefit of another's labor. The suggestion is that, just as you would enjoy the picnic more if you had prepared the basket yourself, so also would you get more out of church participation if you had helped in the building up of the "life" of one church. The weakness in this analogy is that it's not clear that everyone would mind eating out of other people's picnic baskets. So there is no basis for the inference to the conclusion about church participation. In fact, it's not clear that the conclusion itself is true (that people get more reward out of services at their own church). Notice that an unstated comparison rests on the notion that you are mooching off others in each case. On this point the objection is that you are being unfair rather than that you are not helping yourself to the best experience.

Exercises 4.6

1. Obviously, this analogy could be evaluated more thoroughly if it were read within the context of the entire *Science Digest* article. Still, we can see in part what the success of this analogy rests on. At issue is the question of whether a medical or a psychological explanatory model of anxiety is appropriate. The author of the article suggests that the dispute over models "is like a debate on whether eggs or flour is more important in baking a cake." Of course, in baking a cake, each is as necessary as the other. In fact, both are necessary. If the author's intended point is that no account of anxiety is adequate without reference to both perspectives, her analogy is at least somewhat appropriate. However, without eggs or without flour there would be no cake, but without one of the theoretical perspectives in the exploration of anxiety there would still be a coherent and, according to some people, complete account. The interdependence is more obviously necessary in one case than in the other. If the author's intended point is that neither the medical nor the psychological model is more viable than the other, then it is appropriate for her to observe that neither eggs nor flour is more important than the other. If, however, she is merely suggesting that both must be included, then the notion of relative importance should be left out of the analogy.

Skill 10

Exercises 5.1

1. Two wrongs make a right.

South Africa could not be shown to be justified in varying from a "one-man, one-vote" model simply on grounds that the United States also does not measure up in some respects.

2. Contrary-to-fact hypothesis.

In speculating about the results of different historical circumstances (the supposition is that Lincoln did not free the slaves), the writer states the conclusion that the blacks would still be slaves today with unreasonable certainty. In fact, given the presumed ripeness of the times and our recent social development, it seems highly improbable that there would still be slaves. Perhaps someone else would have issued the kind of proclamation that Lincoln did, and perhaps violent revolution would have yielded a similar result.

3. Attacking the person or questionable cause.

   President Eisenhower's view that nonmilitary goods may safely be sold to the Soviets deserves a rational response. Mr. Will should say why this is a dangerous idea. Instead, he simply suggests that Eisenhower's idea (and presumably Eisenhower himself) is dumb. He attacks the source instead of addressing the point and rejects the opponent's position on that basis. Thus, he commits the fallacy of attacking the person. Mr. Will might also be committing the fallacy of questionable cause. If a sufficient number of farm state legislators would have voted the same way even if it weren't an election year, then Mr. Will has named a questionable cause for the passage of the grain legislation.

4. Begging the question.

   The premise "no one else represents our company" is relevant to the conclusion "no one else can give you such low rates" only if we assume that the special characteristic of our company is that its rates are lower. Thus, the arguer assumes with an unstated premise the very point that is offered as a conclusion.

Exercises 5.2

1. Look-alike for fallacy of argument from ignorance.

   The columnist is skeptical of the suggestion that Justice Bird has exhibited prejudice in interpreting the Constitution. He writes, "If that is true, it has not been proved to me." He does not claim that his own view is true and that lack of proof establishes it as true. This is what it would take to commit the fallacy. He would have to write, "That is not true because it has not been proven to me."

2. Look-alike for the fallacy of contrary-to-fact hypothesis.

   This *Newsweek* quotation of Dr. Stanley Weiss falls short of the definition of contrary-to-fact hypothesis in two ways. First, the fallacy occurs only when we speculate about a past event that did not occur. In Dr. Weiss's comment, the reference is to a future event that may not occur. Second, the fallacy occurs only when the results are stated with unreasonable certainty. That is not the case here.

3. Look-alike for the fallacy of questionable cause.

   Ritual is a questionable rather than a necessary cause for the bone structure. Still, the fallacy is not committed because Professor Soffer only suggests ritual as a possible cause: The bone structure *"may have been* the result of ritual. . . ."

4. Look-alike for the fallacy of contrary-to-fact hypothesis.

   If, indeed, Arlene had gone into financial planning, she would not be in a profession in which she would be subject to charges of medical malpractice.

5. Look-alike for the fallacy of attacking the person.

   The claim that, with his teaching, Augustine "weighed down Christianity with his pessimism" might simply be regarded as a relevant claim—true or false— about the history of Christian doctrine. Even if Guitton's charge is taken to be unnecessarily sharp in tone, it's hard to argue that there are separable statements, one of which is a factual claim offered as a conclusion and the other of which is an irrelevant personal attack offered as a premise.

Exercises 5.3

1. Attacking the person.

 The daughter rejects her mother's advice with only a reference to the mother's now unfashionable girls'-school background. Instead, she could have expressed relevant concerns about the advice itself.

2. Look-alike for the fallacy of argument from ignorance.

 The simple claim that "no link to the shuttle explosion had been established" does not imply that the debris and the explosion are unconnected. It allows for the possibility that a link may yet be established or that, even if no link is found, there is nonetheless a connection.

3. Begging the question.

 "He meant to," "he intended to," and "it was his purpose" are synonymous expressions. Since they are interchangeable in this context, each premise has simply restated the conclusion.

4. Attacking the person and questionable cause.

 This is a combination of two fallacies. Attacking the person is committed because the physician's reasoning is rejected on the grounds that he or she is a physician rather than on grounds that relate to the reasoning itself. Questionable cause is committed because money-making is identified as the sole cause for physician opposition to DRGs.

Skill II

Exercises 6.1 and 6.2

There are often several correct ways to map an argument. In each of the following cases, one of those correct ways is shown.

1.

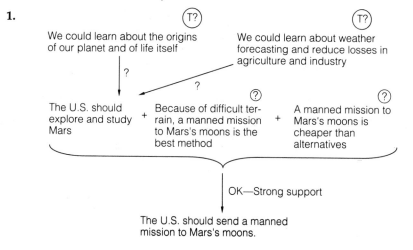

2.

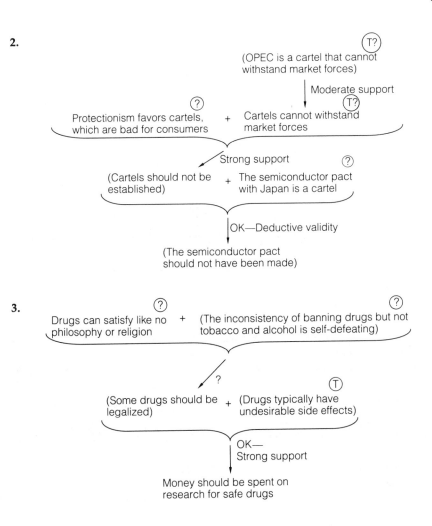

3.

Skill 12

Exercises 7.1

1. Ambiguity. Are horses or cattle to be ridden?
2. Ambiguity. Is it the infection or the disclosure of the infection that is not to be withheld?
3. Ambiguity. Is the witness drunk or is the witness planning a crime?
4. Vagueness. The response gives only a very general sense of the kind of reaction that was observed.

   The questioner almost certainly desired a more specific description.
5. Ambiguity. Of the 24,600 who develop leukemia this year, 17,200 will eventually die (perhaps in a different year) or 17,200 people, some of whom developed leukemia in a prior year, will die during this year.

Exercises 7.2

These, of course, are only examples of how each statement might be rewritten.

1. The wedding was especially touching because of the personal messages that the bride and groom delivered and because of the personal warmth of the minister.
2. He's a dramatic storyteller, pausing just at the right points and using facial expressions to accentuate the suspense.
3. She's mentally alert but she's physically weak because of the lack of exercise.
4. This newspaper is consistently biased on many social and political issues.
5. I liked the bartender's composure and his articulate response after that customer threw her drink in his face.
6. Everyone was carefree and there was a sense of camaraderie.
7. Her friendliness and self-assurance made her a good salesperson.

Skill 13

Exercises 7.3

1. Broad. The definition includes bullies, some of whom are children, and many common, nonpolitical criminals.
2. Narrow. The definition excludes television journalists and people who write articles for newspapers.
3. Broad. The definition includes many other emotions, including jealousy.
4. Narrow. The definition excludes officials who have no White House assignment.
5. Broad. The definition includes members of the U.S. House of Representatives.

Exercises 7.4

After your best effort, look up each word in a large dictionary. In some cases, you may find that you have not been precise enough. In other cases, you may find that you have identified an aspect of the expression's correct use that was missing in the dictionary definition.

Skill 14

Exercises 7.5

1. Earlier in this century both national laws and the medical Hippocratic oath supported an anti-abortion position. No one then questioned that abortion was an unacceptable termination of human life.
2. The news is full of spy cases, creating considerable worry about the nation's legitimate secrets and how to protect them. Unfortunately, Congress is reacting emotionally with short-term solutions that do not promise to stop the spying but may compromise basic civil liberties.
3. In recent months the Right has made great headway in the use of force to further what it takes to be U.S. interests in Nicaragua.

Skill 15

Exercises 8.1

These, of course, are only examples of hypotheses that might be identified.

1. A. These restrooms are cleaned more often.
   B. Fewer people use the officers' restrooms.
2. A. Males are genetically advantaged for math skills.
   B. Expectations and role models for boys encourage boys to develop math skills.
3. A. The child abusers have learned this way of dealing with children as a result of their own childhood experience.
   B. The emotional trauma caused by having been abused is being vented when these people abuse their own children.
4. A. Children with middle-class backgrounds usually attend better schools than children with economically poorer backgrounds.
   B. Children with middle-class backgrounds are more typically encouraged by their parents to be serious about their schoolwork, and they are rewarded in various ways for success in school.

Exercises 8.2

The personal analysis depends on your choice of topic and hypothesis. The second part of the exercise depends on your answers to Exercises 8.1.

Skill 16

Exercises 8.3

1. The claim that Chrysler is the fastest-growing car and truck company in America is based on a comparison of one year's sales (1985) with the previous year's sales (1984). If 1984 was a weak sales year for Chrysler, this is not necessarily a significant claim. To establish a definite trend, the data would have to cover a longer period of time.

   Notice that the claim is based on a market share increase, not on the number of vehicles sold.
2. Since the compared figures are so close (84.63 and 84.73), we should know the margin for error.
3. The people who responded to the magazine advertisements might, being the sort of person who would pursue such a thing, contribute to an unrepresentative sample, even though a balance was established on the bases of region, ethnic group, age, education, and gender. We can also wonder about those who turned down the opportunity after being identified through the phone book.
4. Congressman Packard's rhetoric in voter mailing is strongly pro-president. Who decided to respond to his mail-in survey rather than to junk the mailer? It was those who agreed with his stand. This is not surprising, and we can expect that the sample was unrepresentative.

Exercises 8.4

1. What other factors might be influencing the death rate? Higher safety standards

and air-bag technology have influenced it, as well as campaigns and legislation directed against drunk drivers. This is indicated later in the same article from *Newsweek On Health*.

2. Do the young people who engage in extracurricular activities remain in school because they participate in those activities, or are they participating because this is characteristic of the types of students who do not drop out?

3. What other factors are influencing the increase in joint proprietorships? What proportion of those new joint proprietorships is filed by spouses together? There may not be a fourfold increase, and there may not even be a significant increase.

Skills 17 Through 20

These are process skills. The exercises that cover these skills in Chapters 9 and 10 require the creative application of research and thinking skills. There is no answer key for these chapters.

Skill 21

Exercises A.1

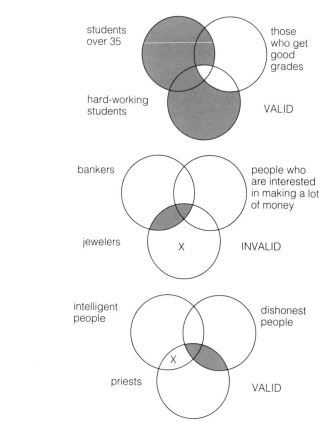

1. students over 35 / those who get good grades / hard-working students / VALID

2. bankers / people who are interested in making a lot of money / jewelers / X / INVALID

3. intelligent people / dishonest people / priests / X / VALID

Exercises A.2

1. Some logical people are not people who like to discuss controversial topics.
2. All people are people with a price.

   (Although it is preferable not to repeat a key term from the subject category when wording the predicate category, it is necessary here.)
3. No Greek gods are representations of supreme good.
4. All conditional arguments are arguments that involve a conditional statement.
5. Some people under hypnosis are people who could hypnotically recall details of the babyhood experience.

Exercises A.3

1.

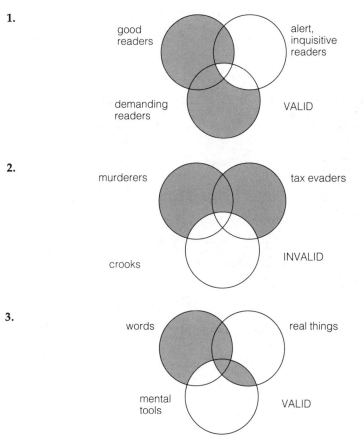

Bibliography

Adler, Mortimer J. *How to Speak, How to Listen*. New York: Macmillan, 1983.

Barash, David P. *The Arms Race and Nuclear War*. Belmont: Wadsworth, 1987.

Barry, Vincent E. *Invitation to Critical Thinking*. New York: Holt, Rinehart and Winston, 1984.

Beardsley, Monroe C. *Thinking Straight*. Englewood Cliffs: Prentice-Hall, 1975.

Bellamy, Edward. *Looking Backward*. Putney, Vt.: Hendricks House, 1946.

Cederblom, Jerry, and David W. Paulson. *Critical Reasoning*. Belmont: Wadsworth, 1986.

Copi, Irving M. *Introduction to Logic*. New York: Macmillan, 1986.

Damer, T. Edward. *Attacking Faulty Reasoning*. Belmont: Wadsworth, 1987.

Engel, S. Morris. *With Good Reason: An Introduction to Informal Fallacies*. New York: St. Martin's Press, 1986.

Evans, Jonathan St. B. T. *Thinking and Reasoning: Psychological Approaches*. London: Routledge & Kegan Paul, 1983.

Fogelin, Robert J. *Understanding Arguments*. San Diego: Harcourt Brace Jovanovich, 1987.

Govier, Trudy. *A Practical Study of Argument*. Belmont: Wadsworth, 1985.

Hamblin, C. L. *Fallacies*. Suffolk: Methuen & Co., 1970.

Huck, Schuyler W., and Howard M. Sandler. *Rival Hypotheses: Alternative Interpretations of Data Based Conclusions*. New York: Harper & Row, 1979.

Huff, Darrell, *How to Lie with Statistics*. New York: W. W. Norton & Co. 1954.

Hurley, Patrick J. *A Concise Introduction to Logic*. Belmont: Wadsworth, 1982.

Johnson, R. H., and J. A. Blair. *Logical Self-Defense*. Toronto: McGraw-Hill Ryerson Limited, 1983.

Kahane, Howard. *Logic and Contemporary Rhetoric: The Use of Reason in Everyday Life*. Belmont: Wadsworth, 1988.

Katz, William. *Your Library: A Reference Guide*. New York: Holt, Rinehart and Winston, 1984.

Katzer, Jeffrey, Kenneth H. Cook, and Wayne W. Crouch. *Evaluating Information: A Guide for Users of Social Science Research*. Reading, Mass.: Addison-Wesley, 1982.

Kaufman, Roger. *Identifying and Solving Problems*. San Diego: University Associates, 1976.

Kepner, Charles H., and Benjamin B. Tregoe. *The Rational Manager*. Princeton: Kepner-Tregoe, 1976.

Key, V. O., Jr. *A Primer of Statistics for Political Scientists*. New York: Thomas Y. Crowell, 1966.

Kimble, Gregory R. *How to Use (and Misuse) Statistics*. Englewood Cliffs: Prentice-Hall, 1978.

McBurney, Donald H. *Experimental Psychology*. Belmont: Wadsworth, 1983.

McCain, Garwin, and Erwin M. Segal. *The Game of Science*. Monterey: Brooks/Cole, 1977.

Moore, Brooke Noel, and Richard Parker. *Critical Thinking: Evaluating Claims and Arguments in Everyday Life*. Palo Alto: Mayfield, 1986.

Moore, David S. *Statistics: Concepts and Controversies*. New York: W. H. Freeman and Co., 1985.

Moore, W. Edgar, Hugh McCann, and Janet McCann. *Creative and Critical Thinking*. Boston: Houghton Mifflin, 1984.

Quine, W. V., and J. S. Ullian. *The Web of Belief*. New York: Random House, 1978.

Radner, Daisie, and Michael Radner. *Science and Unreason*. Belmont: Wadsworth, 1982.

Ray, William, and Richard Ravizza. *Methods Toward a Science of Behavior and Experiment*. Belmont: Wadsworth, 1985.

Richards, Tudor. *Problem Solving Through Creative Analysis*. New York: John Wiley & Sons, 1974.

Robertshaw, Joseph E., Stephen J. Mecca, and Mark N. Rerick. *Problem Solving: A Systems Approach*. New York: Petrocelli Books, 1978.

Rubinstein, Moshe F., and Kenneth Pfeiffer. *Concepts in Problem Solving*. Englewood Cliffs: Prentice-Hall, 1980.

St. Aubyn, Giles. *The Art of Argument*. Buchanan, N. Y.: Emerson Books, 1962.

Sanderson, Michael. *Successful Problem Management*. New York: John Wiley & Sons, 1979.

Skyrms, Brian. *Choice and Chance: An Introduction to Inductive Logic*. Belmont: Wadsworth, 1986.

Tanur, Judith M., et al. *Statistics: A Guide to Political and Social Issues*. San Francisco: Holden-Day, 1977.

Thomas, Stephen Naylor. *Practical Reasoning in Natural Language*. Englewood Cliffs: Prentice-Hall, 1986.

Toulmin, Steven, Richard Rieke, and Allan Janik. *An Introduction to Reasoning*. New York: Macmillan, 1984.

Toulmin, Steven Edelston. *The Uses of Argument*. London: Cambridge University Press, 1958.

Wallis, W. Allen, and Harry V. Roberts. *The Nature of Statistics*. New York: Collier Books, 1962.

Whimbey, Arthur, and Jack Lochhead. *Problem Solving and Comprehension: A Short Course in Analytical Reasoning*. Philadelphia: The Franklin Institute Press, 1980.

Williams, Frederick. *Reasoning With Statistics*. New York: Holt, Rinehart and Winston, 1979.

Zeisel, Hans. *Say It with Figures*. New York: Harper & Row, 1968.

Index